Oracle Business Intelligence with Machine Learning

Artificial Intelligence Techniques in OBIEE for Actionable BI

Rosendo Abellera
Lakshman Bulusu

Apress®

Oracle Business Intelligence with Machine Learning

Rosendo Abellera
Aetna St. Tarzana, California
USA

Lakshman Bulusu
Priceton, New Jersey
USA

ISBN 978-1-4842-3254-5 ISBN 978-1-4842-3255-2 (eBook)
https://doi.org/10.1007/978-1-4842-3255-2

Library of Congress Control Number: 2017963641

Cover image by Freepik (www.freepik.com)

Managing Director: WelmoedSpahr
Editorial Director: Todd Green
Acquisitions Editor: Celestin Suresh John
Development Editor: Matthew Moodie
Technical Reviewer: Shibaji Mukherjee
Coordinating Editor: Sanchita Mandal
Copy Editor: Sharon Wilkey
Compositor: SPi Global
Indexer: SPi Global
Artist: SPi Global

Distributed to the book trade worldwide by Springer Science+Business Media New York, 233 Spring Street, 6th Floor, New York, NY 10013. Phone 1-800-SPRINGER, fax (201) 348-4505, e-mail `orders-ny@springer-sbm.com`, or visit `www.springeronline.com`. Apress Media, LLC is a California LLC and the sole member (owner) is Springer Science + Business Media Finance Inc (SSBM Finance Inc). SSBM Finance Inc is a **Delaware** corporation.

For information on translations, please e-mail `rights@apress.com`, or visit `www.apress.com/rights-permissions`.

Apress titles may be purchased in bulk for academic, corporate, or promotional use. eBook versions and licenses are also available for most titles. For more information, reference our Print and eBook Bulk Sales web page at `www.apress.com/bulk-sales`.

Any source code or other supplementary material referenced by the author in this book is available to readers on GitHub via the book's product page, located at `www.apress.com/978-1-4842-3110-4`. For more detailed information, please visit `www.apress.com/source-code/`.

Printed on acid-free paper

Contents

About the Authors

With a proven track record of successful implementations continuously through several decades, **Rosendo Abellera** ranks among the nation's top practitioners of data warehousing (DW), business intelligence (BI), and analytics. As a SME and expert practitioner, he has architected DW/BI and big-data analytic solutions and worked as a consultant for a multitude of leading organizations including AAA, Accenture, Comcast, ESPN, Harvard University, John Hancock Financial, Koch Industries, Lexis-Nexis, Mercury Systems, Pfizer, Staples, State Street Bank, and the US Department of the Interior (DOI). Moreover, he has held key management positions to establish the DW and BI practices of several prominent and leading consulting firms.

Rosendo founded BIS3, an Oracle Partner firm specializing in business intelligence, as well as establishing a data science company and big-data analytics platform called Qteria. Additionally, Rosendo is certified by Oracle in Data Warehousing, OBIEE, and WebLogic and keeps up with the latest advancements to provide both strategic and tactical knowledge toward successful implementation and solutions delivery. He has authored several books and is a frequent speaker at business intelligence and data events.

Rosendo is a veteran of the US Air Force and the National Security Agency, where he served worldwide as a cryptologist and linguist for several languages. With these beginnings in the US intelligence community more than 30 years ago, Rosendo Abellera provides unique insight and knowledge from his life-long career of utilizing data and information as a critical and vital asset of any organization. He shares these in his books.

Lakshman Bulusu is a Senior Oracle Consultant with 23 years of experience in the fields of Oracle RDBMS, SQL, PL/SQL, EDW/BI/EPM, Oracle-related Java, and Oracle-related R. As an enterprise-level data warehouse and business intelligence solution architect/technical manager in the ORACLE RDBMS space, he focused on a best-fit solution architecture and implementation of the Oracle Industry Data Model for telecom. He has worked for major clients in the pharma/healthcare, telecom, financial (banking), retail, and media industry verticals, with special emphasis on cross-platform heterogeneous information architecture and design.

He has published eight books on Oracle and related technologies, all published in the United States, as well as four books on English poetry. He serves on the development team of Qteria.com and Qteria Big Data Analytics. Bulusu is OCP certified and holds an Oracle Masters credential. He was selected as a FOCUS Expert for several research briefs on FOCUS.com. He has written a host of technical articles and spoken at major Oracle conferences in the United States and abroad.

About the Technical Reviewer

Shibaji Mukherjee is a senior technology professional with more than 20 years of technology development, strategy, and research experience. He has worked on designing and delivering large-scale enterprise solutions, data integration products, data drivers, search engines, large repository Indexing solutions, large complex databases, data analytics, and predictive modelling. He has worked in early-stage start-ups, big product MNCs, services, and consulting firms as product manager, architect, and group head. The major companies he has worked for include I-Kinetics, SeeBeyond, SUN Microsystems, Accenture, Thomson Reuters, and Oracle.

He has research experience in bioinformatics, machine learning, statistical modeling, and NLP and has worked on applications of machine-learning techniques to several areas. He also has extensive research experience in theoretical physics and has been a speaker at conferences and workshops.

Shibaji is a senior industry professional with over 20 years of industry and academic experience in areas of distributed computing, enterprise solutions, machine learning, information retrieval, and scientific modelling.

He holds a master's degree in theoretical physics from Calcutta University in India and from Northeastern University in Boston.

Acknowledgments

I acknowledge and dedicate this book to my mother, Violeta Mendoza Abellera, who embodies sheer determination and perseverance and showed me that it is never too late to reach your goal. You have been a shining example for all your kids and grandkids to never give up hope.

Special thanks to Eric Perry for developing the Qteria POC with machine learning and real-time streaming analytics. Also, to Chien-Ming Tu and Miguel Gamis for contributing research.

—Rosendo Abellera

Thanks to all the readers of my previous books for their invaluable comments and feedback that have enabled me to overcome challenges as I ventured into the trending landscape of AI meets BI.

—Lakshman Bulusu

Introduction

It's an exciting new era for business intelligence as we usher in artificial intelligence and machine learning. Imagine. What if this new technology can actually help us to augment our thinking and provide capabilities that are normally not humanly possible. Should we take a chance and bank on this new technology? Can it really help give us a competitive advantage with our data? Can it make the right recommendations? Are we ready for this?

For several decades now, we have been developing and implementing data-centric solutions. I'd like to say that "we've seen it all," but the industry never ceases to amaze me as new advances are made and exciting new technologies break new ground—such as with artificial intelligence and machine learning. This one promises to be a game changer, and I can't wait to get my hands on it. But wait! How do I successfully incorporate this into my busy schedule? How do I implement is successfully? We have the same old excuses.

With each new advancement in technology, we always seem to go through a ritual before adopting it. First, there is the doubt and denial. We ask, "Could this be real?" or "Is this the Holy Grail that we've been waiting for?" This prompts endless discussions and debates. Lines are drawn, and divisions are made, where people are pitted against each other. Sometimes, a brave soul steps out and goes through the motions of trial and error, where experience (through some success) softens the pangs of doubt and disapproval. When the dust settles, confident players finally arrive at attempting to incorporate the new technology into their plans. These rituals are a far cry from the days when every technologist and developer would jump to become the beta tester for new software.

So that's what it has become—no matter whether the new technology seems fascinating. "Once bitten, twice shy," they say, as we struggle through new technologies. So we wait until we see proven success and are able to repeat it successfully. Then it becomes a tried-and-true approach that practitioners can trust and use in their projects. Finally, confidence takes over, knowing that others have paved the way.

One way to circumvent that experience is to have a mentor go through the implementation with you step by step and show you how it's done. As consultants, we offer that of, course, and we would love to always be in the trenches with you, ready for action. But because that may not be feasible, we give you the next best thing: our book as a guide. Here we have captured our proven successes and demonstrate our code.

With the subject being so fresh, we wrote this book to encompass both a strategic and tactical view, to include machine learning into your Oracle Business Intelligence installation. For practitioners and implementers, we hope that the book allows you to go straight to the parts you need to get your system up and running.

If business intelligence and machine learning are new to you, you may want to go through the entire book (but skimming through the actual code) to get a sense of where this new technology can provide the best advantage in your particular environment. Doing so will provide you with a good overview and basic knowledge of business intelligence and machine learning to get you started. Therefore, if you are a project manager or director in charge of analytics, this would be the method suggested for you. Then perhaps, you can pass it on to your development team to incorporate the R code to get the most out of this book. For the purposes we have described, we have purposely written some chapters purely centered around the code, while others help shape the discussion surrounding the topic.

Moreover, if taken as a whole, each chapter builds onto the previous ones. The book starts with an introduction to artificial intelligence and machine learning in general. Then it introduces Oracle Business Intelligence. Finally, it progresses to some coding and programming, culminating with an actual use case to apply the code. This progressive nature of the book is purposeful and mimics a software development life cycle approach as we go from planning and analysis all the way to implementation.

We hope you find this book helpful and wish you success in implementing this new and exciting technology.

Happy data hunting.

CHAPTER 1

Introduction

"I think, therefore I am." Just as this concept has fueled discussions in philosophy classes about man's existence, it can now certainly apply to an exploration of what it really means to be a *thinking entity*. Moreover, it sparks today's discussions about what artificial intelligence (AI) is as it pertains and compares to human intelligence. Is the aim of artificial intelligence the creation of an object that emulates or replicates the thinking process of a human being? If so, then the Western philosopher Descartes' famous phrase takes on a whole new meaning in terms of existence and the ability to think and—perhaps equally important, especially in machine learning—the ability to doubt, or to interpret that something is uncertain or ambiguous.

Beyond philosophy, this seemingly simple notion can be applied now to our capabilities in analytics and machine learning. But it certainly begs a very direct question: can we actually emulate the way that a human being thinks? Or at the very least, can a machine come up with logic as does a human—and if so, does it classify then as a *thinking* entity? Then again, do we really need to make this comparison? Or are we merely searching for any way to replicate or affect outcomes resulting from a thought or decision?

Indeed, the intelligence and analytical industry is undergoing drastic changes. New capabilities have been enabled by new technologies and, subsequently, new tools. Look around you. Machine learning is already being applied in obvious ways. It's the technology behind facial recognition, text-to-speech recognition, spam filters on your inbox, online shopping, viewable recommendations, credit card fraud detection, and so much more. Researchers are combining statistics and computer science to build algorithms that can solve more-complex problems, more efficiently, using less computing power. From medical diagnosis to social media, the potential of machine learning to transform our world is truly incredible—and it's here!

At the center of it all is machine learning, which tries to emulate the process that humans use to learn things. How do we, as humans, have the ability to learn and get better at tasks through experience? When we are born, we know almost nothing and can do almost nothing for ourselves. But soon, we're learning and becoming more capable each and every day. Can computers truly do the same? Can we take a machine and program it to think and learn as a human does? If so, what does that mean? This book will explore that capability and how it can be effectively applied to the world of business intelligence and analytics. You'll see how machine learning can change an organization's decision-making with actionable knowledge and insight gained through artificial intelligence techniques.

R. Abellera and L. Bulusu, *Oracle Business Intelligence with Machine Learning*,
https://doi.org/10.1007/978-1-4842-3255-2_1

■ **Note** The main focus of this book is applying artificial intelligence (machine learning) to real applications in the business world. It is not enough to revel in the technology itself. Instead, we're interested in how it can change processes and functionality for the good of an organization. In terms of business intelligence, that can clearly point to the ability to gain a competitive edge.

With its anticipated prevalence in our daily lives, you probably want to know a little about artificial intelligence and machine learning. Let's start with a few definitions to introduce our topic (`www.oracle.com/technetwork/issue-archive/2016/16-jul/o46ai-3076576.html`):

- *Artificial intelligence*: The ability of a machine to execute a task without its being programmed specifically for that task. AI is now closely associated with robotics and the ability of a machine to perform human-like tasks, such as image recognition and natural language processing.
- *Machine learning*: An algorithm or set of algorithms that enable a computer to recognize patterns in a data set and interpret those patterns in actionable ways.
- *Supervised learning*: A machine-learning model that focuses its interpretation of a data set within specific parameters. A spam filter is a familiar example.
- *Unsupervised learning*: A machine-learning model that encompasses a complete data set when performing its interpretation. Data mining uses this technique.
- *Predictive analytics*: A machine-learning model that interprets patterns in data sets with the aim of suggesting future outcomes. Note: Not all predictive analytics systems use machine learning or AI-based techniques.

Artificial Intelligence and Machine Learning

It is said that Aristotle, the great thinker of the Western world, was looking for a way to represent how humans reason and think. It took 2,000 years for the publication of *Principia Mathematica* to then lay the foundation for mathematics. Subsequently, this work allowed Alan Turing to show in 1942 that any form of mathematical reasoning can be processed by a machine by using 1s and 0s. This, in turn, has led to some philosophical thoughts on the impact of machines on humankind.

Relying heavily on the theories of those early philosophers, the development of AI accelerated in the latter half of the last century as commercial interest arose in applying AI in a practical manner. [1] At the center of this evolution were advances made in computing power and in capabilities surrounding the effective handling of data via databases and business intelligence—and consequently now with big data. With each technological advancement, we are closer to being able to fully utilize artificial intelligence.

■ **Note** Systems that were designed based on early philosophies and logic failed mainly because of a lack of computing power, less access to large amounts of data, and an inability to describe *uncertainty* and *ambiguity*. [1]

Let's broadly define AI as "the field that studies the synthesis and analysis of computational agents that act intelligently." [2] From this standpoint, our focus is on a computational agent that has the ability to act intelligently. For the purposes of our discussion, we need not be concerned about the fascinating human-like robots that carry out AI—which is usually the focus. We'll simply agree that all of AI aims to build intelligent and autonomous agents that have a goal.

In this AI context, we'll focus on what the agent is to accomplish. Mainly, AI aims to operate autonomously so as to come up with the best expected outcome. In the context of this book, that expected outcome is to improve decision-making and aid in predictive analytics.

So how does the agent go about being intelligent and performing its goal successfully? The answer lies in representation and reasoning.

In building a system for AI, you must do the following:

- Acquire and represent knowledge about a domain (representation)
- Use that knowledge to solve problems in that domain (reasoning)

The agent can develop a representation of the current environment through past experiences of previous actions and observations. This and other data provide the inputs for which it can formulate reasoning. As part of designing a program to solve problems, we must define how the knowledge will be represented and stored by an agent. Then, we must decide on the goal and what counts as a solution for that goal. In other words, we want to do the following:

- Represent the problem in a language that the computer can understand (representation)
- Program the computer to compute the output (use knowledge and reasoning)
- Translate the output as a solution to the problem

The learning aspect of artificial intelligence determines whether knowledge is given or is learned. If the knowledge is learned, then we move to the subcategory of artificial intelligence called *machine learning*. [2]

Overview of Machine Learning

Machine learning brings together several disciplines dealing with computer science and statistics. In simple terms, artificial intelligence deals with the problem of extracting features from data and forming statistics so as to solve predictive tasks. Machine learning takes a unique approach to accomplishing that goal. It approaches the design of the machine learning agent able to make predictions without necessarily providing clear, concise instructions for doing it.

Essentially, machine learning allows the computer to "learn" by trying to find a function that will be able to predict outcomes. In this way, the main focus of machine learning is on the discovery and exploration of data that is provided. That is where it has great use in an enterprise business driven by data: in searching large amounts of data and discovering a certain structure or statistical pattern. In this way, machine learning allows us to take on data problems that were previously too difficult to solve or that we had no way of knowing how to solve. In the past, even the sheer volume of the data itself posed difficulties in terms of processing and extracting vital pieces of information. Later chapters cover in detail how machine learning can be applied and then implemented in an organization via enterprise business intelligence (BI) and advanced analytical solutions.

In simple terms, machine learning enables computers (machines) to learn from a certain stated task and patterns discovered in data. Moreover, it does this without being programmed with the specific steps needed to perform that task—much like a human can decipher and analyze an experience to improve a task. In other words, the computer learns how to best perform a task rather than being programmed with specific steps and instructions to accomplish the task. This is extraordinary, to say the least, because machines are mimicking humans in being able to learn. Let's take this a step further and apply this concept.

With the goal of solving many tasks and providing the correct output, machine learning extracts features from input with hopes of being directed to a desired point. Consider that as a toddler recognizes a flower as a flower by looking at its distinct structure; the input to the toddler's brain comprises the photons perceived through sight that the toddler's brain processes. But a toddler isn't born with the knowledge that a flower is a flower. The toddler learns it by seeing flowers over and over again and recognizing distinct features such as a stem, petals, and its circular symmetry. Machine-learning AI is similar, in that it learns and improves at performing a task (such as recognizing flowers) from experience.

The key here is that the algorithm for recognition is not specifically designated by the designer or the programmer. Rather, it is created by repeated data and statistical methods and training the AI agents of machine learning need to be trained. As part of this training, a large volume of historical data must be provided. [5]

As the use of machine learning permeates the landscape more and more, algorithms will be created that prove to be highly effective and easy to use in analytics. One example of a simple yet highly effective algorithm is one that finds the optimal line that separates and classifies data according to a given category. In this case, the category can be specified in accordance with your features and characteristics. As the computer inputs more and more images. it can begin to check whether that feature falls within your learned attribute. Perhaps even before then, it can scan a picture and determine whether the object in the picture is human or not. The machine-learning algorithm can begin there and perhaps identify humans in the photograph. It learns whether the image is of a human or not. A virtual line is determined that indicates whether the object is indeed human. Perhaps the machine goes even further to look specifically for faces or facial features.

Patterns, Patterns, Patterns

A vital and important branch of machine learning is *pattern recognition*. Patterns and regularities in data help form meaningful labels. This pattern recognition mimics how we, as humans, categorize and classify things as we observe them. Through time and repetitive reinforcement, we begin to identify a pattern in our observations, and thus begin a process of learning from those patterns. This works much the same way for machines in today's world of big data; that repetition can now be readily provided at an accelerated pace as computers sift through massive amounts of data to learn and recognize patterns.

Take, for instance, being able to distinguish faces in a social media application. The application is fed images and begins to formulate information based on data points. A computer programmed to learn will seek statistical patterns within the data that enable it to recognize and then represent that information, numerically organizing it in space. But, crucially, it's the computer, and not the programmer, that identifies those patterns and establishes the algorithm by which future data will be sorted. Of course, there can be mistakes. The more data the computer receives, the more finely tuned its algorithm becomes, and the more accurate it can be in its predictions. Applied to "recognizing" a face, definitive points are determined to distinguish and identify similarities.

But what if the data points are fuzzy and not so definitive? Could a machine distinguish a likeness or even a representation of a person (for example, in a painting)?

The answer to this question may contain the very essence of what differentiates human reasoning and machine learning, and provides a glimpse of what the future may hold if we enter the ability to reason. A person can recognize a certain likeness of Elvis in an abstract painting by applying knowledge of his facial features (even though here they're somewhat vague) and of the way Elvis may have looked as he sang intensely, with eyes closed, into the microphone. Through past experience and observations, we have learned and come to know that Elvis had a certain pose, and so we apply and reason and accept that this is indeed a representation of him. On the other hand, without this reasoning, and with a reliance on definitive data points, a machine may not even come close to correlating the image in the painting with the familiar face of Elvis as in the following depiction:

Figure 1-1. *Blue Elvis by Roz Abellera (`https://roz-abellera.pixels.com/blogs/blue-elvis.html`)*

We can reason that the likeness is close enough for us to even make an educated guess about the painting, and that a machine would not be able to pick up the pattern in order to learn and recognize the resemblance. We can then begin to understand how exactly a machine can learn, and how pattern recognition is the key to this ability.

Machine learning can be divided into three main types. Two of those main categories are supervised and unsupervised. These are most applicable and pertinent to today's big data.

With *unsupervised learning*, the agent can pick up patterns in the input that is provided. Moreover, no explicit feedback or instruction is given. The most common unsupervised learning task is *clustering*, which deals with detecting potentially useful clusters of input examples. [1] Let's apply this concept to people. Children don't need to be told that something is a flower in order to recognize it as something distinct; when repeatedly seen, the flower is mentally registered as a visual pattern by the child. Without specific instruction, the child can recognize the flower as a thing that belongs in a group. The association with the word *flower* is made later, and is just a classification of this thing that the child's mind already grouped. With enough data that covers all possibilities, grouping can be done. Clustering is the most common type of grouping.

Contrast this to *supervised learning*, where the agent is provided a direct input to home in on as it attempts to clarify and classify items accordingly.

Furthermore, along with supervised/unsupervised learning, we have *reinforcement learning*. Here the agent learns (in either a supervised or unsupervised manner) from a series of reinforcements in the form of rewards or punishments. A binary result is the focus, as each respective reward or punishment signals to the machine that it may have done something right or wrong, respectively. It is then up to the agent to decide which of the actions prior to the reinforcement were most responsible for it. [1] In turn, the machine uses this information to further learn and move toward a certain outcome.

This is a small sample of some of the methods covered in machine learning. In later chapters, we will discuss and even apply these methods to a real use case. However, we don't attempt to explain machine learning in its entirety in this book; we focus only on major topics such as knowledge discovery and classification. However, we will continue to cover this subject in our blog at `www.bis3.com`, where we cover the latest in business intelligence software, service, and solutions.

Machine-Learning Vendors

In a race to provide artificial intelligence and machine learning to the mainstream, a multitude of vendors have clamored to the market to offer premiere tools. In 2016, artificial intelligence and machine learning exploded onto the scene, becoming a reality in many facets of our daily lives—especially in the Internet world, including Google and Facebook, for instance. From a corporate standpoint, some of the leaders thus far have been those organizations that led the software and database application revolution in the past, such as Oracle, which offers a complete, holistic enterprise reporting and analytics offering.

Build or Buy?

This new trend in analytics is resulting in a barrage of unique partnerships. Even some strange bedfellows are looking to collaborate in order to offer capable services or products in the new BI and big-data analytics market. If the past strategies of major software companies hold true, I can easily predict that if some of these vendors can't develop their own software, they will end up acquiring their missing pieces.

In terms of this book, the real questions we need to answer are as follows:

- What improvements do vendors need to offer in order to satisfy capabilities in this space for the future?
- Is Oracle Business Intelligence the right platform and technology to provide a foundation for what is to come with artificial intelligence?

Numerous industry analysts make predictions about which vendors will win the race to deliver the best offering. Many look for Oracle to be a leader in this area. With its latest offering relying heavily on artificial intelligence and machine learning, it will be interesting to see what Oracle can develop, or perhaps which companies and technologies it will acquire to complete its offering.

With this push from some of the world's largest and most advanced corporations in the world, artificial intelligence and machine learning have made their way into the corporate world. Access to these tools and technologies has permeated into all levels of the enterprise and corporate ladder. No longer are artificial intelligence and machine learning reserved for just the most sophisticated statistics operations or matters of strategy. Now everyone in the organization is in on the game. Only one thing stands between accessing a wealth of enterprise data and knowledge, and that is how easy a user can get to and use the data. Naturally, this issue of user-friendliness and self-service has caused a lot of angst and has been a catalyst for many vendors, including Oracle, to revamp their strategies and toolsets accordingly.

Introduction to Machine-Learning Components in OBIEE

Oracle Corporation has long been in the business of data management. And with every advancement in data and knowledge management, new capabilities have led users to more—and even advanced—features of business intelligence. With Oracle's introduction of Oracle Business Intelligence Enterprise Edition (OBIEE) a decade ago, and its subsequent adoption and popularity, users wanted to gain more control of their data and any capabilities that their analytical tool could offer.

So began this need for self-service BI. It was exactly this functionality that users sought in a BI system that would allow some degree of independence and capability for users to do their own analysis. I'm sure that almost all would agree that this idea of self-service BI is perhaps the true overall vision and essence of what a business intelligence solution should offer. Indeed, the industry has come a long way to be able to offer all the technologies that enable a person to access and readily use large amounts of data. In recent years, the industry has introduced new tools and technologies, such as big data and artificial intelligence, to help realize self-service BI and beyond.

Oracle BI and Big Data

Self-service BI revolves around the fact that using data for decision-making is aided, in particular, by interactive and business-user-driven interfaces to that underlying data. Data today consists not only of structured data, but also of *unstructured data*—which is often referred to as *big data*. The analysis of big data demands fast processing as well as an integrated approach to the analysis of online transaction processing (OLTP) and online analytical processing (OLAP) data and the discovery of new information from that data. Big data for decision-making must support new data, new analytics, and new metrics that involve past performance analytics along with predictive analytics.

Self-service and, more important, the resulting actionable analytics, can become a reality as the latest technologies and business analysis processes (such as mobile device management, visual discovery, and spreadsheet analysis) become business-user driven, with no disconnect across all needed data points. Oracle's concentration on the enterprise is making this possible.

OBIEE combined with Oracle Essbase provides a holistic solution that enables predictive analytics, operational BI, and self-service reporting on structured data. Similarly, Oracle offerings for analytics and big data can help extend BI beyond relational data and its multidimensional analysis, which in turn allows self-service analytics on gig data. This can answer what we call the *who, what, when, why,* and even *how* of big data in near-real-time, with results easily served via a dashboard and various visualizations of the data to expose the vital information discovered.

Later chapters examine how advances in Oracle's data visualization and data preparation tools, technologies, and artificial intelligence components are changing the way we handle and utilize data in today's world of advanced analytics.

R for Oracle BI

Perhaps the biggest enabler and game changer in today's analytical space is the introduction of the R language for statistics into various BI and analytical products. Beginning in 2012, Oracle made a major leap into artificial intelligence when it announced Oracle Advanced Analytics for big data. This package integrated the R statistical programming language into the Oracle Database (version 11g at the time), and bundled Oracle R Enterprise with Oracle Data Mining. Since then, Oracle has continued to add R and its capabilities in its suite of BI tools. Oracle also has committed to using it for machine learning to fine-tune and improve its own products, including its flagship database offering, being dubbed as a self-healing database system.

Introduced in 1995 as an open source project, R has been adopted by millions of users for statistical analysis. Oracle has integrated it and enabled its functionality to be utilized by its applications and systems. Oracle customers can utilize this analytical functionality to explore and discover valuable information from all the data gathered in their Oracle systems.

This book later provides an example of applying R and machine-learning techniques to create and develop actionable BI and analytics.

Summary

This chapter provided an introduction to artificial intelligence and machine learning—rom their early history and evolution, to today's world as a game changer in our daily lives. A multitude of algorithms have already been written as well as applications that successfully use machine-learning techniques. From the early automation of tasks found in industries such as agriculture and manufacturing, we have now reached an age in which new applications are being sought to automate tasks for knowledge workers.

One such area of automation is in decision support systems (DSSs) and enterprise data warehouses (EDWs) specifically in an organization. It is here where the power of computing and the capability to handle volumes of data are being put to the test with new applications of AI-powered technologies. The basic goal of the EDW is to find a trend in the data that has been integrated and stored. Often, it is only in the EDW that an organization has data that is completely gathered, integrated, and further cleansed; this enables the delivery of a usable set of data that can provide historical insight into the enterprise and expose trends. Applying AI and machine learning can extend the EDW even further by supplying missing or unknown data.

Machine-learning application algorithms that can discover trends and basic patterns lend themselves to the exact focus and purpose of an EDW. OBIEE is the perfect AI-powered technology for the enterprise business and commercial world of the future.

With Oracle's OBIEE suite, capabilities have now entered the realm of artificial intelligence. This book provides step-by-step instructions for setting up R and machine learning. Moreover, this book provides a case study as an example of applying machine learning to the business world.

Citations

Russell, S. J., & Norving, P. (2010). Artificial Intelligence: A modern Approach. New Jersey: Pearson. [1]

Artificial Intelligence: Foundations of Computational Agents by David L. Poole and Alan K. Mackworth [e-textbook] http://artint.info/html/ArtInt.html#cicontents [2]

https://www.forbes.com/sites/mikhailnaumov/2016/12/30/2017-guide-for-deep-learning-business-applications/#6a0217147b84 [3]

https://journalofbigdata.springeropen.com/articles/10.1186/s40537-014-0007-7 [4]

http://docs.aws.amazon.com/machine-learning/latest/dg/training-ml-models.html [5]

Rainbird, August 12, 2016, The History of Artificial Intelligence (AI), AI - The Cognitive Reasoning Platform [6]

CHAPTER 2

Business Intelligence, Big Data, and the Cloud

In our first book together, written around 2015, we described how a complete, holistic BI solution involved three main classifications of reporting and analytics in general. In that book we labeled them as:

- Operational Reporting
- Operational BI
- Analytical BI

At the time, we focused on mainly describing the elements in an enterprise business intelligence solution—that is, one that involves structured data. Although we wrote a few chapters about it, we almost purposely ignored the changes in the industry that were happening at the time with the emergence of big data and the cloud. Since then, we can no longer ignore their presence and dominance in what is to become the future of business intelligence and analytics. This book covers these components along with artificial intelligence (machine learning) that enable advanced analytics and even big-data analytics.

Now with the new capabilities advanced by today's latest technologies such as big data, artificial intelligence, and cloud computing, a new classification in the reporting and analytics realm has taken the forefront and grabbed a lot of attention. That new classification comprises data discovery and exploration and even big-data analytics in general. In this new classification, even the area of business intelligence as a whole takes on an entirely new role. Business intelligence has transformed into a totally different level of functionality, with capabilities to provide insights about and interactions with the intelligence gathered from the data. This next level of business intelligence—being fueled by artificial intelligence—is called *actionable intelligence.*

The Goal of Business Intelligence

We've come a long way when it comes to business intelligence. We, as practitioners and implementers, have seen a lot of changes and added functionalities. Some were not even feasible in the early days of the industry, mainly because of deficiencies in the

R. Abellera and L. Bulusu, *Oracle Business Intelligence with Machine Learning*,
https://doi.org/10.1007/978-1-4842-3255-2_2

technologies that were needed. Take, for instance, real-time or near-real-time analytics. The challenge was that by the time the data reached the right person, the intelligence would no longer be fresh or worth utilizing. A line manager or director in charge of such operations would not even have access to that type of information (and related insights) in order to affect the operational process; this lack of information could prevent businesses from gaining a competitive edge.

So it was that real-time business intelligence did not even come into play until the tools and technologies became sophisticated enough to move data to and from the source in a way that was conducive to using that data to gain a competitive edge. The mere act of gathering data within your organization in order to utilize it posed a big challenge. For many decades, just the idea of being able to store all that information together in one place was a big issue. There was simply no effective way of moving data to and from one system to another. Several approaches were studied to determine the most effective method of creating intelligence and analytics from raw data. Let's discuss an early solution to moving data around.

A great deal of the evolution in capabilities to collect and use data was initiated by companies such as Informatica, which focused on delivering data from one source to a target. With Oracle-Based Optimization Engine (OBOE), we already had methods of moving data by, for example, writing SQL scripts and using SQL *Loader with Oracle. But there just wasn't a sophisticated way of moving data from one system to another. Even if you were able to collect all the data, you'd still have the challenge of cleaning it, transporting it, and converting it. This problem was addressed by companies such as Informatica, which automated the process by creating what is now called extract, transform, and load (ETL). An entire market grew around this new technology as executives were able to focus on business intelligence and analytics.

Although ETL was effective for managing the process, it still left a void in being able to handle large amounts of disparate data and, especially the unstructured data we now call big data. There simply was no effective way of moving data around, not even with powerful ETL tools. This issue opened up a whole new paradigm for handling large amounts of data. We will discuss this new approach for data preparation later in this chapter.

Big-Data Analytics

There are differences between business intelligence and big-data analytics. Although today the two terms are often used interchangeably. However, with new advancements in technology, data architectures, and strategies—and specifically in advanced analytics—I expect that the two will eventually converge to be one and the same.

In the early days, starting with reporting, the capability to access data for use transactionally was the main focus. However, it was not really capable of gaining any kind of insight analytics based on history—at least not automatically. Reporting was really just a means to access whatever data your transactional system had. Any kind of analytics thereafter was done by a different system, often referred to as a decision support system (DSS) or an online analytical processing (OLAP) system.

In today's world of advanced analytics with artificial intelligence, moving from reporting to analytics is becoming more seamless. If we were to separate the various types of systems that are available, we could talk about reporting versus analytics (which as a whole are encompassed by what is now referred to as *business intelligence*). But with each advancement of the tools and technology that deliver reporting and analytics capabilities seamlessly, new subcategories arise that have their own sets of success criteria and requests.

In terms of big-data analytics, a whole new set of goals has arisen related to actionable business intelligence. We aim to push analytical systems to go further, to be predictive and prescriptive. If we were to truly change the success of this industry, we would have to point to these recent advancements as the impetus for an evolution that would then take business intelligence and analytics truly to the next level, where information and intelligence provides valuable insights that can then be totally actionable.

With the cloud, we come closer to this goal of actionable business intelligence, as this ubiquitous solution clearly offers several advantages (see Figure 2-1).

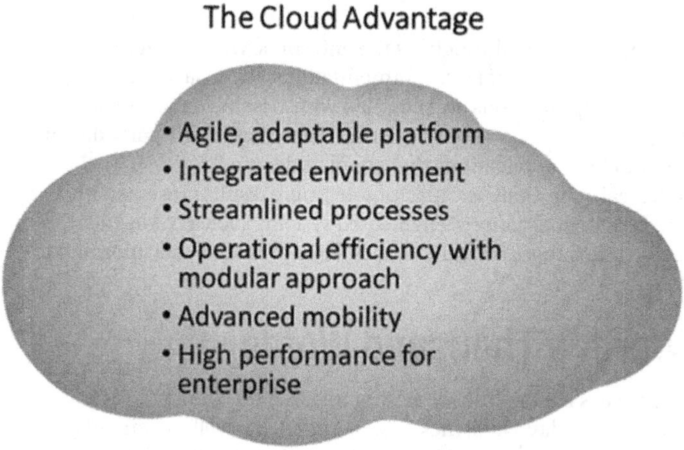

The Cloud Advantage
• Agile, adaptable platform
• Integrated environment
• Streamlined processes
• Operational efficiency with modular approach
• Advanced mobility
• High performance for enterprise

Figure 2-1. *The cloud advantage*

In 2016, a popular data visualization vendor wrote a white paper titled "Top 10 Cloud Trends for 2016." The paper stated the following:

> *In 2015, the cloud technology landscape changed in ways that only a highly disruptive market can. From watershed innovation announcements to unexpected business moves, 2015 drove any last shred of doubt from the minds of skeptics that the cloud revolution is permanent. At the eye of this storm is the growing realization that data as a critical business asset can be very efficiently (and cost-effectively) stored in the cloud. The database, integration, and analytics markets are now in a race to understand how each can ultimately capitalize on this shift.*

But Why Machine Learning Now?

The argument in favor of machine learning is quite simple: we want to access as much data as possible in one repository and be able to analyze that data in order to find certain patterns that may be useful. These might be patterns that would not be humanly possible to derive without the use of a supercomputer. Therefore, we can argue that only through artificial intelligence, which is machine learning, can we even get to the results.

Until now, technology has not provided us the means to be able to use all the data that is now being produced. Without these new tools and technologies, we would have a sea of endless data that we, as humans, couldn't possibly analyze and process.

In 2016, Oracle announced its future strategy and next generation of cloud infrastructure called Cloud at Customer. In response to the public's acceptance and adoption of its previous cloud offerings, Oracle centered its new strategy on its customers and the advantages that new technologies can bring to the table for its ERP programs (for example, EBS) that cover every aspect of the enterprise, from human resources to supply-chain management.

Cloud at Customer combines data throughout the enterprise with multiple sources, and uses machine learning to make recommendations. Artificial intelligence is embedded into the software applications and coupled with Oracle's data. Oracle describes the products as "software-as-a-service offerings that blend third-party data with real-time analytics to create cloud applications that adapt and learn."

Moreover, with its the real-time analytics, machine-learning results presented in user-friendly displays, and data visualizations, engineered systems such as Cloud at Customer can offer users so much more insight into their enterprise data and information.

A Picture Is Worth a Thousand Words

What is *data visualization*? Let's explore the increasing role that this tremendously popular technique is playing in today's analytics. *Visualization*, by itself, is defined as the transformation of information to visual objects such as points, lines, and bars, with the goal of communicating that information to viewers more efficiently. The information can be a set of numerical data or even abstract ideas, processes, or concepts. *Data visualization*, in technology, refers to the display of information that can be stored in computers, with the goal of explaining or exploring patterns, trends, and correlations. In a broader sense, this can be seen as relations of numbers. Undoubtedly, using charts or graphs (or some other form of data visualization) is an easier means to process large amounts of complex data, as opposed to having to process the data laid out in a tabular form stored as spreadsheets.

We have all heard the popular quip that "a picture is worth a thousand words," or should we say in today's business intelligence and analytics world that "a visualization is worth a thousand data points." Data visualization can compress rows of data into a pictorial representation, allowing viewers to quickly access a lot of information efficiently. It is designed to engage its viewers and hold an audience's attention. This is because images are easier to absorb and interpret than tabular data; the human brain has better perception for images, as compared to words and numbers.

In addition to being visual, words and numbers are encoded units of information that we learn throughout our lives. Having many numbers presented all at once requires a lot of mental processing, as well as mathematical and statistical expertise, to see their relationships. In contrast, patterns, correlations, outliers, and trends are much easier recognize visually.

In terms of using data visualization for explanatory purposes, images are also easier to retain than words and numbers. Moreover, data visualization can answer questions in a more complete way that shows the bigger picture. For example, say you have a quantitative question, such as which month had the lowest amount of sales. An answer presented through data visualization would show a complete picture, enabling you to see the distribution of sales throughout the year as well as how much smaller that minimum was compared to other months. In contrast, an answer from simple query-based software would give you only the direct value. Data visualization also provides an ease of access to data and new insights that encourages follow-up questions, which in turn lead to new insights. For instance, the same data answering a monthly pattern can also answer a yearly pattern if aggregated.

Business managers need to pinpoint issues and opportunities in their businesses, but also to quickly figure out why and how they are occurring in order to make reactionary decisions. Business analysts need to find key variables that influence these issues and these opportunities in order to formulate the right solutions. [1] The effect that data visualization has on analytics is dictated by the continuing needs of businesses for BI and analytics. Businesses rely on analytics to put actionable information in the hands of line-of-business users quickly by providing self-service access to data and custom analysis on the fly to empower decision makers. [2]

Recognizing the need to combine visualization solutions with data analysis and data-mining front ends, a new discipline has emerged from information visualization, scientific visualization, and data-mining communities: visual analytics. *Visual analytics* focuses on the entire so-called sense-making process that starts with data acquisition, continues through a number of repeated and refined visualization scenarios (during which interaction allows users to explore various viewpoints, or test and refine numerous hypotheses), and ends by presenting the users' insight about the underlying phenomena of interest. As such, visual analytics typically focuses on processes or data sets that are either too large or too complex, by a single static or image. The goal of visual analytics is to provide techniques and tools that support end users in their analytical thinking. [3]

A further fundamental feature of visualizations is their interactive aspect. The visualization process is rarely a static one. In most applications, there is a need to visualize a large amount of data that would not fit on a single screen, a high-dimensional data set containing many independent data values per data point, or both. In such cases, displaying a static image that contains all the data is typically not possible. Moreover, even when this is possible, there usually are many ways of constructing the data-to-image mapping, which the user might like to try out in order to better understand the data at hand. All of these aspects benefit from the use of interactive visualizations. Such applications enable the user to modify several parameters (ranging from the view angle, zoom factor, and color usage to the type of visualization method used) and to observe the changes in the produced image.

But larger amounts and more complex forms of data are emerging from today's devices and computers. A popular statement and big-data line is that "90% of all digital data in the Internet today was generated in the past two years" [4]. Data scientists or data miners often require the analytics team to have expertise in statistics and data science in order to perform more complex exploratory analysis to process big data. So the business thinkers may need to consult with the data team before getting a clear answer to questions about their data.

Visualization is a continuous process. Large amounts of data cannot all be summed up in one, or even just a few, images; big data is too vast, and each data point has too many attributes of value. For example, rows of data for a sales transaction for a department store chain has many attributes: the price sold, profit margin, date, location of sale, time, and even more attributes originating both from the product and the buyer. All these attributes cannot all be summed up into one or a few forms of visualization. Different variables need to be isolated, omitted, and filtered in a continuous process to gain new insights.

In a way, visual analytics has become the user-friendly interface for business thinkers to access big data. Business thinkers can take the initiative and be analysts. With quick and interactive access to data, business thinkers can freely explore data without necessarily having a specific question to answer or an issue to solve. Visibility of data for easier and quicker recognition of patterns, correlations, trends, and outliers backed with the business expertise to reason about these observations becomes a very powerful commodity for businesses. For this reason, many enterprise software providers are now adopting visual analytics as a necessity.

In today's landscape of business intelligence and knowledge management, data visualization has become such an essential—and even the most powerful—tool for analytics. For that reason, many vendors have focused on it and marketed how it should be done effectively. There are many who say data visualization is an intricate blend of science and art. Its appealing and effective interface experience has become an essential part of the big-data analytics equation, and many vendors have recognized its role.

In conclusion, data visualization tools are transforming business intelligence, as many vendors in the marketplace have gone to market primarily around their data visualization tools. Some vendors have recently risen to popularity by riding this data visualization and discovery wave and have seen a new chance to compete by focusing on their product's data visualization capabilities. Many of these were small "departmental" tools. On the other hand, the major players of business intelligence are also now in the game, such as Oracle with its most recent version of OBIEE 12c. In this case, they have released visualization capabilities to complement their traditional and already popular suites of tools.

CITATIONS

www.sas.com/en_ca/insights/analytics/what-is-analytics.htm [1]

http://bluehillresearch.com/business-intelligence-data-visualization-and-the-brain/ [2]

Telea, Alexandru. Data Visualization: Principles and Practice. Boca Raton: CRC, Taylor & Francis Group, 2015. Print. [3]

SINTEF. "Big Data, for better or worse: 90% of world's data generated over last two years." ScienceDaily. ScienceDaily, 22 May 2013. www.sciencedaily.com/releases/2013/05/130522085217.htm. [4]

Data Modeling

The direction now in working with data is to turn unstructured data into structured data automatically. With the Oracle Analytics Cloud platform, Big Data Services will use a lightweight model and then use the Data Preparation with artificial intelligence to read the data from any data store and add it to the model. The focus is shifted toward the business and analytics modelers to apply their model on top of the data that is already prepared and ready for analysis, and the real work that is needed.

Another feature is Oracle Big Data SQL, which has the ability to send out a query of any format and standards that are not native, such as NoSQL databases. Furthermore, SQL with R will be used to do analytics.

It's important to understand that two different structures and architectures are needed to support a transactional system and a decision support system. Simply speaking, one type of architecture can't effectively satisfy both. As a data architect, you must understand how and when to apply the proper architecture to each respective system. To this day, I still encounter organizations that do not understand this basic notion and fail miserably at constructing a proper solution. Even worse, I have recently encountered organizations that took it upon themselves to create yet another structure (explaining it as a hybrid) that supports neither transactional nor decision support solutions effectively. What they end up with is yet another structure to maintain that costs a tremendous amount of money and resources to create, and yet still leaves a void in offering a proper solution. Furthermore, any future advancements aided by artificial intelligence and machine learning would be further confused by the patterns of the data structures and thus could not be utilized.

To illustrate this, try optimizing a transactional system the same way you do a decision support system, and vice versa. You will find that you end up with futile results. For instance, the index you create for a transactional system focuses on data manipulation (inserts, updates, and deletes) and will surely be different from one created for decision support, in which the main focus is for fast retrieval and querying. How great it would be to be able to hit your transactional system directly for querying, without any other type of work needed. Indeed, when technology catches up to a point where transactional systems and decision support systems can use the same database structure in the back, then there will be no need for data architects and their expertise. With machine learning, that day might have just arrived.

By using data points, we can create aggregates and summaries from the data that paint a picture of facts and behavior (which could be expected or unexpected). Moreover, through artificial intelligence and machine learning, anomalies can be identified based on baseline data in order to predict certain future actions. This predictive and prescriptive function is the ultimate aim for machine learning, which focuses on real-time analytics and automated anomaly detection in data.

This technology could be used not only to look for data anomalies but also to "learn" of certain changes and then to suggest a recommendation based on the patterns of the data and the changes. Machine learning can learn from the data metrics, identify the anomalies, alert users, and provide recommendations. Then beyond that, it can identify what we, as humans, failed to ask or couldn't have possibly known to ask. Like a most trusted advisor, artificial intelligence can help us in ways that we are not even aware of. The future is wide open for applying artificial intelligence in our daily lives as well as in business.

The Future of Data Preparation with Machine Learning

Artificial intelligence has changed the future of analytics in Oracle by changing the way we create an analytical solution. One of the most significant changes has been in preparing data for generating reports. The term *data preparation* is becoming more and more important and could be the game changer we've been looking for all along.

Let me set the background for why this is significant. When building a solution from the ground up, the traditional method for implementation what's the first put into place the data foundation needed to support the application your solution. In general, this endeavor involved a tremendous amount of time and effort between business and technical resources to come up with the proper data foundation. As such, data architects have been tasked with coming up with the day model and subsequent database, and the whole development process is dependent on it.

For over two decades, my expertise has been repeatedly utilized. It has been my personal observation that, although an extremely important skillset for developers of data-centric applications, it seems to be one that was forgotten or even set aside. As a result, I've seen projects that were unsuccessful due to the lack data architecture and data modeling skillsets. The fact is that laying down the foundation is probably the single most important piece of a data-centric and data-driven solution. Without the proper foundation, downstream applications would have to "muscle" a solution and try to make up for problems in the day model. It took me years of experience to finally be able to provide the expertise over and over again. So what if this expertise could be packaged up in a way that could be readily used to create a solution? That application would act as a data architect, armed with the appropriate design techniques needed to come up with a proper data model and foundation. Essentially, you would be able to deliver a solution on the fly because it would be readily handled with automation.

Enter today's paradigm for creating a data model, which has shifted considerably. Timing is an equally important factor in today's process. In starting a solution, instead of having a data model specified fully up front, machine learning enables us to identify certain data elements and objects that are missing and append them to a model that is already in place. This eliminates common obstacles that data modelers and architects encounter when attempting to set the right foundation correctly in the first attempt. So how does this affect development? Implementation can be considerably shortened by only having to set into place a baseline foundation and then letting AI continue the development by identifying missing components. In other words, through machine learning, a simple schema can be read and utilized by your machine-learning algorithm in order to determine the proper storage of data as it comes into your landing area. Consequently, via the machine-learning algorithm, the mechanism can recommend and even create the proper attributes in accordance with the data sampling to automatically create a new schema.

So what does that mean for data modeling? It means that you no longer have to make sure that your schema is currently specified with your database and subsequent RPD. Machine learning will help to automatically include any data that is beyond the structured schema, by adding it as a recommendation based on the patterns found in the data.

To sum this up, a suggested process for creating the proper data model is to use a canonical model that specifies a base foundation for any entity. Then, using machine-learning algorithms, any subsequent additional attributes that are needed can be automatically added to the schema and structures.

Oracle Business Intelligence Cloud Service

In 2014, Oracle released one of the first BI platforms on the cloud as part of its Oracle Analytics Cloud offering. It was a full-fledged cloud application that at the time was relatively new. For those practitioners familiar with OBIEE, it essentially offered the features of 11g.

In 2016, I was implementing OBIEE 12c for a US government agency, but also presented the BICS product at one of the Oracle Application User Group conferences. I noted that the data visualization feature and components came in a separate offering. I sensed that it was only a matter of time before Oracle integrated everything between OBIEE, Visual Analyzer, and big-data analytics. That time has now come, and I urge those who are interested and tried it before to give it another try.

Oracle Analytics Cloud

Leading up to the Oracle Analytics Cloud that we have today, BICS was the first generation of the BI application on the cloud. As previously mentioned, it included in its suite package the tools needed to develop reporting and analytics from the ground up, including a database service, a modeling tool, a data loader, and dashboards. From an industry standpoint, it was one of first on the cloud, and its feature set was more like 11g.

Oracle Analytics Cloud, the second-generation analytics product, is essentially the "latest and greatest" version (12c) of Oracle's cloud solution. Moreover, as a go forward strategic, Oracle will update the cloud version first with new features and the on-premises version will follow suit.

In terms of features, the Standard version concentrates on visualization (to compete against data visualization tools such as Tableau, Qlikview, and PowerBI. The enterprise includes everything to make it a complete holistic solution, including the Big Data Lake Edition with big data and artificial intelligence components. In addition, it has BI Publisher for reporting. For advanced analytics, R and mapping are built in. A content pack is provided free in order to help bootstrap development. Through machine-learning approaches programmed in R, corrective actions are suggested by the analytics. Subsequently, the analytics project can be published, exported, and imported to be shared with others or to embed in a web page to share.

Oracle Database 18c

Oracle announced in October 2017 that the latest version (version 18c) of its flagship product, the Oracle relational database management system, now uses machine learning to automatically maintain, administer, and troubleshoot the system. This includes upgrades, patching, and tuning itself. This technology is able to baseline the system and then, using machine- learning approaches and techniques, learn what is not "normal" and suggest ways to correct or modify itself accordingly.

Oracle Mobile Analytics

As an integral part of Oracle's overall strategy, it has incorporated programs and applications to tie in today's mobile devices. Day by Day and Synopsis are mobile applications that are part of its next generation of mobile apps that are integrated with the enterprise layer seamlessly.

ANALYTICS ON THE GO

Oracle Business Intelligence Mobile is the only mobile app that provides a full range of functionality—from interactive dashboards to location intelligence—and lets you initiate business processes right from your mobile device. The app enables you to do the following:

- Make business intelligence as easy to use as any consumer mobile app
- View, analyze, and act on all your Oracle Business Intelligence content on the Apple iPhone and iPad
- Instantly access new or existing content on mobile devices; no design changes required
- Increase the use of business intelligence in your organization with an intuitive and easy-to-use mobile application

`www.oracle.com/solutions/business-analytics/business-intelligence/mobile/bi-mobile/index.html`

The user would use the voice interface through the mobile device, which, in turn, goes through the semantic layer of the Enterprise BI and Big Data Lake layer, and then finally build a visualization in response to your inquiry.

Summary

Oracle, with its recent offering of the Oracle Analytics Cloud platform, has provided a complete, holistic, analytical solution encompassing business intelligence, big data, and artificial intelligence all on the ubiquitous cloud.

The two main features of machine learning are as follows:

- Data visualization
- Data preparation

These are game changers offering a whole new paradigm for providing business intelligence with advanced analytics.

Through machine learning, insights are possible. Some of these insights involve things that we, as humans, couldn't even have thought of. Even when it comes to effectively handling the sheer amount of data coming from big data or even from an enterprise data warehouse, artificial intelligence can help identify patterns in the data that we would not normally be able to do.

CHAPTER 3

The Oracle R Technologies and R Enterprise

Advances in artificial intelligence (AI) have extended the domain of business intelligence (BI) to areas of machine learning and predictive analytics as well as big-data analytics. This has resulted in an expansive set of machine-learning algorithms that can be used to solve real-world BI problems. One of the most popular and widely used languages for machine learning and statistical computing is the R open source language. Its extensive set of algorithms, coupled with its support for rich graphics and data visualization, has made it the language of choice for data analysis and data science.

This chapter focuses on R technologies for the enterprise. It also outlines the use of some of the expansive sets of open source R packages as well as the use of R scripts and Oracle R Enterprise in the Oracle database from a machine-learning perspective. The chapter explains how Oracle R Enterprise can be used with OBIEE. Finally, it explains how to perform big-data advanced analytics by using machine learning with the R ecosystem.

R Technologies for the Enterprise

R is an open source scripting language for machine and statistical learning and advanced graphics functionality. For the purposes of this chapter, R technologies can be broadly classified into two categories: open source R and Oracle's R technologies.

Open Source R

Open source R consists of a rich set of compiled code, functional routines, and related data in the form of packages and views, called CRAN views, or CRAN task views. *CRAN* is an acronym for *Comprehensive R Archive Network* and consists of user-defined packages published to its web site, `http://cran.r-project.org`. Each task view consists of a web page specific to a functional domain and the details of the corresponding packages for that domain. Examples of CRAN task views are Genetics, Clinical Trials, and Medical Imaging in the Health Care Domain; Machine Learning; Statistical Learning; Time Series Analysis; and Financial Analysis.

R. Abellera and L. Bulusu, *Oracle Business Intelligence with Machine Learning*,
https://doi.org/10.1007/978-1-4842-3255-2_3

R is extensible and comprehensive with the ability to add custom functionality in the form of new packages. R can be further extended with out-of-the-box features in the form of *knobs* that help in additional customization. Either the R project web site or the CRAN web site can be used to download and install R for free.

■ **Note** Details of the R open source project can be found at `www.R-project.org`.

Table 3-1 describes the widely used CRAN task views for machine learning. These can also be found at `https://cran.r-project.org/web/views/MachineLearning.html`.

Table 3-1. *CRAN Task Views for Machine Learning*

View Name	Description
Neural Networks and Deep Learning	Stuttgart Neural Network Simulator (RSNNS) User-extensible artificial neural networks (FCNN) Deep learning—darch, deepnet, RcppDL, h2o TensorFlow
Recursive Partitioning	Tree-structured models for regression, classification, and survival analysis; rule-based models and boosting; recursive partitioning
Random Forests	Regression and classification, ensemble learning, reinforcement learning trees
Regularized and Shrinkage Methods	Linear, logistic, and multinomial regression models; gene expression analysis
Boosting and Gradient Descent	Gradient boosting and learning models based on gradient descent for regression tasks
Support Vector Machines	Interface to SVMLIB and and SVMLight (only for one-against-all classification)
Bayesioan Methods	Bayesian Additive Regression Trees (BART), genetic algorithms, etc.
Associative Rules	Mining frequent itemsets, maximal itemsets, closed frequent itemsets and association rules
Fuzzy Rule-Based Systems	Fuzzy rule-based systems from data for regression and classification, rough set theory, and fuzzy rough set theory
Meta Packages	Building predictive models (caret), GBM, GLM (with elastic net regularization), mlr, and deep learning (feed-forward multilayer networks)
GUI	Graphical user interface for data mining in R

(*continued*)

Table 3-1. *(continued)*

View Name	Description
Visualization	Various plots and graphs for visualization in R including scatter plots, feature sets, ggplots, pairs plots, plots for exploratory data analysis, trellis charts, and plots for learning models including random forests and SVMs, prediction functions, etc.
Statistical Learning	Various alogirthms based on statistics and probability for data mining, inference, and prediction
Miscellaneous	Model selection and validation algorithms, evidential classifiers that quantify the class of test pattern, classification models for determining and handling missing values and numerical data, feature-based and graph-based data for prediction of a response variable

Oracle's R Technologies

Oracle's R technologies consist of the following:

- Oracle R Distribution
- ROracle
- Oracle R Enterprise (ORE)
- Oracle R Advanced Analytics for Hadoop

Each is descibed in the subsections that follow.

Oracle R Distribution

Oracle R Distribution is a free R software redistribution of open source R. This contains functionality to dynamically load math libraries for high-performance computations and learning, including multithreaded execution. The primary math libraries include Intel Math Kernel Library, AMD Core Math Library, and Solaris Sun Performance Library. Mathematical functions such as matrix functions, component analysis, fast Fourier series transformations, and vector analysis can be transparently done using these libraries. Oracle R Distribution also comes with enhancements to open source R and is available on Oracle Enterprise Linux, Solaris, AIX, and Windows. Oracle Support is included for customers of the Oracle Advanced Analytics option and Big Data Appliance as well as Oracle R Enterprise. Use of Oracle R Distribution also enables scalability across the client and database for embedded R execution. As of this writing, the latest version of Oracle R Distribution is 3.3.0.

ROracle

ROracle is a database-interface-compliant Oracle driver for R using Oracle Call Interface (OCI) libraries. Reengineered and optimized for connectivity between R and Oracle DB, ROracle is an open source R CRAN package managed by Oracle. It primarily enables execution of SQL statements from the R interface and transactional support for data manipulation language (DML) operations. ROracle is also used by Oracle R Enterprise to connect between R and Oracle DB. ROracle connectivity is faster while reading from Oracle table to R data.frame, and writing from R data.frame to Oracle table, as compared to RODBC and RJDBC. ROracle also is scalable across all data types (primarily, Oracle `NUMBER`, `VARCHAR2`, `TIMESTAMP`, and `RAW` data types) as well as large resultsets. As of this writing, ROracle 3-1.11 is the latest version of ROracle.

■ **Note** ROracle can be used to connect to Oracle DB from the Oracle R Distribution. Either the Oracle Instant Client or the Oracle standard Database Client *must be installed* for ROracle to be used. The SQL*Plus SQL interface can also be used with Oracle Instant Client when connecting using ROracle. There is no need to create `ORACLE_HOME` when Oracle Instant Client is used.

To use the ROracle package, first the Oracle Database must be installed. Then Oracle R must be installed, followed by installation of the ROracle package and database interface (DBI) package. Once this setup has been done, a connection can be established between Oracle DB and Oracle R by first loading the ROracle library and the Oracle DB driver, and then creating a database connection. Once this is completed, standard DDL, DML, and/or commit/rollback operations can be executed. When you're finished using database operations, the DB connection needs to be closed and the database driver unloaded. Listing 3-1 gives an example of using ROracle; the codeloads the ROracle package and then retrieves results from an Oracle schema table. The built-in RConsole can be used to run ROracle methods.

Listing 3-1. Connecting to and Retrieving Results from an Oracle DB Table by Using ROracle from Oracle R

```
SQL> alter user testr quota unlimited on users;
User altered.
```

This allocates unlimited quota to the user testr on the tablespace users.

```
SQL> create table temp_tab(cd varchar2(10 char) constraint temp_tab_pk
primary key,
  2 descr varchar2(30 char) not null,
  3 eff_start_date date not null,
  4 eff_end_date date);

Table created.
```

The following script must be executed in the R console.

```
library(ROracle)
drvr <- dbDriver("Oracle")
conn <- dbConnect(drvr, username = "myusername", password = "mypassword")
select_resultset <- dbSendQuery(conn, "select * from myusername.temp_tab")
fetch(select_resultset)
row_cnt <- dbGetRowCount(select_resultset)
if (row_cnt == 0) {
        warning("No results returned!")
}
dbClearResult(select_resultset)
dbDisconnect(conn)
dbUnloadDriver(drvr)
```

Here is the output of the code executed in RGui in:

```
> library(ROracle)
Loading required package: DBI
Warning messages:
1: package 'ROracle' was built under R version 3.3.0
2: package 'DBI' was built under R version 3.2.5
> drvr <- dbDriver("Oracle")
> conn <- dbConnect(drvr, username = "testr", password = "testr")
> select_resultset <- dbSendQuery(conn, "select * from testr.temp_tab")
> fetch(select_resultset)
[1] CD              DESCR           EFF_START_DATE EFF_END_DATE
<0 rows> (or 0-length row.names)
> row_cnt <- dbGetRowCount(select_resultset)
> if (row_cnt == 0) {
+ warning("No results returned!")
+ }
Warning message:
No results returned!
> dbClearResult(select_resultset)
[1] TRUE
> dbDisconnect(conn)
[1] TRUE
> dbUnloadDriver(drvr)
[1] TRUE
>
```

An Oracle instance can also be specified in dbConnect by using the DB instance name attribute, as as shown here:

```
conn <- dbConnect(drvr, username = "myusername", password = "mypassword",
dbname="mydbinstance")
```

Instead of using `dbDriver("Oracle")`, the Oracle method `Oracle()` can be used to instantiate an Oracle instance:

```
drvr <- Oracle()
```

Additionally, two other arguments, SYSDBA and `external_credentials`, can be set to connect as SYSDBA and external authentication, respectively. They are specified as `SYSDBA = TRUE|FALSE` and `external_credentials=TRUE|FALSE`. These are supported in the ROracle 1-1.11 version.

Listing 3-2 gives example code for writing data from an R data.frame to an Oracle table, and subsequently reading from the same table into an R data.frame and displaying it.

Listing 3-2. Connecting to and Writing Data from an R data.frame into an Oracle DB Table, and Reading the Same Table Data into an R data.frame and Displaying It Using ROracle from Oracle R

```
library(ROracle)
drvr <- dbDriver("Oracle")
conn <- dbConnect(drvr, username = "testr", password = "testr",
dbname="orcl")
insertStr <- "insert into testr.temp_tab values (:1, :2, :3, :4)";
cd <- "CD13";
descr <- "Description for Code 13";
eff_start_date <- "2017-01-01";
eff_start_date <- as.POSIXct(eff_start_date);
eff_end_date <- "2017-12-31";
eff_end_date <- as.POSIXct(eff_end_date);
# The TZ env variable in R must be set as also the corresponding ORA_SDTZ
# env var to the same value
Sys.setenv(TZ = "EST")  # EST value is obtained from SESSIONTIMEZONE value
# in Oracle
Sys.setenv(ORA_SDTZ = "EST")
dbGetQuery(conn, insertStr, data.frame(cd, descr, eff_start_date, eff_end_
date));
dbCommit(conn)

# Selecting data into R data.frame and displaying it
select_resultset <- dbSendQuery(conn, "select * from testr.temp_tab")
data <- fetch(select_resultset)
dim(data)
data
dbClearResult(select_resultset)
dbDisconnect(conn)
dbUnloadDriver(drvr)
```

Here's the output of running the code in Listing 3-2:

```
> library(ROracle)
Loading required package: DBI
Warning messages:
1: package 'ROracle' was built under R version 3.3.0
2: package 'DBI' was built under R version 3.2.5
> drvr <- dbDriver("Oracle")
       > conn <- dbConnect(drvr, username = "testr", password = "testr",
       dbname="orcl")
> dbListTables(conn)
       [1] "TEMP_TAB"
> Sys.timezone()
[1] "EST"
> Sys.setenv(TZ = "EST")
> Sys.setenv(ORA_SDTZ = "EST")
> dbGetQuery(conn, insertStr, data.frame(cd, descr, eff_start_date, eff_end_
date));
[1] TRUE
> dbCommit(conn)
[1] TRUE
> select_resultset <- dbSendQuery(conn, "select * from testr.temp_tab")
> data <- fetch(select_resultset)
> dim(data)
[1] 1 4
> data
    CD                    DESCR EFF_START_DATE EFF_END_DATE
1 CD13 Description for Code 13     2017-01-01   2017-12-31
> dbClearResult(select_resultset)
[1] TRUE
> dbDisconnect(conn)
[1] TRUE
> dbUnloadDriver(drvr)
[1] TRUE
>
```

A set of rows based on bind parameter values (that is, the actual values substituted for `:1`, `:2`, `:3`, `:4` when the code in Listing 3-2 is executed) can also be read from the Oracle table into an R data.frame and displayed. Listing 3-3 gives the example code.

Listing 3-3. Connecting to and Writing Data from an R data.frame into an Oracle DB Table, and Reading the Same Table Data into an R data.frame and Displaying it Using ROracle from Oracle R

```
library(ROracle)
drvr <- dbDriver("Oracle")
```

```
conn <- dbConnect(drvr, username = "testr", password = "testr",
dbname="orcl")
dbListTables(conn)

# Selecting data based on code value CODE13 into R data.frame and displaying
it
select_resultset <- dbSendQuery(conn, "select * from testr.temp_tab where cd
= :1", data = data.frame(cd='CODE13'))
data1 <- fetch(select_resultset)
dim(data1)
data1
dbClearResult(select_resultset)
dbDisconnect(conn)
dbUnloadDriver(drvr)
```

Here's the output of running the code in Listing 3-3:

```
> library(ROracle)
> drvr <- dbDriver("Oracle")
> conn <- dbConnect(drvr, username = "testr", password = "testr",
dbname="pdborcl")
> dbListTables(conn)
[1] "TEMP_TAB"
> select_resultset <- dbSendQuery(conn, "select * from testr.temp_tab where
cd = :1", data = data.frame(cd='CD13'))
> data1 <- fetch(select_resultset)
> dim(data1)
[1] 1 4
> data1
    CD                    DESCR EFF_START_DATE EFF_END_DATE
1 CD13 Description for Code 13     2017-01-01   2017-12-31
> dbClearResult(select_resultset)
[1] TRUE
> dbDisconnect(conn)
[1] TRUE
> dbUnloadDriver(drvr)
[1] TRUE
>
```

Oracle R Advanced Analytics for Hadoop

Oracle R Advanced Analytics for Hadoop (ORAAH) is a component of the Oracle Big Data Connectors software suite. The latest version of ORAAH is 2.7.0. It integrates Hadoop and Apache Hive inside a Hadoop cluster with Oracle Database (with the Advanced Analytics option) and R (via an R interface that includes the R engine and open source R packages). Working on data in the Hadoop Distributed File System (HDFS) can be done using

Hive-based Hibernate Query Languuage (HQL) and also via HDFS data mappings as direct input to machine-learning routines. The latter can then be executed as MapReduce jobs that call custom R mappers and/or reducers, or by using Apache Spark. Hive-based HQL enables data preparation, joins, and view creation. Source data can be in the form of an HDFS comma-separated values (CSV) data set or Hive tables, or an HDFS CSV data set cached into Apache Spark as a resilient distributed dataset (RDD). ORAAH Spark-based algorithms perform better compared to Spark MLlib-based algorithms, as also is the case with ORAAH Spark-based algorithms vs. corresponding MapReduce algorithms.

Table 3-2 shows the primary algorithms in a Hadoop cluster that are supported by the latest release of ORAAH. These algorithms are for machine and statistical learning and enable parallized and distributed execution. In addition, the GLM and LM algorithms have the ability to work on big data and scale across the enterprise and are faster than corresponding Apache Spark's MLlib models.

Table 3-2. *Primary Machine-Learning Algorithms Supported by ORAAH*

Algorithm Name	Description
Linear regression	For regression—both Spark and MapReduce based
Logistic regression LM	For classification, based on Apache Spark MLlib
Mult-layer perception feed-forward neural networks (MLP NN) with Spark caching enabled	For regression, based on Apache Spark MLlib and MapReduce
Generalized linear models (GLM) with Spark caching enabled	For classification, based on MapReduce and Spark as of v 2.7.0
Principal component analysis (PCA)	For attribute importance, based on Spark and MapReduce
k-means	For clustering, based on Spark and MapReduce
Non-negative matrix factorization (NMF) Low-rank matrix factorization (LMF)	For feature extraction, based on MapReduce For feature extraction, based on MapReduce
Gaussion mixture model	*New in version 2.7.0,* based on Apache Spark MLlib
Correlation and covariance matrix computations	For statistical computation and learning, based on MapReduce
Least absolute shrinkage and selection operator (LASSO)	Based on Spark
Decision trees	Based on Spark
Random forest	Based on Spark
Support vector machines	Based on Spark

■ **Note** Further information about ORAAH, including the various alogrithms supported and benchmarking, can be found at Oracle's web site: `www.oracle.com/technetwork/database/database-technologies/bdc/r-advanalytics-for-hadoop/overview/index.html`.

Examples of real-world use cases implementing some of these alogrithms using Hive and ORAAH can be found at `https://blogs.oracle.com/R/entry/oracle_r_advanced_analytics_for`.

Oracle R Enterprise

Oracle R Enterprise (ORE) is by far the most important of the Oracle R technologies and comes with the Oracle Advanced Analytics option of Oracle Database. ORE boosts and extends open source R execution by leveraging Oracle in-database computing on stored data directly, thereby resulting in reduced latency, high-performance computing, multithreaded parallel execution of data and tasks, scalability, and reduced or minimal memory usage.

From an architectural standpoint, ORE consists of the following:

- Database server machine with Oracle DB installed that has libraries and PL/SQL programs to support the ORE client
- R engine installed on Oracle DB that supports embedded R execution and executes in-database statistics and machine-learning functions. Each DB R engine ORE server and ORE client packages. The Oracle DB spawns multiple R engines for data parallelism. The in-DB R engine has a native Oracle DB feature-set that is capable of tight SQL integration and DBMS package-based functionality
- Oracle R Distribution
- R Oracle for database connectivity
- Client R engine with client ORE packages, open source R (or Oracle R Distribution) and ROracle
- Database R script repository that stores R scripts inside Oracle Database that can be called by name directly from SQL
- Database R datastore that stores R objects inside Oracle DB

Figure 3-1 gives an overview of the ORE architecture.

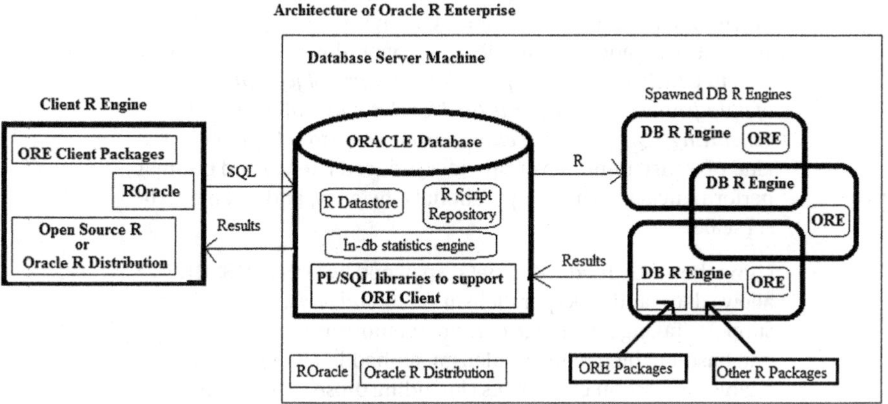

Figure 3-1. *An overview of Oracle R enterprise architecture*

From an enhancement perspective, ORE extends open source R in the following manner:

- ORE transparency layer
- Embedded R execution (via the embedded R engine)—both R interface and SQL interface
- Predictive analytics

As of this writing, the latest version of Oracle R Enterprise is 1.5.0.

Note Additional information about ORE, including enhancements in ORE 1.5.0, can be found at `www.oracle.com/technetwork/database/database-technologies/r/r-enterprise/overview/index.html`.

From an enterprise standpoint, ORE has the following characteristics:

- ORE provides the required optimization in terms of memory allocation and multithreaded execution without the hassle of supplemented packages, as it enables in-database execution of R scripts and models directly on data in Oracle DB. Large data-sets can be loaded into memory and run using function invocation without copies of the data being made, thereby eliminating R's call-by-value semantics. This is also true while executing open source R packages from the CRAN set.

- The in-database computation and analysis of data through R is done transparently. Basic R operations can be coded as R data. frames. The corresponding R functions are exposed as overloaded function definitions, and their execution is pushed to Oracle DB. The statistical and machine-learning operations are executed on data in Oracle tables. *ORE provides ore.frame objects (a subclass of data.frame) that get substituted for database tables, thereby generating SQL, for in-DB execution on data stored in Oracle.* This kind of transparency layer provides reduced latency and optimal performance in terms of operational efficiency, and at a big-data set scale.
- Using the embedded R engine(s) spawned by Oracle DB, ORE allows data- and task- parallelism via its *embedded R execution* support. Taking advantage of more memory availability and database-enabled data parallelism, embedded R execution enables execution of R scripts (including those that are based on open source CRAN packages) embedded in SQL and PL/SQL routines. This type of processing is called *lights-out processing.* The R scripts can be stored in the database R script repository and invoked by name in calling SQL statements. This can be done dynamically too. Embedded R execution is exposed through both R and SQL APIs. The output of such execution can be structuredd data, XML representations of R objects and graphics, or PNG graphics via BLOB columns in Oracle table(s). The latter allows seamless integration with other applications such as OBIEE RPDs and dashboards by passing results from R for business intelligence and advanced analytics. Table 3-3 lists these APIs (both R interface and SQL interface) for ORE v1.5.0.
- ORE also allows interfacing with in-DB predictive analytics algorithms through R. Examples include OREeda (exploratory data analysis), OREdm (data mining) and OREpredict. OREeda can implement linear models, stepwise regression, generalized linear models, neural networks, and random forest algorithms as well as base SAS equivalent functionality.

Table 3-3. *ORE Embedded Execution API (for R Interface and SQL Interface)*

API R Interface	API SQL Interface	Description
`ore.doEval`	`rqEval`	Executes function `f` without input data argument.
`ore.tableApply`	`rqTableApply`	Executes function `f` with `ore.frame` input data argument provided via first parameter to `f` (as `data.frame`).
`ore.groupApply`	`rqGroupApply`	Executes function `f` by partitioning data as per values in an index column. Each data partition is provided as a `data.frame` argument to the first parameter of `f`. Parallel execution of each call of `f` is enabled.
`ore.rowApply`	`rqRowEval`	Executes function `f` by passing a chunk of rows of the provided input data. Each input chunk of data is passed as a `data.frame` to the first parameter of `f`. Parallel execution of each call of `f` is enabled.
`ore.indexApply`	N/A	Executes function `f` without input data argument but with an index of the execution calls 1 through n, where n is the number of function calls. Parallel execution of each call of `f` is enabled.
`ore.scriptCreate`	`sys.rqScriptCreate`	Stores the R script into the ORE R script repository with the given name and the associated function.
`ore.scriptDrop`	`sys.rqScriptDrop`	Drops the R script from the ORE R script respository with the given name.
`ore.scriptLoad`		Loads the R script with the given name from the ORE R script repository for subsequent execution of the function associated with the R script.

In the Description column, the function f refers to the R function associated with each API.

OREeda consists of database-enabled ORE versions of R models for linear and stepwise regression, generalized linear models, neural networks, and random forest classification in parallel. It exposes these via the functions: `ore.lm()` for linear regression and least squares regression, `ore.stepwise()` for stepwise least squares regression, `ore.glm` for generalized linear models and logistic regression, `ore.neural()` for neural network models for pattern recognition, and `ore.randomForest()` for classification, respectively. All of these work on data in an `ore.frame` and can be used to create R models based on data in Oracle DB.

OREdm has Oracle Data Mining algorithms equivalent to implementing classification, regression, clustering, attribute importance, association rules, feature extraction, and anomaly detection. These algorithms be used to build models with data in Oracle tables. Here's a list of the alorithms:

- Classification
    - Decision tree
    - GLM classification—binary logistic regression
    - Naïve Bayes
    - Support vector machine
    - Random forest—new in ORE V1.5.0
- Regression
    - GLM regression (linear regression and ridge regression)
    - Support vector machine
- Clustering
    - k-means (a distance-based clustering algorithm)
    - Orthogonal partitioning cluster, or O-Cluster (`ore.odmOC`)
- Attribute importance (minimum descriptor length—`ore.odmAI`)
- Association rules
    - Apriori (`ore.odmAssocRules`)
- Feature extraction
    - Non-negative matrix factorization (`ore.odmNMF`)
    - Principal component analysis—new in V1.5.0
    - Singular value decomposition—new in V1.5.0
- Anamoly detection
    - Support vector machine

OREpredict gives the ability to use select R models to score in-DB data in an `ore.frame` object. Normally, data to score using R models must be in R `data.frame`. ORE allows for these native R models to be transparently translated into SQL during scoring operation. Examples are in-DB SQL and R predictive models for behaviorial analytics. OREpredict has the following algorithms:

- Linear model
- Generalized linear model
- Negative binomial generalized linear model
- Multinomial log linear model
- k-means clustering
- Hierarchical clustering
- Neural network
- Recursive partitioning and regression tree

ORE provides the backup, recovery, and security of the data needed to be analyzed at the enterprise level.

ORE inherently takes care of the semantic data mappings from Oracle tables into R data.frames, and vice versa, that would otherwise have been needed for direct database access using RODBC, RJDBC, and ROracle packages or during analytical model creation involving R.

Table 3-4 lists the primary Oracle R Enterprise packages

Table 3-4. *Primary ORE Packages*

Package	Functionality
DBI	Supplemental packages for database interface for R
ORE	Oracle R Enterprise
OREbase	Functionality related to R's base package
OREgraphics	Functionality related to R's graphics package
OREstats	Functionality related to R's statistics package
OREeda	Package for exploratory data analysis
OREdm	Package for data mining (Oracle Data Mining)
OREpredict	Package for scoring data in Oracle database using R model predictions
ORExml	Functionality for XML generation within R
bitops	Functions for bitwise operations
png	Supplemental package for read/write PNG images from/to R and Oracle DB
OBIEEAdvanced Analytics	Advanced analytics and machine learning R functions supported in ORE for integration with OBIEE

OBIEE integration with R graphics also includes parameter controls that can be used to customize graphs such as graph plots and charts.

Using ORE for Machine Learning and Business Intelligence with OBIEE: Start-to-Finish Pragmatics

This section details the end-to-end pragmatics of using a machine-learning algorithm with ORE and the subsequent incorporation of its output for business intelligence via OBIEE dashboards. We will first show an example of an R program that uses the `randomForest()` algorithm to predict the origin of wine. Next, we'll show an example of how this program can be modified to exhibit embedded R execution in Oracle DB using the ORE R interface. Then we'll demonstrate an example of using the same program to exhibit embedded R execution using the SQL interface. This example explains how to obtain output from ORE including a structured table, XML, and a graph (PNG). Finally, we'll detail how the output from ORE execution can be integrated within OBIEE dashboards for predictive analytics.

Using the ORD randomForest Algorithm to Predict Wine Origin

This is done using the random forest R model, which is an extension of the decision tree model.

■ **Note** A good explanation of decision trees and random forests can be found at `https://medium.com/towards-data-science/decision-trees-and-random-forests-df0c3123f991` and `https://medium.com/towards-data-science/decision-trees-and-random-forests-for-classification-and-regression-pt-1-dbb65a458df`. A comparative use of decision trees and random forests can be found at `http://whrc.org/wp-content/uploads/2016/02/DecisionTrees_RandomForest_v2.pdf`.

Listing 3-4 gives example code for this. It builds the R model and subsequently tests the built model on test data to predict the origins of wines depending on the `Wine` class. It outputs a table of the predicted results as well as PNG graph that displays the predicted wine origin output vis-à-vis the output table. The source data for this consists of modifying the Wine data set obtained at `https://archive.ics.uci.edu/ml/machine-learning-databases/wine/wine.data`. Also, the article at `https://datascienceplus.com/predicting-wine-quality-using-random-forests/` was referred to as a sample example for this.

Listing 3-4. Using R randomForest Model to Predict Wine Origin (R code along with its output)

```
> library(randomForest)
randomForest 4.6-12
Type rfNews() to see new features/changes/bug fixes.
Warning message:
package 'randomForest' was built under R version 3.2.5
> winedata <- read.csv("winedata.csv", header=TRUE, sep=',') # The file
# winedata.csv is present in the working directory from where the R
# interface was invoked
> head(winedata)
  class Alcohol Malic.acid  Ash Alcanility.of.ash Magnesium Total.phenols
  Flavanoids
1     1   14.23       1.71 2.43              15.6       127          2.80       3.06
2     1   13.20       1.78 2.14              11.2       100          2.65       2.76
3     1   13.16       2.36 2.67              18.6       101          2.80       3.24
4     1   14.37       1.95 2.50              16.8       113          3.85       3.49
5     1   13.24       2.59 2.87              21.0       118          2.80       2.69
6     1   14.20       1.76 2.45              15.2       112          3.27       3.39
  Nonflavanoid.phenols Proanthocyanins Color.intensity  Hue OD280.OD315.
  of.diluted.wines
1                 0.28            2.29            5.64 1.04                 3.92
2                 0.26            1.28            4.38 1.05                 3.40
3                 0.30            2.81            5.68 1.03                 3.17
4                 0.24            2.18            7.80 0.86                 3.45
5                 0.39            1.82            4.32 1.04                 2.93
6                 0.34            1.97            6.75 1.05                 2.85
  Proline
1    1065
2    1050
3    1185
4    1480
5     735
6    1450
> winedata$origin <- ifelse(winedata$class == 1, 'Origin1',
+                    ifelse(winedata$class == 2, 'Origin2',
+                    ifelse(winedata$class == 3, 'Origin3', '')))
> winedata$origin <- as.factor(winedata$origin)
> head(winedata$origin)
[1] Origin1 Origin1 Origin1 Origin1 Origin1 Origin1
Levels: Origin1 Origin2 Origin3
> table(winedata$origin)
```

```
Origin1 Origin2 Origin3
    489     549     336
> set.seed(123)
> sample_size <- 0.70 * nrow(winedata)
> sampledata <-sample(seq_len(nrow(winedata)), sample_size)
> training_data <- winedata[sampledata, ]
> test_data <- winedata[-sampledata, ]
> wine.rf <- randomForest(origin ~ . - class, data = training_data)
> wine.rf
Call:
 randomForest(formula = origin ~ . - class, data = training_data)
              Type of random forest: classification
                    Number of trees: 500
No. of variables tried at each split: 3

        OOB estimate of  error rate: 0%
Confusion matrix:
        Origin1 Origin2 Origin3 class.error
Origin1     349       0       0           0
Origin2       0     387       0           0
Origin3       0       0     225           0
> origin_pred <- predict(wine.rf, newdata = test_data)
> table(origin_pred, test_data$origin)

origin_pred Origin1 Origin2 Origin3
    Origin1     140       0       0
    Origin2       0     162       0
    Origin3       0       0     111
> pairs(table(origin_pred, test_data$origin), main="Wine Origin Predictors")
>
```

Figure 3-2 shows the graph from Listing 3-4.

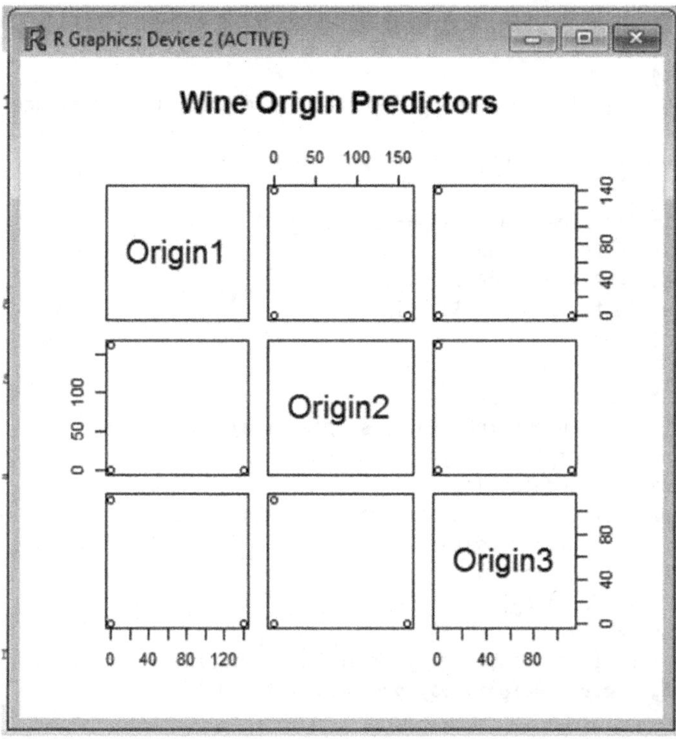

Figure 3-2. PNG graph output of the pairs plot on the Wine Origin Predictors table data

Using Embedded R Execution in Oracle DB and the ORE R Interface to Predict Wine Origin

In this section, we'll modify Listing 3-4 to use the ORE embedded R execution function for the R interface. It uses the `ore.doEval()` function for the same functionality. The modified code is given in Listing 3-5 and the corresponding PNG graph is shown in Figure 3-3. As you can see, both the outputs of using `ore.doEval()` and the original R program are the same. The difference is that the `ore.doEval()` ORE function is executed in-database and the results passed to the R terminal on the user's console.

Listing 3-5. Using ORE to Build and Test a randomForest() Model

```
library(ORE)
ore.connect(user="testr", sid="orcl", host="localhost", password="testr")
ore.doEval(function () {
library(randomForest)
# The file winedata.csv is in the working directory from where ORE interface
# was invoked
winedata <- read.csv("winedata.csv", header=TRUE, sep=',')
head(winedata)
winedata$origin <- ifelse(winedata$class == 1, 'Origin1',
ifelse(winedata$class == 2, 'Origin2',
ifelse(winedata$class == 3, 'Origin3', '')))
winedata$origin <- as.factor(winedata$origin)
head(winedata$origin)
set.seed(123)
sample_size <- 0.70 * nrow(winedata)
sampledata <-sample(seq_len(nrow(winedata)), sample_size)
training_data <- winedata[sampledata, ]
test_data <- winedata[-sampledata, ]
wine.rf <- randomForest(origin ~ . - class, data = training_data)
origin_pred <- predict(wine.rf, newdata = test_data)
table(origin_pred, test_data$origin)
library(AppliedPredictiveModeling)
transparentTheme(trans = .4)
pairs(table(origin_pred, test_data$origin), main="Wine Origin Predictors")
}, ore.graphics=TRUE, ore.png.height=600, ore.png.width=500)
```

Here are the steps to follow:

1. Open an Rterminal using ORE.
2. Connect to the database. This step is needed to use ORE, even if no DB-related functions are used.
3. Load the ORE library.
4. Code an `ore.doEVal` function that does the following:
    a. Loads the library randomForest.
    b. Retrieves the wine data set from source CSV file into the data.frame named `winedata`.
    c. Displays the first few rows to verify that the data frame consists of the loaded data.
    d. Creates a wine origin classifier variable, `winedata$origin`, based on the first column class in the `winedata` data set.

e. Splits the data in `winedata` into a training data set and test data set. Approximately 70% of data gets sampled as training data, and the remaining as test data.

f. Applies the `randomForest()` model on the training data set, resulting in a wine predictor class called `wine.rf`. The model output shows three predictors at each split, namely, Origin1, Origin2, and Origin3. The output also shows a table of the prediction vs. actual values.

g. Displays the Test the model by using `predict()` on the test data, and displays the output of the prediction as a table based on the predict output and `test_data$origin` classifier variable

h. Plots a pairs graph by using the the predictor table as the input data. The PNG graph is displayed in a separate graph display window.

Here's the output of the code in Listing 3-5:

```
> library(ORE)
Loading required package: OREbase
Loading required package: OREcommon

Attaching package: 'OREbase'

The following objects are masked from 'package:base':

    cbind, data.frame, eval, interaction, order, paste, pmax, pmin,
    rbind, table

Loading required package: OREembed
Loading required package: OREstats
Loading required package: MASS
Loading required package: OREgraphics
Loading required package: OREeda
Loading required package: OREmodels
Loading required package: OREdm
Loading required package: lattice
Loading required package: OREpredict
Loading required package: OREXml
> ore.connect(user="testr", sid="orcl", host="localhost", password="testr")
> ore.doEval(function () {
+ library(randomForest)
+ winedata <- read.csv("winedata.csv", header=TRUE, sep=',')
+ head(winedata)
+ winedata$origin <- ifelse(winedata$class == 1, 'Origin1',
+ ifelse(winedata$class == 2, 'Origin2',
```

```
+ ifelse(winedata$class == 3, 'Origin3', '')))
+ winedata$origin <- as.factor(winedata$origin)
+ head(winedata$origin)
+ set.seed(123)
+ sample_size <- 0.70 * nrow(winedata)
+ sampledata <-sample(seq_len(nrow(winedata)), sample_size)
+ training_data <- winedata[sampledata, ]
+ test_data <- winedata[-sampledata, ]
+ wine.rf <- randomForest(origin ~ . - class, data = training_data)
+ origin_pred <- predict(wine.rf, newdata = test_data)
+ table(origin_pred, test_data$origin)
+ library(AppliedPredictiveModeling)
+ transparentTheme(trans = .4)
+ pairs(table(origin_pred, test_data$origin), main="Wine Origin Predictors")
+ }, ore.graphics=TRUE, ore.png.height=600, ore.png.width=500)

origin_pred Origin1 Origin2 Origin3
    Origin1     140       0       0
    Origin2       0     162       0
    Origin3       0       0     111
>
```

Figure 3-3 shows the corresponding PNG graph.

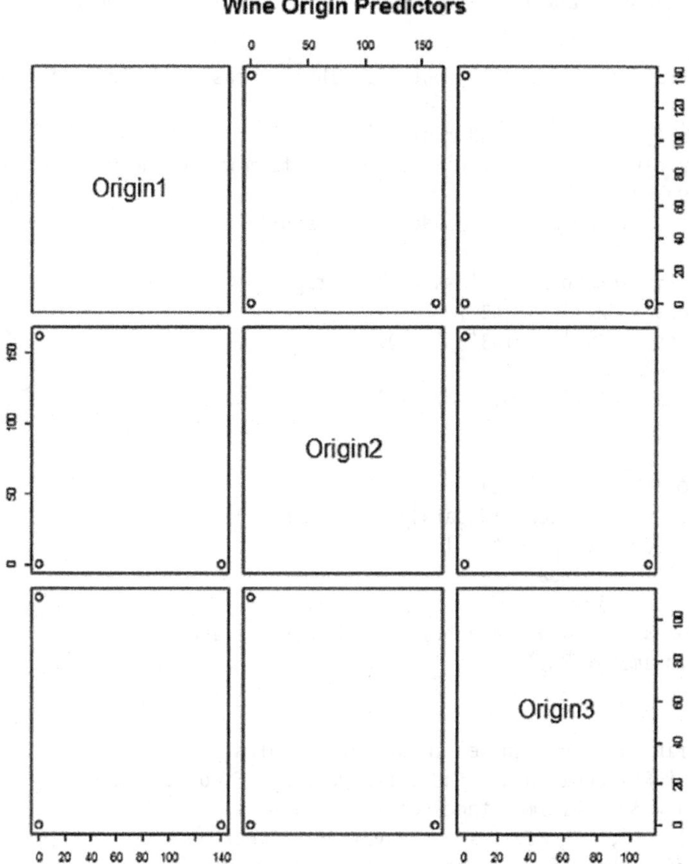

Figure 3-3. *PNG graph output of the pairs plot on the Wine Origin Predictors table data*

Listing 3-6 shows a detailed version of building a random forest model by using ORE. It depicts details such as printing the RF model to see important features after building it using the `print()` R function, plotting the RF model to see the corresponding RF model graph using the `plot()` function, printing the importance output of the model after building it using the `importance()` function, and plotting the importance variables after building it using `varIMpPLot()` function. Also, the margin of error for accuracy is plotted using the output of the `margin()` function with the model and origin classifier obtained from scoring the RF model on `test_data` as arguments to it. These outptuts, along with the original table and pairs plot output, are shown immediately after Listing 3-6.

Listing 3-6. Using ORE to Build and Test a randomForest() Model— Detailed Version

```
library(ORE)
ore.connect(user="testr", sid="orcl", host="localhost", password="testr")
ore.is.connected()
ore.doEval(function () { library(randomForest)
# The file winedata.csv is in the working directory from where the ORE
# interface was invoked
winedata <- read.csv("winedata.csv", header=TRUE, sep=',')
head(winedata)
winedata$origin <- ifelse(winedata$class == 1, 'Origin1',
ifelse(winedata$class == 2, 'Origin2',
ifelse(winedata$class == 3, 'Origin3', '')))
class(winedata$origin)
winedata$origin <- as.factor(winedata$origin)
head(winedata$origin)
set.seed(123)
sample_size <- 0.70 * nrow(winedata)
sampledata <-sample(seq_len(nrow(winedata)), sample_size)
training_data <- winedata[sampledata, ]
test_data <- winedata[-sampledata, ]
formula <- origin ~ . - class
wine.rf <- randomForest(formula, data=training_data,ntree=100,
importance=TRUE, proximity=TRUE)
head(wine.rf)
class(wine.rf)
print(wine.rf) # Print RF model to see important features
plot(wine.rf) # Plot RF Model to see the corresponding RF model graph
importance(wine.rf) # See the importance of the variables
varImpPlot(wine.rf) # Plot RF Model see the variable Importance
origin_pred <- predict(wine.rf, newdata = test_data)
head(origin_pred)
table(origin_pred, test_data$origin)
plot(margin(wine.rf, test_data$origin)) # Plot margin of error for accuracy
library(AppliedPredictiveModeling)
transparentTheme(trans = .4)
pairs(table(origin_pred, test_data$origin), main="Wine Origin Predictors")
}, ore.graphics=TRUE, ore.png.height=600, ore.png.width=500)
```

The two primary outputs of the code in Listing 3-6 are `print(wine.rf)` and `importance(wine.rf)`, shown here:

```
> print(wine.rf)

Call:
 randomForest(formula = formula, data = training_data, ntree =
100,      importance = TRUE, proximity = TRUE)
```

```
               Type of random forest: classification
                     Number of trees: 100
No. of variables tried at each split: 3

        OOB estimate of  error rate: 0%
Confusion matrix:
        Origin1 Origin2 Origin3 class.error
Origin1     349       0       0           0
Origin2       0     387       0           0
Origin3       0       0     225           0
> plot(wine.rf)
> importance(wine.rf) # See the importance of the variables
                            Origin1   Origin2   Origin3         MeanDecrease
                                                                    Accuracy
Alcohol                     11.105535 9.526838  7.123277          12.129635
Malic.acid                  4.839083  6.448424  4.905585           6.960896
Ash                         4.326631  6.724472  5.399456           7.243023
Alcanility.of.ash           4.527594  6.332050  4.863168           6.958164
Magnesium                   6.467083  6.776471  4.327440           7.301142
Total.phenols               6.739080  6.357134  6.025438           7.877900
Flavanoids                  8.465542  8.610455 11.318216          12.551384
Nonflavanoid.phenols        2.866508  4.082630  3.718137           4.484671
Proanthocyanins             2.909023  5.907274  5.583297           7.075015
Color.intensity             12.855845 12.054849 12.554351         17.634433
Hue                         5.896908  7.500771  8.471345           9.225476
OD280.OD315.of.diluted.wines 6.017725  7.304052 8.207104           9.652773
Proline                     12.374653 8.791325  6.200598          13.307739
                             MeanDecreaseGini
Alcohol                             80.459884
Malic.acid                          15.259082
Ash                                  8.053578
Alcanility.of.ash                   14.141569
Magnesium                           19.983451
Total.phenols                       42.076450
Flavanoids                          96.234232
Nonflavanoid.phenols                 6.998323
Proanthocyanins                     14.879801
Color.intensity                    109.622069
Hue                                 50.237897
OD280.OD315.of.diluted.wines        52.182508
Proline                            114.973278
```

Next is the output of running the code in Listing 3-6, followed by the four graphs produced from in Figures 3-4 to 3-7.

```
> library(ORE)
Loading required package: OREbase
Loading required package: OREcommon

Attaching package: 'OREbase'

The following objects are masked from 'package:base':

    cbind, data.frame, eval, interaction, order, paste, pmax, pmin,
    rbind, table

Loading required package: OREembed
Loading required package: OREstats
Loading required package: MASS
Loading required package: OREgraphics
Loading required package: OREeda
Loading required package: OREmodels
Loading required package: OREdm
Loading required package: lattice
Loading required package: OREpredict
Loading required package: OREXml
> ore.connect(user="testr", sid="orcl", host="localhost", password="testr")
> ore.doEval(function () {
+ library(randomForest)
+ winedata <- read.csv("winedata.csv", header=TRUE, sep=',')
+ head(winedata)
+ winedata$origin <- ifelse(winedata$class == 1, 'Origin1',
+ ifelse(winedata$class == 2, 'Origin2',
+ ifelse(winedata$class == 3, 'Origin3', '')))
+ class(winedata$origin)
+ winedata$origin <- as.factor(winedata$origin)
+ head(winedata$origin)
+ set.seed(123)
+ sample_size <- 0.70 * nrow(winedata)
+ sampledata <-sample(seq_len(nrow(winedata)), sample_size)
+ training_data <- winedata[sampledata, ]
+ test_data <- winedata[-sampledata, ]
+ formula <- origin ~ . - class
+ wine.rf <- randomForest(formula, data=training_data,ntree=100,
importance=TR$
+ print(wine.rf)
+ plot(wine.rf)
+ importance(wine.rf)
```

```
+ varImpPlot(wine.rf)
+ origin_pred <- predict(wine.rf, newdata = test_data)
+ table(origin_pred, test_data$origin)
+ plot(margin(wine.rf, test_data$origin)) # PLot margin of error for
accuracy
+ library(AppliedPredictiveModeling)
+ transparentTheme(trans = .4)
+ pairs(table(origin_pred, test_data$origin), main="Wine Origin Predictors")
+ }, ore.graphics=TRUE, ore.png.height=600, ore.png.width=500)
NULL
>
```

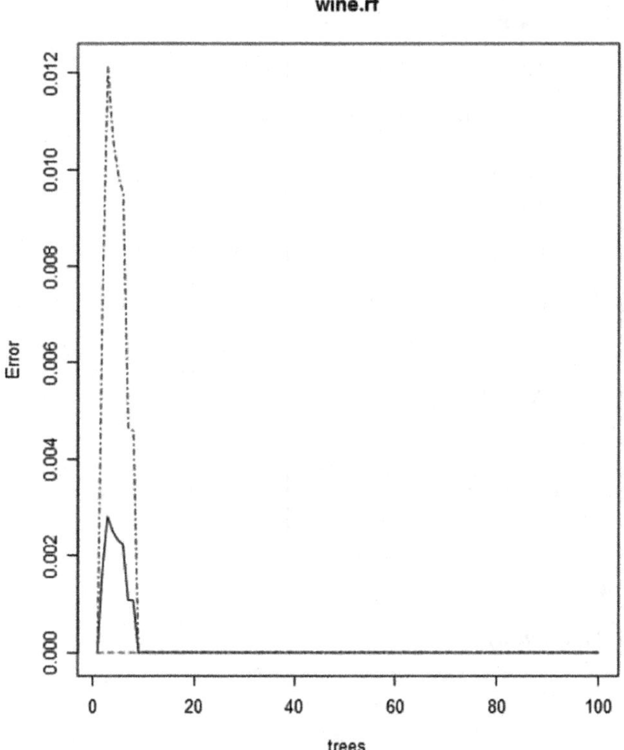

Figure 3-4. *Output of plot(wine.rf)*

Note that the number of trees on the x-ais extend up to 100, as defined by the `ntree` parameter value in the call to the `randomForest` model in Listing 3-6.

In regards to the the importance outputs from the `ranDomForest` model, these are `MeanDecreaseAccuracy` and `MeanDecreaseGini`. These appear on the x-axis of Figure 3-5.

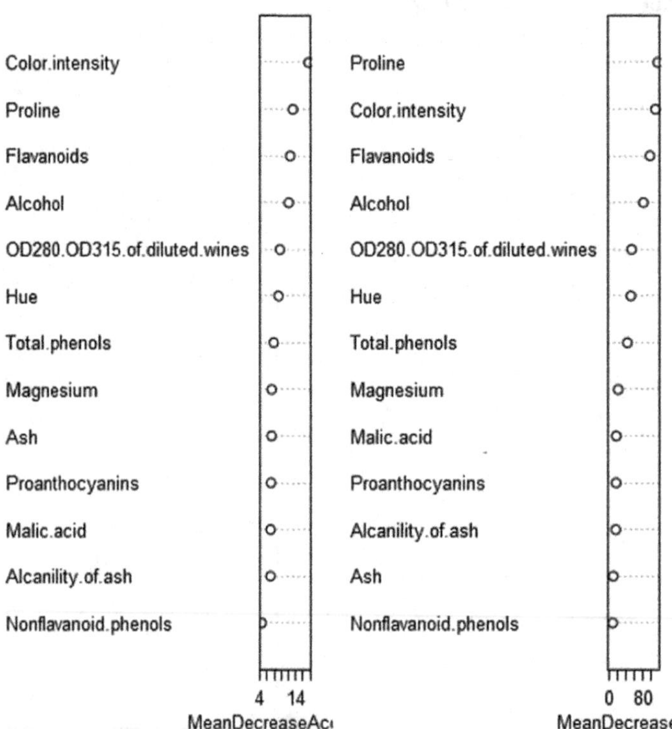

Figure 3-5. *Output of varImpPlot(wine.rf)*

The importance variables shown in Figure 3-6 are `MeanDecreaseAccuracy` and `MeanDecreaseGini`, respectively.

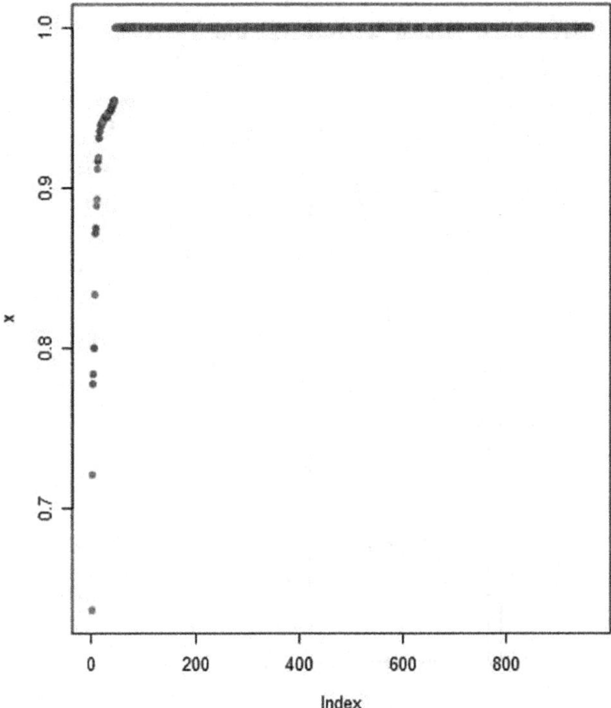

Figure 3-6. *Output of plot(margin(wine.rf, test_data$origin))*

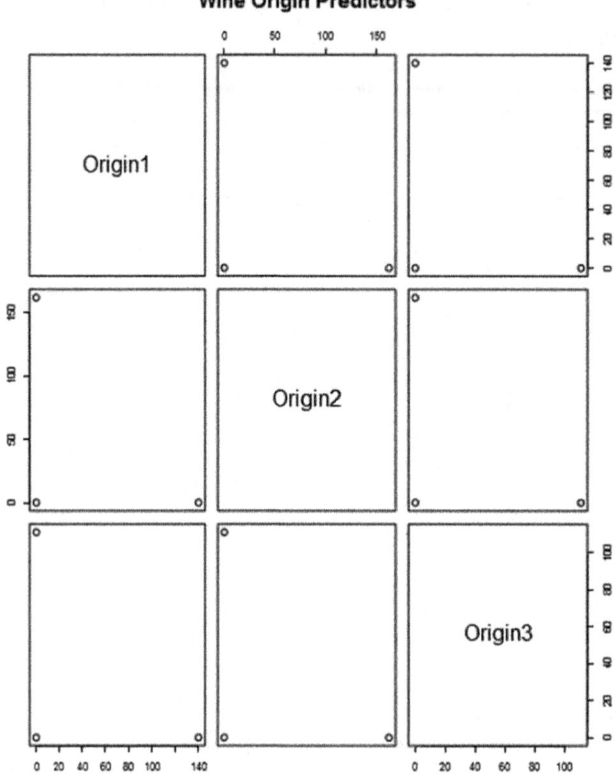

Figure 3-7. *Output of pairs(table(origin_pred, test_data$origin), main="Wine Origin Predictors")*

Using ore.randomForest Instead of R's randomForest Model

This subsection demonstrates how ORE's `ore.randomForest` function can be used to build and score the random forest model for predicting wine origin. We've modified the code in Listing 3-4 to use `ore.randomForest`; Listing 3-7 provides the modified code, and its execution output is shown in the code that follows the listing.

Listing 3-7. Use of ore.randomForest to Predict Wine Origin

```
library(ORE)
ore.connect("testr","orcl","localhost","testr")
library(OREmodels)
# The file winedata.csv is in the working directory frm which ORE interface
# was invoked
winedata <- read.csv("winedata.csv", header=TRUE, sep=',')
```

```
head(winedata)
winedata$origin <- ifelse(winedata$class == 1, 'Origin1',
ifelse(winedata$class == 2, 'Origin2',
ifelse(winedata$class == 3, 'Origin3', '')))
class(winedata$origin)
winedata$origin <- as.factor(winedata$origin)
class(winedata$origin)
head(winedata$origin)
table(winedata$origin)
set.seed(123)
sample_size <- 0.70 * nrow(winedata)
sampledata <-sample(seq_len(nrow(winedata)), sample_size)
training_data <- winedata[sampledata, ]
class(training_data)
TRAINING_DATA <- ore.push(training_data)
class(TRAINING_DATA)
test_data <- winedata[-sampledata, ]
TEST_DATA <- ore.push(test_data)
class(TEST_DATA)
head(TRAINING_DATA)
head(TEST_DATA)
wine.rf <- ore.randomForest(origin ~ . - class, TRAINING_DATA)
class(wine.rf)
tree15 = grabTree(wine.rf, k = 15, labelVar = TRUE)
origin_pred <- predict(wine.rf, TEST_DATA, type = "all", supplemental.
cols="origin")
res <- table(origin_pred$origin, origin_pred$prediction)
library(AppliedPredictiveModeling)
transparentTheme(trans = .4)
pairs(table(origin_pred$origin, origin_pred$prediction), main="Wine Origin
Predictors")
res
```

Here's the output of executing the code in Listing 3-7:

```
> library(ORE)
Loading required package: OREbase
Loading required package: OREcommon

Attaching package: 'OREbase'

The following objects are masked from 'package:base':

    cbind, data.frame, eval, interaction, order, paste, pmax, pmin,
    rbind, table
```

```
Loading required package: OREembed
Loading required package: OREstats
Loading required package: MASS
Loading required package: OREgraphics
Loading required package: OREeda
Loading required package: OREmodels
Loading required package: OREdm
Loading required package: lattice
Loading required package: OREpredict
Loading required package: ORExml
> ore.connect("testr","orcl","localhost","testr")
> library(OREmodels)
> winedata <- read.csv("winedata.csv", header=TRUE, sep=',')
> head(winedata)
  class Alcohol Malic.acid  Ash Alcanility.of.ash Magnesium Total.phenols
1     1   14.23       1.71 2.43              15.6       127          2.80
2     1   13.20       1.78 2.14              11.2       100          2.65
3     1   13.16       2.36 2.67              18.6       101          2.80
4     1   14.37       1.95 2.50              16.8       113          3.85
5     1   13.24       2.59 2.87              21.0       118          2.80
6     1   14.20       1.76 2.45              15.2       112          3.27
  Flavanoids Nonflavanoid.phenols Proanthocyanins Color.intensity  Hue
1       3.06                 0.28            2.29            5.64 1.04
2       2.76                 0.26            1.28            4.38 1.05
3       3.24                 0.30            2.81            5.68 1.03
4       3.49                 0.24            2.18            7.80 0.86
5       2.69                 0.39            1.82            4.32 1.04
6       3.39                 0.34            1.97            6.75 1.05
  OD280.OD315.of.diluted.wines Proline
1                         3.92    1065
2                         3.40    1050
3                         3.17    1185
4                         3.45    1480
5                         2.93     735
6                         2.85    1450
> winedata$origin <- ifelse(winedata$class == 1, 'Origin1',
+ ifelse(winedata$class == 2, 'Origin2',
+ ifelse(winedata$class == 3, 'Origin3', '')))
> class(winedata$origin)
[1] "character"
> winedata$origin <- as.factor(winedata$origin)
> class(winedata$origin)
[1] "factor"
> head(winedata$origin)
[1] Origin1 Origin1 Origin1 Origin1 Origin1 Origin1
Levels: Origin1 Origin2 Origin3
> table(winedata$origin)
```

```
Origin1 Origin2 Origin3
    489     549     336
> set.seed(123)
> sample_size <- 0.70 * nrow(winedata)
> sampledata <-sample(seq_len(nrow(winedata)), sample_size)
> training_data <- winedata[sampledata, ]
> class(training_data)
[1] "data.frame"
> TRAINING_DATA <- ore.push(training_data)
> class(TRAINING_DATA)
[1] "ore.frame"
attr(,"package")
[1] "OREbase"
> test_data <- winedata[-sampledata, ]
> TEST_DATA <- ore.push(test_data)
> class(TEST_DATA)
[1] "ore.frame"
attr(,"package")
[1] "OREbase"
> head(TRAINING_DATA)
     class Alcohol Malic.acid  Ash Alcanility.of.ash Magnesium Total.phenols
396      3   12.60       2.46 2.20              18.5        94          1.62
1083     3   13.45       3.70 2.60              23.0       111          1.70
562      2   11.82       1.72 1.88              19.5        86          2.50
1211     2   11.82       1.47 1.99              20.8        86          1.98
1289     3   12.70       3.55 2.36              21.5       106          1.70
63       2   13.67       1.25 1.92              18.0        94          2.10
     Flavanoids Nonflavanoid.phenols Proanthocyanins Color.intensity  Hue
396        0.66                 0.63            0.94            7.10 0.73
1083       0.92                 0.43            1.46           10.68 0.85
562        1.64                 0.37            1.42            2.06 0.94
1211       1.60                 0.30            1.53            1.95 0.95
1289       1.20                 0.17            0.84            5.00 0.78
63         1.79                 0.32            0.73            3.80 1.23
     OD280.OD315.of.diluted.wines Proline  origin
396                          1.58     695 Origin3
1083                         1.56     695 Origin3
562                          2.44     415 Origin2
1211                         3.33     495 Origin2
1289                         1.29     600 Origin3
63                           2.46     630 Origin2
> head(TEST_DATA)
   class Alcohol Malic.acid  Ash Alcanility.of.ash Magnesium Total.phenols
4      1   14.37       1.95 2.50              16.8       113          3.85
6      1   14.20       1.76 2.45              15.2       112          3.27
8      1   14.06       2.15 2.61              17.6       121          2.60
20     1   13.64       3.10 2.56              15.2       116          2.70
21     1   14.06       1.63 2.28              16.0       126          3.00
24     1   12.85       1.60 2.52              17.8        95          2.48
```

```
   Flavanoids Nonflavanoid.phenols Proanthocyanins Color.intensity  Hue
4        3.49                 0.24            2.18            7.80 0.86
6        3.39                 0.34            1.97            6.75 1.05
8        2.51                 0.31            1.25            5.05 1.06
20       3.03                 0.17            1.66            5.10 0.96
21       3.17                 0.24            2.10            5.65 1.09
24       2.37                 0.26            1.46            3.93 1.09
   OD280.OD315.of.diluted.wines Proline  origin
4                          3.45    1480 Origin1
6                          2.85    1450 Origin1
8                          3.58    1295 Origin1
20                         3.36     845 Origin1
21                         3.71     780 Origin1
24                         3.63    1015 Origin1
> wine.rf <- ore.randomForest(origin ~ . - class, TRAINING_DATA)
> class(wine.rf)
[1] "ore.randomForest" "ore.model"
> tree15 = grabTree(wine.rf, k = 15, labelVar = TRUE)
> origin_pred <- predict(wine.rf, TEST_DATA, type = "all", supplemental.
cols="$
> res <- table(origin_pred$origin, origin_pred$prediction)
> library(AppliedPredictiveModeling)
Warning message:
package 'AppliedPredictiveModeling' was built under R version 3.2.5
> transparentTheme(trans = .4)
> pairs(table(origin_pred$origin, origin_pred$prediction), main="Wine Origin
P$
> res

          Origin1 Origin2 Origin3
  Origin1     140       0       0
  Origin2       0     162       0
  Origin3       0       0     111
>
```

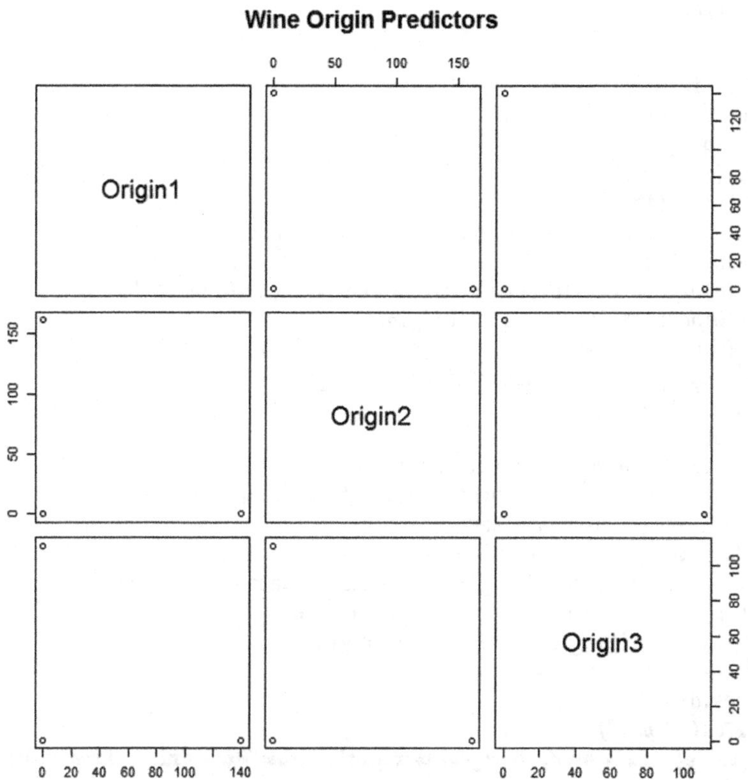

Figure 3-8. Output of pairs plot from Listing 3-7

Notice that the plot of `table(origin_pred$origin, origin_pred.$prediction)` is same as that of `table(origin_pred, test_data$origin)`.

Using Embedded R Execution in Oracle DB with the ORE SQL Interface to Predict Wine Origin

Listing 3-8 shows the SQL interface of the embeddded R execution equivalent of Listing 3-5 that stores the R code in an Oracle database repository script, which in turn is invoked by the following SQL `SELECT` statement. The output image from Listing 3-8 is the same as that obtained from executing the code in Listing 3-5. The R function code is encapsulated in a PL/SQL block and subsequently called from a SQL `SELECT` statement. The image is generated as a PNG file when lines 24 and 25 are executed. The PL/SQL block and the subsequent `SELECT` are saved as a SQL file named `rTestRF.sql`. The image `rTestRF.png` is created in the folder set as the working directory, as shown in line 6 of the code.

To execute the code in Listings 3-8 to 3-13, SQL*Plus can be used. Or a GUI-based interface such as Oracle SQL Developer can also be used. Open SQL*Plus, log in in using the specific username and password, cut and paste the code, and press Enter.

Listing 3-8. Using SQL Interface of Embedded R Execution to Build and Test a randomForest() Model

```
SQL> begin
sys.rqScriptDrop('rTestRF');
sys.rqScriptCreate('rTestRF',
' function () {
library(randomForest)
setwd("F:/testr/")
winedata <- read.csv("winedata.csv", header=TRUE, sep='','')
head(winedata)
winedata$origin <- ifelse(winedata$class == 1, ''Origin1'',
ifelse(winedata$class == 2, ''Origin2'',
ifelse(winedata$class == 3, ''Origin3'', '''')))
winedata$origin <- as.factor(winedata$origin)
head(winedata$origin)
set.seed(123)
sample_size <- 0.70 * nrow(winedata)
sampledata <-sample(seq_len(nrow(winedata)), sample_size)
training_data <- winedata[sampledata, ]
test_data <- winedata[-sampledata, ]
wine.rf <- randomForest(origin ~ . - class, data = training_data)
origin_pred <- predict(wine.rf, newdata = test_data)
res <- table(origin_pred, test_data$origin)
res.df <- as.matrix(res)
head(res.df)
png("rTestRF.png")
pairs(table(origin_pred, test_data$origin), main="Wine Origin Predictors")
dev.off()
res.df
}' );
end;
/
PL/SQL procedure successfully completed.
```

To verify that the script is stored in the Oracle Database R script repository, issue the query from the ORE DB user account, as shown in Listing 3-9.

Listing 3-9. SQL Query to Verify That the Script rTestRF is Created in Oracle RB

```
SQL> select * from user_rq_scripts where name = 'rTestRF';

NAME
--------------------------------------------------------------------------------
-----
SCRIPT
--------------------------------------------------------------------------------
-----
rTestRF
 function () {
library(randomForest)
setwd("F:/testr/")
winedata <- read.csv("winedata.csv", header=TRUE, sep=',')
head(winedata)
winedata$origin <- ifelse(winedata$class == 1, 'Origin1',
ifelse(winedata$class == 2, 'Origin2',
ifelse(winedata$class == 3, 'Origin3', '')))
winedata$origin <- as.factor(winedata$origin)
head(winedata$origin)
set.seed(123)
sample_size <- 0.70 * nrow(winedata)
sampledata <-sample(seq_len(nrow(winedata)), sample_size)
training_data <- winedata[sampledata, ]
test_data <- winedata[-sampledata, ]
wine.rf <- randomForest(origin ~ . - class, data = training_data)
origin_pred <- predict(wine.rf, newdata = test_data)
res <- table(origin_pred, test_data$origin)
res.df <- as.matrix(res)
head(res.df)
png("rTestRF.png")
pairs(table(origin_pred, test_data$origin), main="Wine Origin Predictors")
dev.off()
res.df
}
SQL>
```

Notice that the NAME column value is `rTestRF`, and the SCRIPT clob column shows the definition of the R function, as defined in Listing 3-8.

The preceding script can be invoked from SQL*Plus by using a SQL SELECT statement as follows:

```
select * from table (rqEval(NULL, 'XML', 'rTestRF'));
```

The first argument is NULL, as the function defined in the script does not take any input arguments. The second argument is XML, to specify that the output desired is an XML representation of the R function output, which in this case is an R table. The third argument is the actual R script name that is stored in the ORE database R script repository.

The output of running the preceding SQL statement is shown in Listing 3-10.

Listing 3-10. SQL Interface of Embedded R Execution Based Query Invocation of Script rTestRF Defined in Listing 3-8

```
SQL> set pages 1000
SQL> set long 200000
SQL> select * from table(rqEval(NULL, 'XML', 'rTestRF'));

NAME
--------------------------------------------------------------------------------
VALUE
--------------------------------------------------------------------------------

<root><table_obj><ROW-table_obj><origin_pred>Origin1</origin_pred>
<Var2>Origin1</Var2><Freq>140</Freq></ROW-table_obj>
<ROW-table_obj><origin_pred>Origin2</origin_pred><Var2>Origin1
</Var2><Freq>0</Freq></ROW-table_obj><ROW-table_obj>
<origin_pred>Origin3</origin_pred><Var2>Origin1</Var2><Freq>0
</Freq></ROW-table_obj><ROW-table_obj><origin_pred>Origin1
</origin_pred><Var2>Origin2</Var2><Freq>0</Freq></ROW-table_obj>
<ROW-table_obj><origin_pred>Origin2</origin_pred><Var2>Origin2
</V"ar2><Freq>162</Freq></ROW-table_obj><ROW-table_obj>
<origin_pred>Origin3</origin_pred><Var2>Origin2</Var2><Freq>0
</Freq></ROW-table_obj><ROW-table_obj><origin_pred>Origin1
</origin_pred><Var2>Origin3</Var2><Freq>0</Freq></ROW-table_obj>
<ROW-table_obj><origin_pred>Origin2</origin_pred><Var2>Origin3
</Var2><Freq>0</Freq></ROW-table_obj><ROW-table_obj><origin_pred>
Origin3</origin_pred><Var2>Origin3</Var2><Freq>111</Freq></ROW-table_obj>
</table_obj></root>

SQL>
```

■ **Note** As evident from the preceding XML output, the table representation of the R output from ORE is represented by three columns named `origin_pred`, `Var2`, and `Preq`. These are the column names and the column values. The column values are shown alongside each column name (as indicated in bold italics in the XML). The PNG graph is created in the working directory specified in line 6 of Listing 3-8. The image is generated by execution of lines 24 and 25 of Listing 3-8.

The R table output of Listing 3-8 using the R `View` call is shown in Figure 3-9. The R `View` call is invoked in the R console as follows:

```
View(res.df)
```

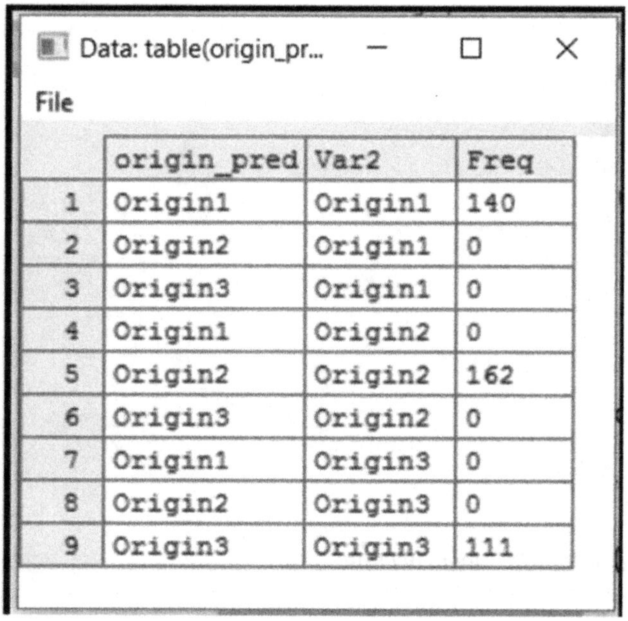

Data: table(origin_pr...

File

	origin_pred	Var2	Freq
1	Origin1	Origin1	140
2	Origin2	Origin1	0
3	Origin3	Origin1	0
4	Origin1	Origin2	0
5	Origin2	Origin2	162
6	Origin3	Origin2	0
7	Origin1	Origin3	0
8	Origin2	Origin3	0
9	Origin3	Origin3	111

***Figure 3-9.** R table output of Listing 3-8 using the `View` R function*

The corresponding XML output of the VALUE column in Listing 3-10 is shown in Figure 3-10.


```
<?xml version="1.0"?>
- <root>
  - <table_obj>
    - <ROW-table_obj>
        <origin_pred>Origin1</origin_pred>
        <Var2>Origin1</Var2>
        <Freq>140</Freq>
      </ROW-table_obj>
    - <ROW-table_obj>
        <origin_pred>Origin2</origin_pred>
        <Var2>Origin1</Var2>
        <Freq>0</Freq>
      </ROW-table_obj>
    - <ROW-table_obj>
        <origin_pred>Origin3</origin_pred>
        <Var2>Origin1</Var2>
        <Freq>0</Freq>
      </ROW-table_obj>
    - <ROW-table_obj>
        <origin_pred>Origin1</origin_pred>
        <Var2>Origin2</Var2>
        <Freq>0</Freq>
      </ROW-table_obj>
    - <ROW-table_obj>
        <origin_pred>Origin2</origin_pred>
        <Var2>Origin2</Var2>
        <Freq>162</Freq>
      </ROW-table_obj>
    - <ROW-table_obj>
        <origin_pred>Origin3</origin_pred>
        <Var2>Origin2</Var2>
        <Freq>0</Freq>
      </ROW-table_obj>
    - <ROW-table_obj>
        <origin_pred>Origin1</origin_pred>
        <Var2>Origin3</Var2>
        <Freq>0</Freq>
      </ROW-table_obj>
    - <ROW-table_obj>
        <origin_pred>Origin2</origin_pred>
        <Var2>Origin3</Var2>
        <Freq>0</Freq>
      </ROW-table_obj>
    - <ROW-table_obj>
        <origin_pred>Origin3</origin_pred>
        <Var2>Origin3</Var2>
        <Freq>111</Freq>
      </ROW-table_obj>
    </table_obj>
  </root>
```


This XML output shows the R output from ORE represented as three individual XML elements <orig_pred>, <Var2>, and <Freq> - children of the node <ROW-table_obj> and the corresponding values for these elements are shown in Bold enclosed by the individual elements tags. For example, the very first set of three individual element values are **Origin1, Origin1**, and **140** respectively. These are shown in the box in the XML output and reflect the actual values in Figure 3-5 for the columns origin_pred, Var2, and Freq.

Figure 3-10. *XML output of the VALUE column in Listing 3-10*

To get the preceding View call output by using SQL SELECT, the res.df output must be converted to a data.frame output. This can be done by adding the following line of code after line 27 in Listing 3-8:

```
res.df.output <- data.frame(res.df)
```

The query in Listing 3-10 can be modified as shown in Listing 3-11 to get a structured (relational) table output.

Listing 3-11. Listing 3-10 Modified to Generate Structured Table Output

```
SQL> select *
     from table(rqEval(
         NULL,
          'select CAST(''a'' as VARCHAR2(50)) "origin_pred",
          CAST(''b'' AS VARCHAR2(50)) "Var2", 1 as "Freq" from dual',
         'rTestRF'));

origin_pred
--------------------------------------------------
Var2                                                    Freq
-------------------------------------------------- ----------
Origin1
Origin1                                                  140

Origin2
Origin1                                                    0

Origin3
Origin1                                                    0

Origin1
Origin2                                                    0

Origin2
Origin2                                                  162

Origin3
Origin2                                                    0

Origin1
Origin3                                                    0

Origin2
Origin3                                                    0

Origin3
Origin3                                                  111


9 rows selected.
```

Instead of generating the image to a PNG file, as in Listing 3-8, the output can be captured in XML format. The difference lies in removing lines 24 and 26 from Listing 3-8 and modifying the SELECT query in Listing 3-10. Listings 3-12 and 3-13 illustrate this change and the corresponding execution output.

Listing 3-12. Listing 3-8 Modified to Capture Image Generated in XML Format

```
SQL> begin
     sys.rqScriptDrop('rTestRF_final1');
     sys.rqScriptCreate('rTestRF_final1',
     ' function () {
     library(randomForest)
     setwd("F:/testr/")
     winedata <- read.csv("winedata.csv", header=TRUE, sep='','')
     winedata$origin <- ifelse(winedata$class == 1, ''Origin1'',
    ifelse(winedata$class == 2, ''Origin2'',
    ifelse(winedata$class == 3, ''Origin3'', '''')))
    winedata$origin <- as.factor(winedata$origin)
    set.seed(123)
    sample_size <- 0.70 * nrow(winedata)
    sampledata <-sample(seq_len(nrow(winedata)), sample_size)
    training_data <- winedata[sampledata, ]
    test_data <- winedata[-sampledata, ]
    wine.rf <- randomForest(origin ~ . - class, data = training_data)
    origin_pred <- predict(wine.rf, newdata = test_data)
    res <- table(origin_pred, test_data$origin)
    pairs(table(origin_pred, test_data$origin), main="Wine Origin Predictors")
    res
    }' );
 end;
 /

PL/SQL procedure successfully completed.

SQL>
```

Listing 3-13. SQL Interface of Embedded R Execution Based Query Invocation of Script rTestRF_final1 Defined in Listing 3-12

```
SQL> set pages 1000
SQL> set long 100000
SQL> select xmltype(a.value).getClobVal() as "XML Output with Image included"
  2  from   table(rqEval( NULL,'XML','rTestRF_final1')) a;

XML Output with Image included
--------------------------------------------------------------------------------
```


```
<root><R-data><table_obj><ROW-table_obj><origin_pred>Origin1</origin_pred>
<Var2>Origin1</Var2><Freq>140</Freq></ROW-table_obj><ROW-table_obj>
<origin_pred>Origin2</origin_pred><Var2>Origin1</Var2><Freq>0</Freq>
</ROW-table_obj><ROW-table_obj><origin_pred>Origin3</origin_pred>
<Var2>Origin1</Var2><Freq>0</Freq></ROW-table_obj><ROW-table_obj>
<origin_pred>Origin1</origin_pred><Var2>Origin2</Var2><Freq>0</Freq>
</ROW-table_obj><ROW-table_obj><origin_pred>Origin2</origin_pred>
<Var2>Origin2</Var2><Freq>162</Freq></ROW-table_obj><ROW-table_obj>
<origin_pred>Origin3</origin_pred><Var2>Origin2</Var2><Freq>0</Freq>
</ROW-table_obj><ROW-table_obj><origin_pred>Origin1</origin_pred>
<Var2>Origin3</Var2><Freq>0</Freq></ROW-table_obj><ROW-table_obj>
<origin_pred>Origin2</origin_pred><Var2>Origin3</Var2><Freq>0</Freq>
</ROW-table_obj><ROW-table_obj><origin_pred>Origin3</origin_pred>
<Var2>Origin3</Var2><Freq>111</Freq></ROW-table_obj></table_obj></R-data>
<images><image><img src="data:image/pngbase64"><![CDATA[iVBORwOKGgoAAAAN....
fBAAAAAElFTkSuQmCC]]></img></image></images></root>
```

The XML output of the modified column in Listing 3-13 is shown in Figure 3-11.

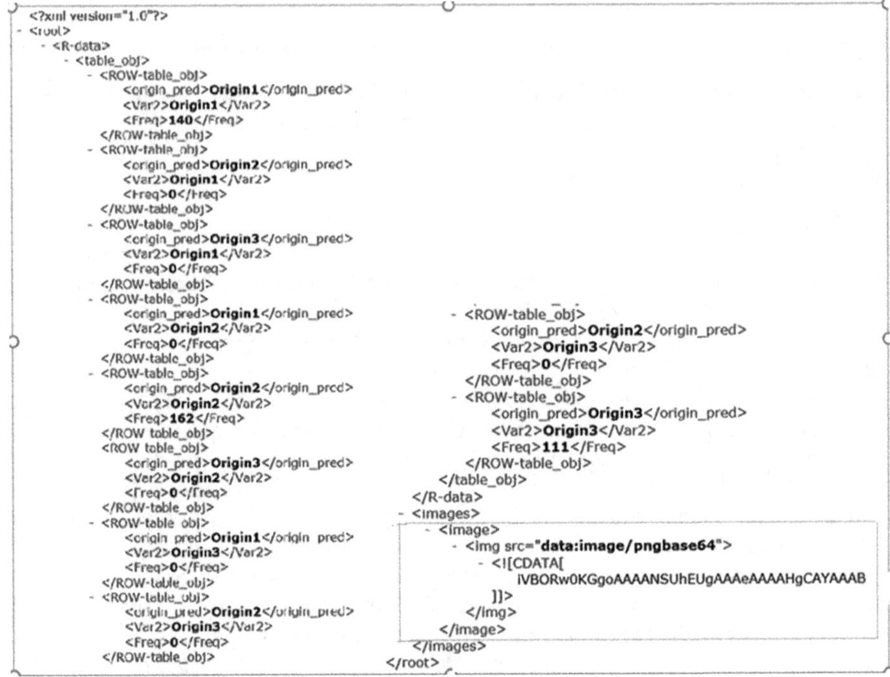

```
<?xml version="1.0"?>
- <root>
  - <R-data>
    - <table_obj>
      - <ROW-table_obj>
          <origin_pred>Origin1</origin_pred>
          <Var2>Origin1</Var2>
          <Freq>140</Freq>
        </ROW-table_obj>
      - <ROW-table_obj>
          <origin_pred>Origin2</origin_pred>
          <Var2>Origin1</Var2>
          <Freq>0</Freq>
        </ROW-table_obj>
      - <ROW-table_obj>
          <origin_pred>Origin3</origin_pred>
          <Var2>Origin1</Var2>
          <Freq>0</Freq>
        </ROW-table_obj>
      - <ROW-table_obj>
          <origin_pred>Origin1</origin_pred>
          <Var2>Origin2</Var2>
          <Freq>0</Freq>
        </ROW-table_obj>
      - <ROW-table_obj>
          <origin_pred>Origin2</origin_pred>
          <Var2>Origin2</Var2>
          <Freq>162</Freq>
        </ROW-table_obj>
        <ROW-table_obj>
          <origin_pred>Origin3</origin_pred>
          <Var2>Origin2</Var2>
          <Freq>0</Freq>
        </ROW-table_obj>
      - <ROW-table_obj>
          <origin_pred>Origin1</origin_pred>
          <Var2>Origin3</Var2>
          <Freq>0</Freq>
        </ROW-table_obj>
      - <ROW-table_obj>
          <origin_pred>Origin2</origin_pred>
          <Var2>Origin3</Var2>
          <Freq>0</Freq>
        </ROW-table_obj>
      - <ROW-table_obj>
          <origin_pred>Origin2</origin_pred>
          <Var2>Origin3</Var2>
          <Freq>0</Freq>
        </ROW-table_obj>
      - <ROW-table_obj>
          <origin_pred>Origin3</origin_pred>
          <Var2>Origin3</Var2>
          <Freq>111</Freq>
        </ROW-table_obj>
      </table_obj>
    </R-data>
  - <images>
    - <image>
      - <img src="data:image/pngbase64">
        - <![CDATA[
            iVBORw0KGgoAAAANSUhEUgAAAeAAAAHgCAYAAAB
          ]]>
        </img>
      </image>
    </images>
  </root>
```


Figure 3-11. XML output of the modified VALUE column in Listing 3-13

Generating PNG Graph Using the ORE SQL Interface and Integrating It with OBIEE Dashboard

In this section, we'll demonstrate how a PNG graph can be obtained by using the ORE SQL interface for the wine origin prediction problem using the `randomForest` R algorithm. As outlined in earlier examples, we first create two scripts that are stored in the Oracle DB R script repository. These are named `BuildandScoreRF` and `validateRF`. The first script, `BuildandScoreRF`, associates an R function that takes input data as an argument and partitions it into two sets based on random sampling—70% as training data set, and 30% as test data set. It builds a random-forest-based model based on the training data set and then scores the model using the `predict` R function based on the test data set.

The `validaterF` script prepares the input data required for the `BuildandScoreRF` script from a CSV file of wine data based on the `Wine` class and other relevant attribuites. It stores this input data in a database table called and then calls the first script, passing the prepared data as input to its corresponding R function.

Listings 3-14 and 3-15 show the code for these two R scripts.

To execute the code in Listings 3-14 to 3-16 and any SELECT statements, open either SQL*Plus or Oracle SQL Developer. Log in, and copy and paste the code. For SQL*Plus, press Enter; for Oracle SQL Developer, click the Run Script icon.

Listing 3-14. BuildandScoreRF Script Using SQL Interface That Builds and Scores the Wine Class Data Using randomForest R Function

```
begin
   sys.rqscriptDrop('BuildandScoreRF');
   sys.rqScriptcreate('BuildandScoreRF',
'function(winedata) {
library(randomForest)
winedata$origin <- ifelse(winedata$class == 1, ''Origin1'',
ifelse(winedata$class == 2, ''Origin2'',
ifelse(winedata$class == 3, ''Origin3'', '''')))
winedata$origin <- as.factor(winedata$origin)
set.seed(123)
sample_size <- 0.70 * nrow(winedata)
sampledata <-sample(seq_len(nrow(winedata)), sample_size)
training_data <- winedata[sampledata, ]
test_data <- winedata[-sampledata, ]
wine.rf <- randomForest(origin ~ . - class, data = training_data)
origin_pred <- predict(wine.rf, newdata = test_data)
res <- table(origin_pred, test_data$origin)
pairs(table(origin_pred, test_data$origin), main="Wine Origin Predictors")
res
}');
end;
/
```

Listing 3-15. validateRF Script Using SQL Interface That Prepares the Input Data and Calls the BuildandScoreRF Script Based R Function

```
begin
  sys.rqScriptDrop('validateRF');
  sys.rqScriptCreate('validateRF',
  'function() {
    library(ORE)
    ore.connect("testr","orcl","localhost","testr")
    setwd("F:/testr/")
    inputdata <- read.csv("winedata.csv", header=TRUE, sep='','')
    ore.drop(table="WINE_DATA")
    ore.create(inputdata, table="WINE_DATA")
```

```
    ore.scriptLoad(name = "BuildandScoreRF")
    res1 <- BuildandScoreRF(inputdata)
    res1.df <- data.frame(res1)
    res1.df
    }');
end;
/
```

To verify that the output of validateRF is accurate, we first query it for SQL tabular output by executing the following query:

```
SQL> select *
     from table(rqEval(
         NULL,
          'select CAST(''a'' as VARCHAR2(50)) "origin_pred", CAST(''b'' AS
          VARCHAR2(50)) "Var2", 1 as "Freq" from dual',
         'validateRF'));

origin_pred
--------------------------------------------------
Var2                                                     Freq
-------------------------------------------------- ----------
Origin1
Origin1                                                   140

Origin2
Origin1                                                     0

Origin3
Origin1                                                     0

Origin1
Origin2                                                     0

Origin2
Origin2                                                   162

Origin3
Origin2                                                     0

Origin1
Origin3                                                     0

Origin2
Origin3                                                     0

Origin3
Origin3                                                   111

9 rows selected.
```

The output is similar to the that obtained from Listing 3-11. Next we execute the query shown in Listing 3-16 that generates an IMAGE column corresponding to the PNG graph output.

■ **Note** The query in Listing 3-16 will be used for integration of the two R scripts and the graph output produced with the OBIEE RPD.

Listing 3-16. SQL Based Query for Obtaining PNG Graph Output of validateRF Script Execution

```
SQL> select *
  2  from table(rqEval(
  3       NULL,
  4       'PNG',
  5       'validateRF'));

NAME
------------------------------------------------------------------------
        ID
----------
IMAGE
------------------------------------------------------------------------

         1
89504E470D0A1A0A0000000D4948445200001E0000001E008060000007DD4BE950000200049444
54789CEDDD7F901BF57DFFF1D706FFA80DC660E3D824181B9FCE105998160A89EF8A99129B727243
0E42AF6EC28F09A15203ADEF8039481ABE43004FA7E4A0D191528F44CA8CA16E2767DC5E2720116C
0A76F1D171301D8C7C98938E40B0030D0E501FBFFC83EEF70F6637924EBA9374BAFDE8C7F331A319
6B6FF7F3794B27EFEB3E9F5DED5AB66DDB0200009EFA8CE902000068440430000000610C000001840
0003006000010C00800104300000610C00000184000030060000010C008001043000000610C00000
184000030060000010C00800104300000610C00000184000030060000010CA35A5B5B655996D2E9B4
BB2C1C0ECBB22CB5B6B666AD6B59962CCB1AF56F2FF4F6F6BA7D3A8FDEDEDEA2B72FA7DE4ABCC6DC
9A9D47EE7B5B69B9B57BFDFB026A01010CA30281802429954AB9CB62B19824696060C05DE6047428
........
SQL>
```

The output of the query in Listing 3-16 when viewed from SQL Developer is shown in Figure 3-12. Notice the BLOB output for the IMAGE column. Double-clicking the IMAGE column and choosing View as Image displays the PNG graph.

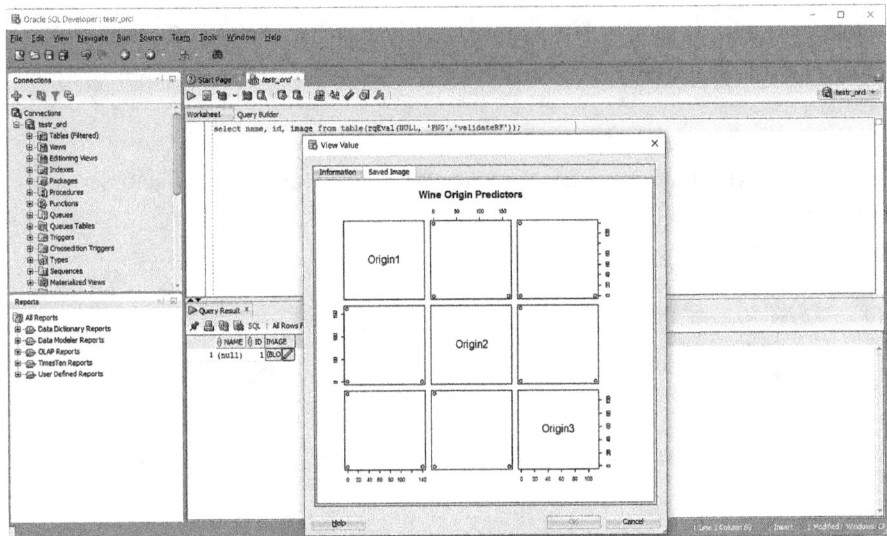

Figure 3-12. *PNG output of the IMAGE column in Listing 3-16*

Integrating the PNG Graph with OBIEE

Integrating the R PNG graph output with OBIEE 12c requires either downloading an existing repository or creating a new repository and integrating it with the OBIEE12c repository. In this section, we'll download the existing `SampleAppLite` repository and modify it to reflect out wine origin prediction graph.

Pre-Steps Required for OBIEE 12c Integration

Before downlaoding the SampleAppLite repository from the OBIEE12c server, a few pre-steps must be done so that OBIEE 12c can communicate with the test database and schema:

1. In the `NQSConfig.INI` file located in the `<FusionMiddlewareHome>\user_projects\domains\bi\config\fmwconfig\biconfig\OBIS` folder, make the following changes:

    a. In the `[ADVANCE_ANALYTICS_SCRIPT]` section. set the value of `TARGET = "ORE";` and set the value of connection pool as `CONNECTION_POOL = "ORCL"."testr/testr:1521";`

   b. Make sure the ORCL alias is defined in the `tnsnames.ora` file of the Oracle DB 12c server.

2. Restart WebLogic Server and the associated services by issuing the `stop.cmd` command followed by `start.cmd` command. These are found in the `<FusionMiddlewareHome>\user_projects\domains\bi\bitools\bin` folder.

3. Restart the Oracle Business Intelligence service (from Task Manager ➤ Services if on Windows).

4. Download the server RPD file corresponding to SampleAppLite by using the following command:

```
<FusionMiddlewareHome>\user_projects\domains\bi\
bitools\bin\datamodel.cmd downloadrpd -O obieenew.
rpd -W Admin123 -U weblogic -P <weblogic_password>
-SI ssi
```

   The RPD is downloaded as the `obieenew.rpd` file.

Customize the Downloaded SampleAppLite RPD for ORE returned PNG Graph Integration

The start-to-finish steps for integrating the Wine Origin Prediction graph with the `obieenew.rpd` file include the Customization of `obieenew.rpd`, which is done in the OBIEE Administration Tool on the client-side.

This consists cf the following primary steps:

1. Creating an Oracle connection pool
2. Creating a Physical layer
3. Creating a Business Model and Mapping layer
4. Creating a Presentation layer

These are described in the sub-sections that follow.

Creating an Oracle Connection Pool

Here are the steps involved:

1. Open `obieenew.rpd` in offline mode in the OBIEE Admin Tool. In the Physical layer, choose New Database. Fill in the details as shown in the dialog box in Figure 3-13.

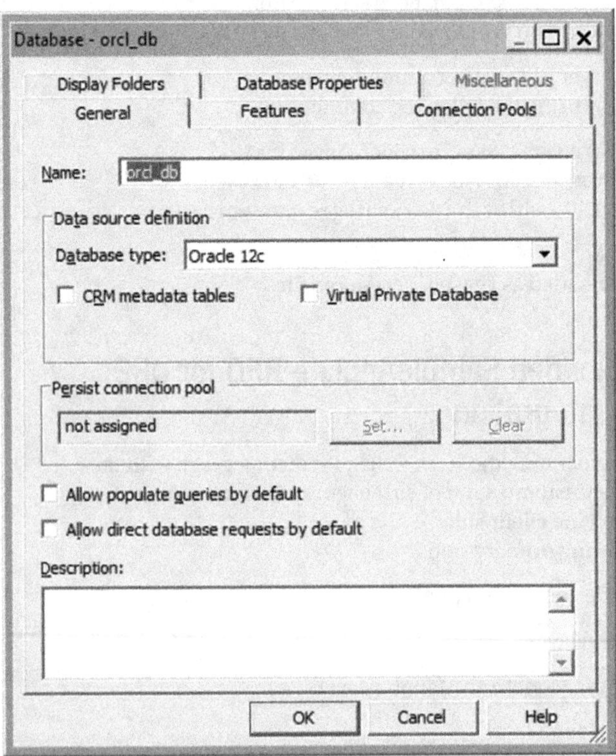

Figure 3-13. *New Database dialog box in OBIEE Admin tool*

2. Click the Connection Pools tab and create a new connection pool with the properties shown in Figure 3-14. The Data Source Name must be specified as the complete connect descriptor string for the tnsnames alias ORCL.

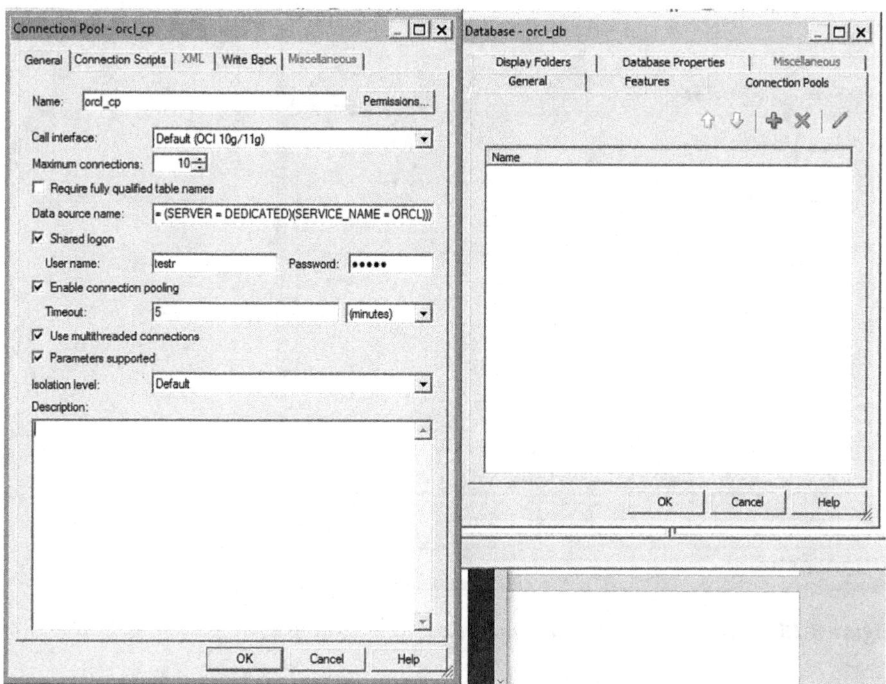

Figure 3-14. *New Connection Pool dialog boxes*

Creating a Physical Layer

Here are the steps involved for creating a Physical layer:

1. Select `orcl_db` and right-click and select New Object ➤ Physical Schema. Specify the Name as TESTR. as shown in Figure 3-15.

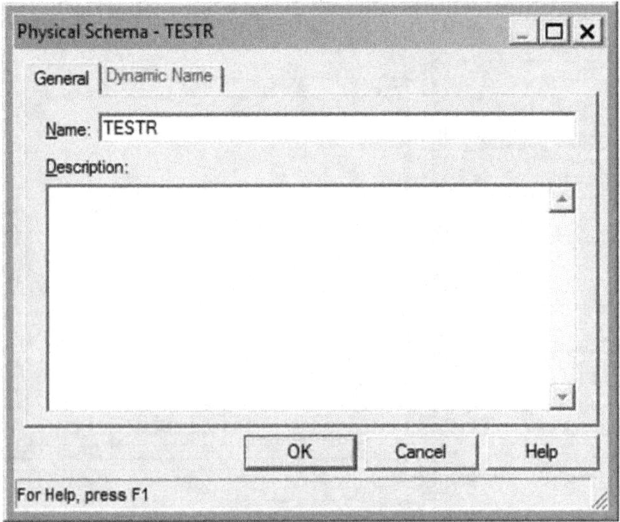

Figure 3-15. *New Physical Schema dialog box*

2. Right-click the TESTR schema and select New Physical Table. A new dialog box appears, as shown in Figure 3-16.

■ **Note** In the Physical Table dialog box, in the General tab, specify the Name as validateRF, the Table Type as Select, and the Default Initialization String as the `SELECT` statement from Listing 3-16, as follows:

```
select id, image from table(rqEval(NULL, 'PNG', 'validateRF'))
```

These are highlighted in Figure 3-16.

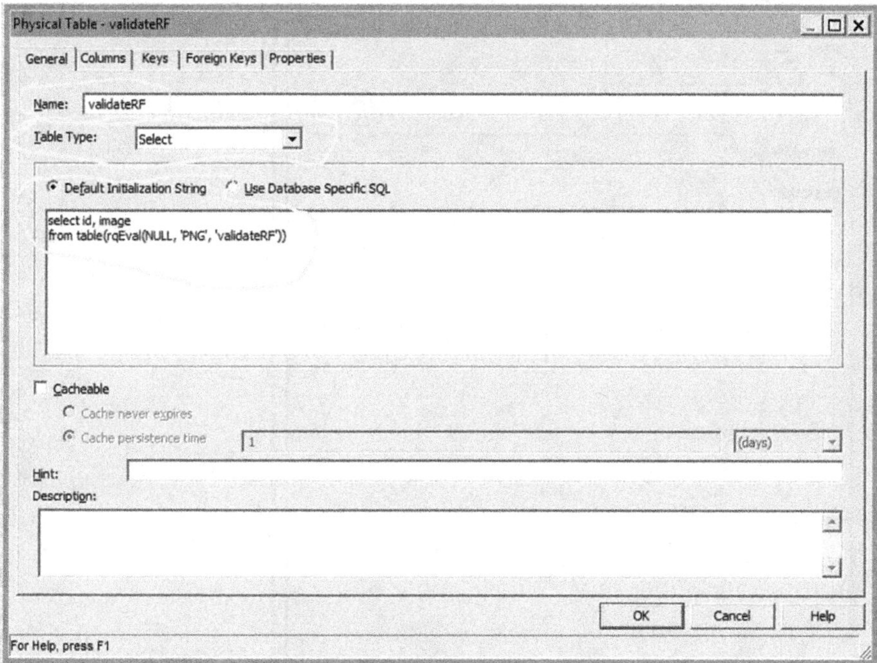

***Figure 3-16.** New Physical Table dialog box*

3. In the Columns tab, define two columns named `Id` and `image`. For the Id column, set the Type too INT and Length for the `Id` column, as shown in Figure 3-17. For the `image` column, set Type to LONGVARBINARY and Length to 32000, as shown in Figure 3-18.

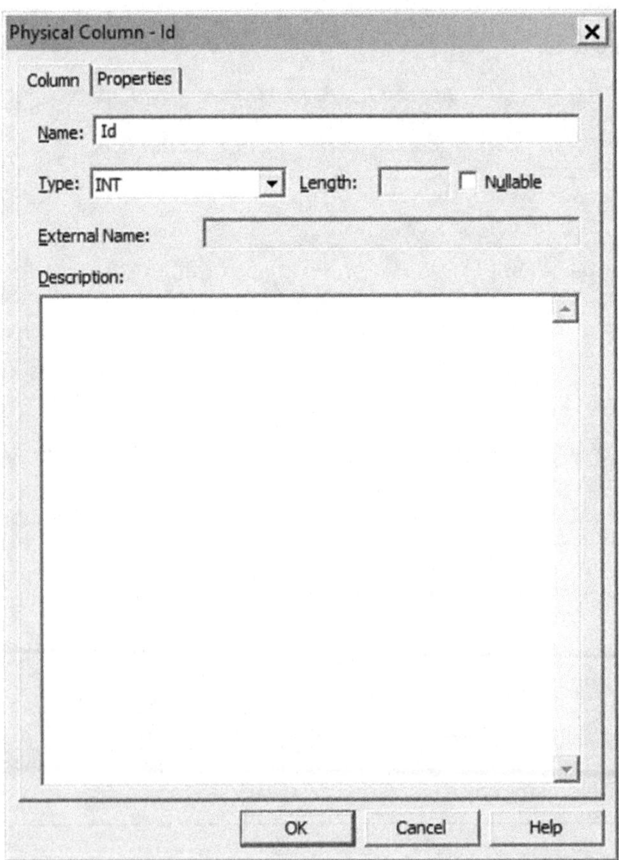

Figure 3-17. *Id column dialog box of New Physical Table validateRF*

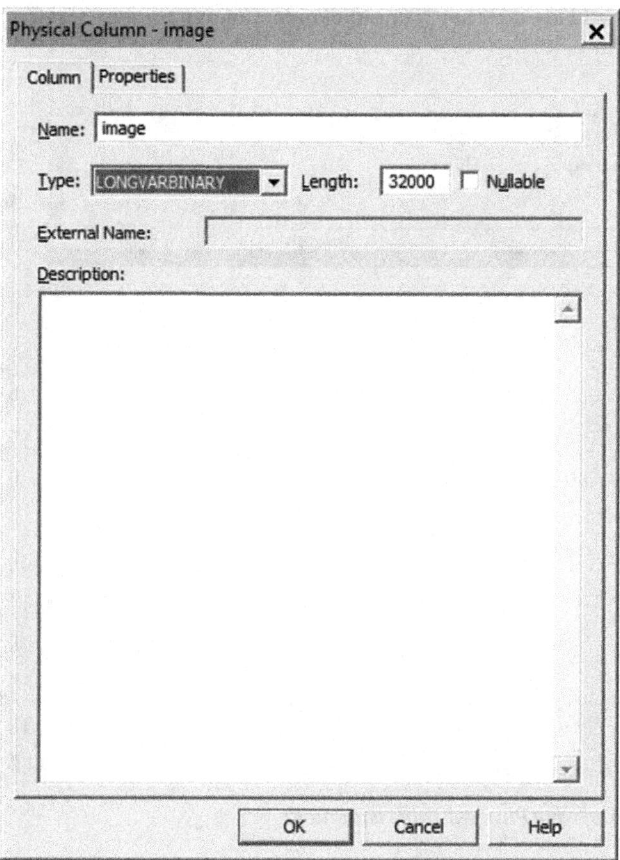

Figure 3-18. *image column dialog box of New Physical Table lidateRF*

4. On the Keys tab, add id under Key Name and under Column, as shown in Figure 3-19.

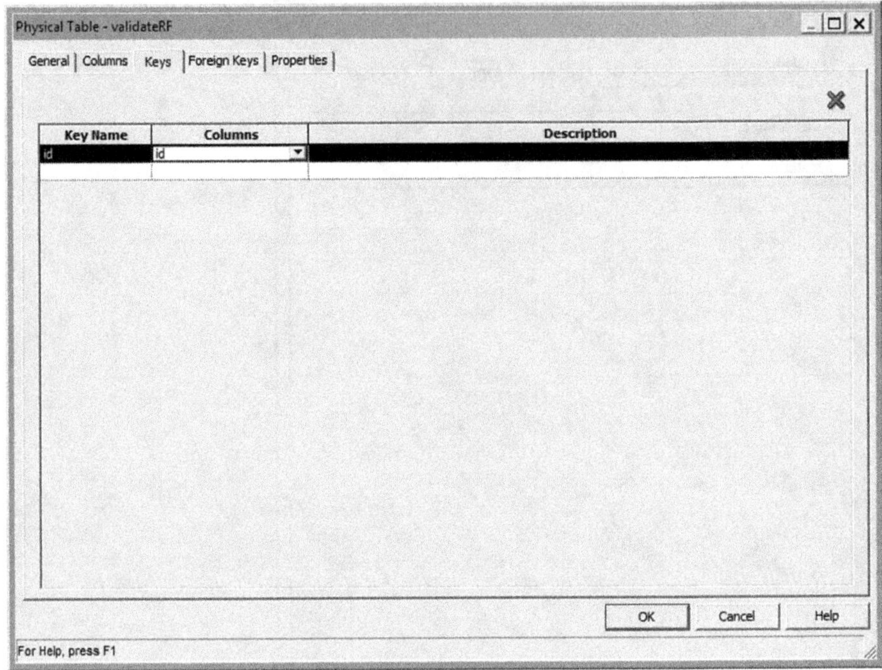

***Figure 3-19.** Keys dialog box of New Physical Table validateRF*

5. Click OK in the main Physical Table dialog box, as shown in Figure 3-20.

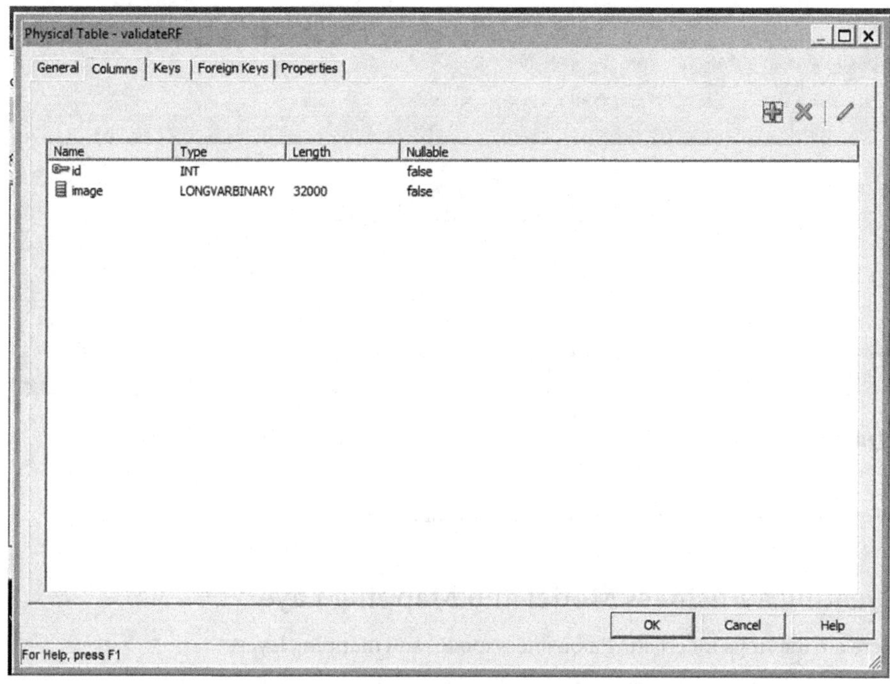

Figure 3-20. *Physical Table dialog box of validateRF table*

6. The Physical Diagram window is displayed, showing the `validateRF` physical table, as shown in Figure 3-21.

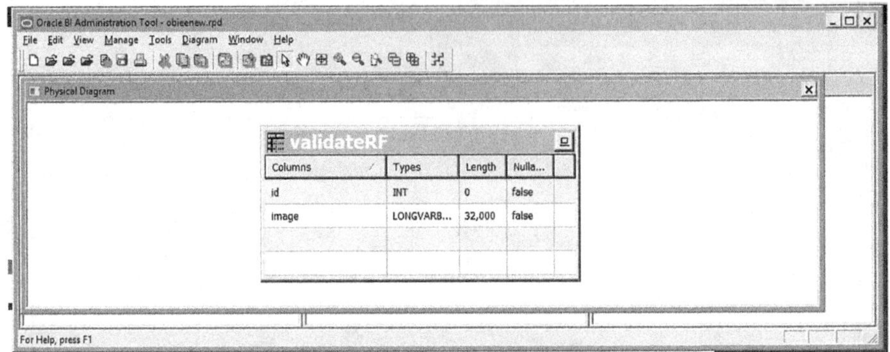

Figure 3-21. *Physical Diagram window showing the validateRF physical table*

7. Save the RPD and close the Physical Diagram window.

Creating a Business Model and Mapping Layer

Here are the steps for creating a business model and mapping layer:

1. Click the TESTRF schema in the Physical layer and drag and drop it into the Business Model and Mapping layer (BMM layer). Figure 3-22 shows the Physical layer with the `validateRF` table and its columns (note that the id column is marked as a key column, as shown by the yellow key icon to its left); and the TESTR schema with the `validateRF` entity in the BMM layer.

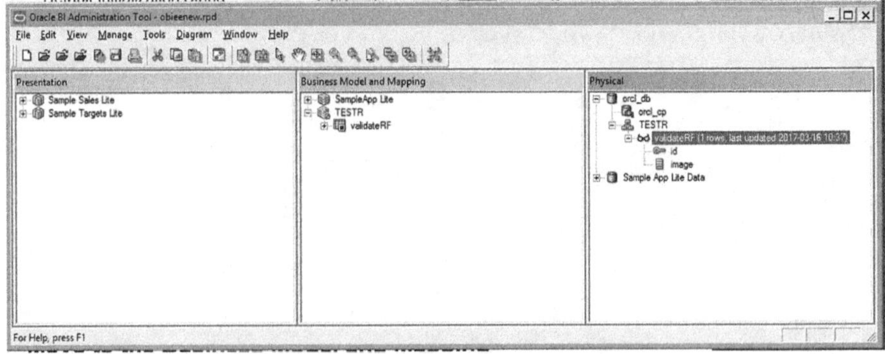

Figure 3-22. *Physical layer and Business Model and Mapping layer showing the TESTR schema with the validateRF table*

2. Right-click the `validateRF` entity in the BMM layer to duplicate it, resulting in `validateRF#1`. This is illustrated in Figure 3-23.

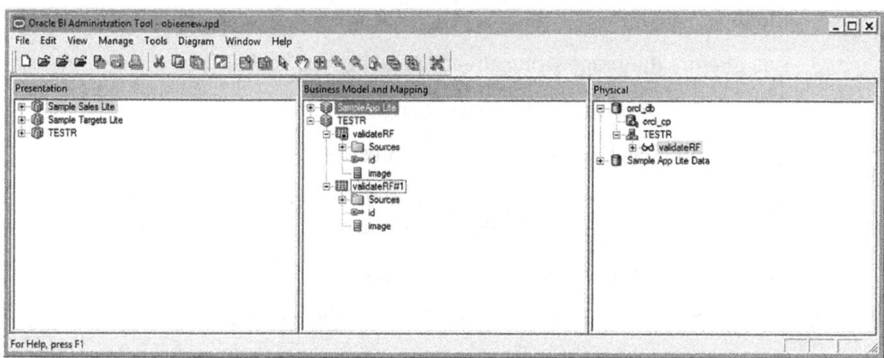

Figure 3-23. *BMM showing duplicated validateRF table appearing as validateRF#1*

3. Expand the `validateRF` table. Double-click id. The Logical Column dialog box for id appears, as shown in Figure 3-24.

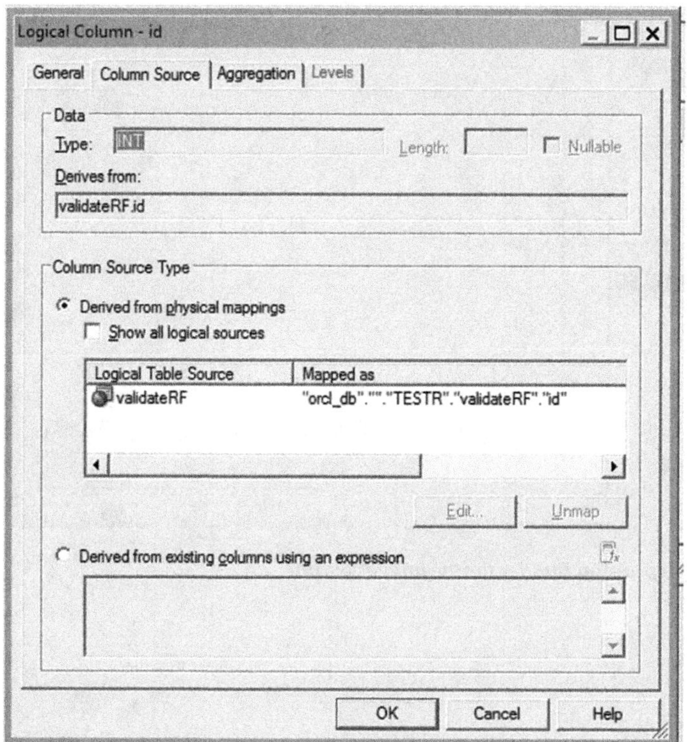

Figure 3-24. *Logical column dialog box for id*

4. In the Column Source tab, double-click Logical Table Source Entry . Here you specify the image lookup column. Click the Edit icon on the right. Specify the lookup expression as follows:

    a. Before the `image` string already present, type `lookup(`.

    b. Add a comma after the `image` string.

    c. Double-click `id` to add it to the expression.

    d. Change the two consecutive dots after the second `orcl_db` to two consecutive double quotes.

    e. Add a closing `)` at the end of the expression.

5. Click OK. The resulting dialog box is shown Figure 3-25.

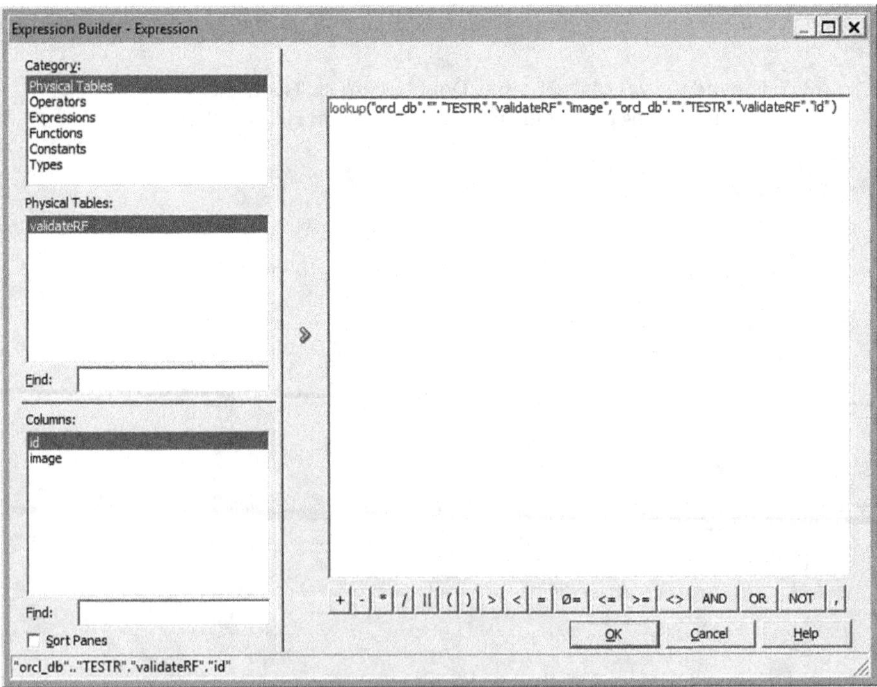

Figure 3-25. *Lookup Expression Builder for the image column*

6. Specify the sort order and descriptor id columns for the image column as follows:

   a. *Double-click image and click Set Corresponding to the Sort Order.*

   b. *Select the id column in the resulting dialog box, as shown in Figure 3-26, and click OK.*

   c. *Repeat this for the descriptor id. The Logical Column dialog box for image now appears, as shown in Figure 3-27.*

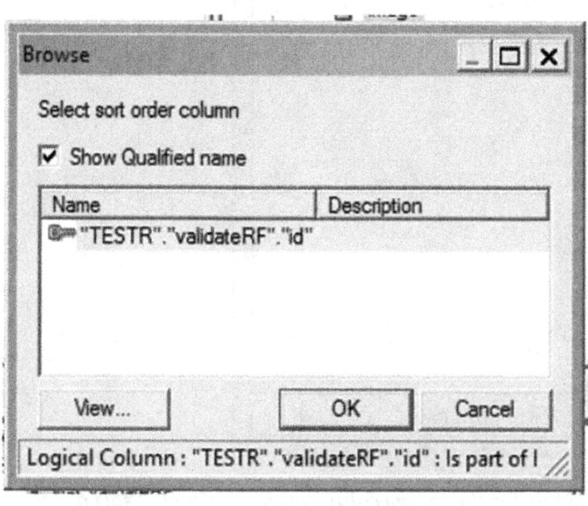

Figure 3-26. *Setting sort order and descriptor id for image column*

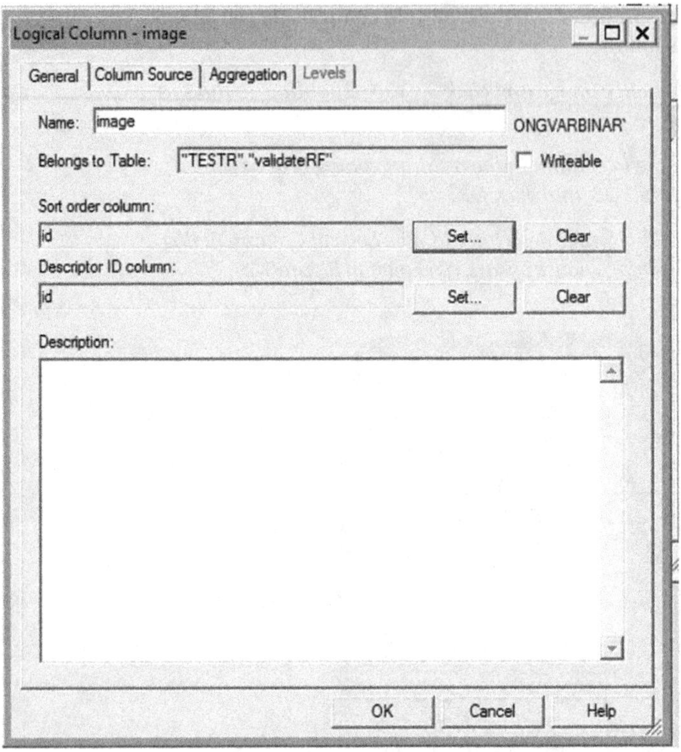

Figure 3-27. Logical Column dialog box for the image column after setting the sort order and descriptor id

At this point, the Physical and BMM layers appear as shown in Figure 3-28.

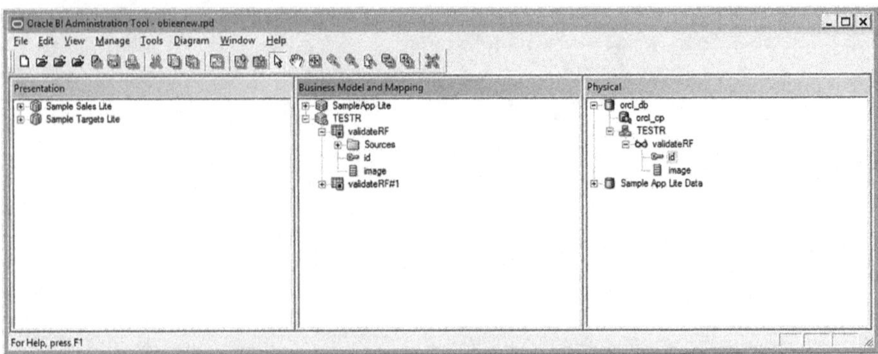

Figure 3-28. Physical and BMM layers corresponding to the TESTR schema with the validateRF table included

7. Rick-click the `validateRF` entity in the BMM layer and select Business Model Diagram ➤ Whole Diagram, as shown in Figure 3-29. The BMM diagram is displayed in a new window. Click the New Join icon in the tool, select the `validateRF` object in the BMM diagram, and drag the cursor to the `validateRF#1` object to form a straight line, subsequently releasing the cursor. The updated BMM diagram appears, as shown Figure 3-30.

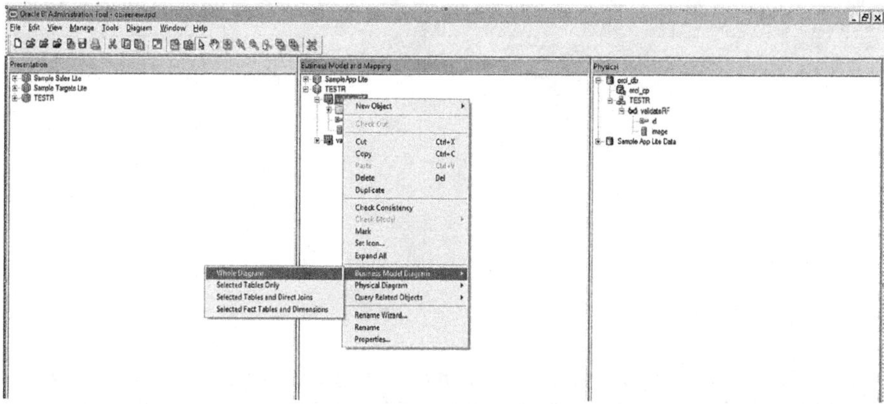

Figure 3-29. *BMM diagram—whole diagram for the TESTR schema*

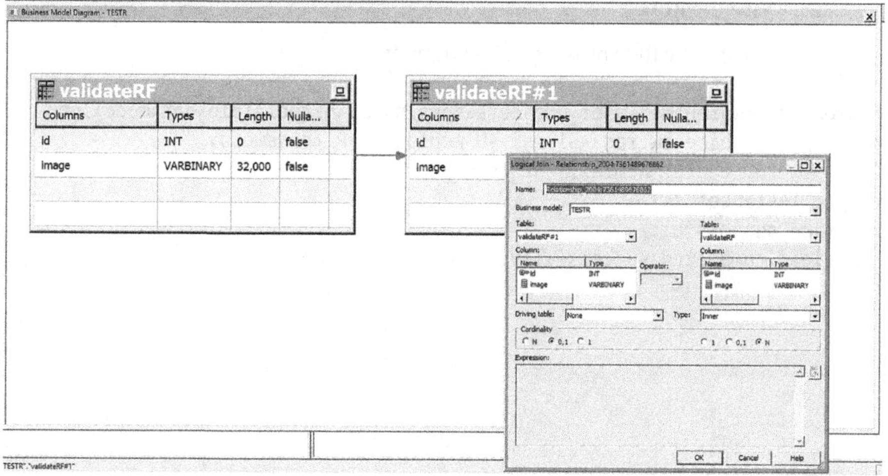

Figure 3-30. *Updated BMM diagram showing join between validateRF and validateRF#*

Creating a Presentation Layer

Here are the steps for creating a Presentation layer:

1. Close the BMM diagram and save the RPD. In the Presentation area, drag and drop the TESTR schema from the BMM layer to create a New Presentation subject area named TESTR. The three modified layers appear as shown in Figure 3-31.

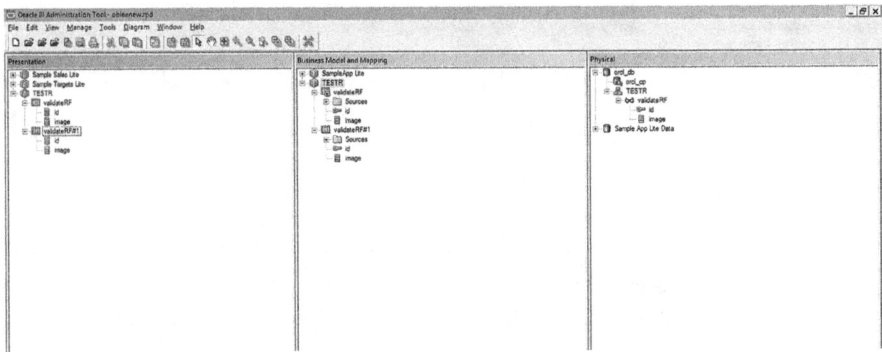

Figure 3-31. *Physical layer, Business Model and Mapping layer, and Presentation layer showing the TESTR schema along with the validateRF and validateRF#1 tables in the Presentation layer*

2. Save the RPD.

   Upload the RPD by using this command:

```
<FusionMiddlewareHome>\user_projects\domains\bi\bitools\bin\datamodel.cmd
uploadrpd -I obieenew.rpd -SI ssi -U weblogic -P <password>
RPD Password: <enter Admin123 at this prompt>
Service Instance: ssi
Operation successful.
RPD upload completed successfully.
```

Creating the OBIEE Analysis and Dashboard with the Uploaded RPD

This means that `obieenew.rpd` will be used to create and customize a new analysis and dashboard in OBIEE 12c Presentation Services.

1. Log in to OBIEE and click on Administration ➤Reload Files and Metadata.

2. Then create an Analysis by clicking New ➤ Analysis. The schema TESTR now appears under the available subject areas. Click it, as shown in Figure 3-32.

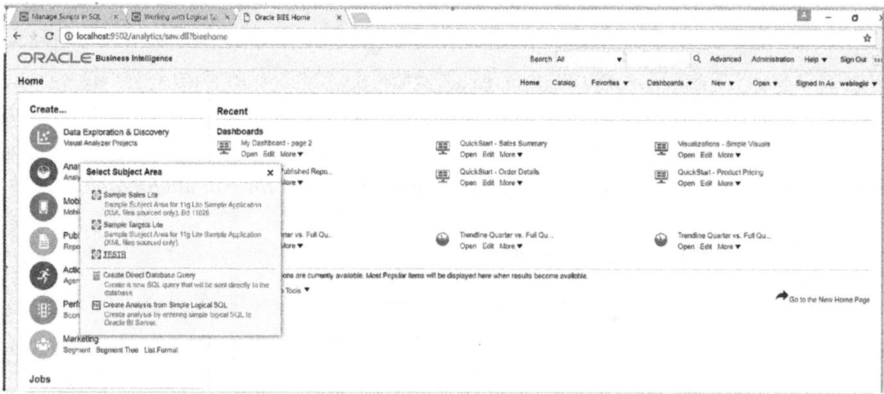

Figure 3-32. *New OBIEE Analysis showing TESTR as one of selectable subject areas*

3. Drag and drop the `id` and `image` columns from the TESTR subject area to the Selected Columns area. Click Results. The pairs plot of Wine Origin Prediction is displayed. This graph is the same as the one generated from the ORE R interface and SQL interface.

4. Save the Analysis by clicking the Save icon at the top.

The analysis and the resulting graph (PNG) are shown in Figures 3-33 and 3-34.

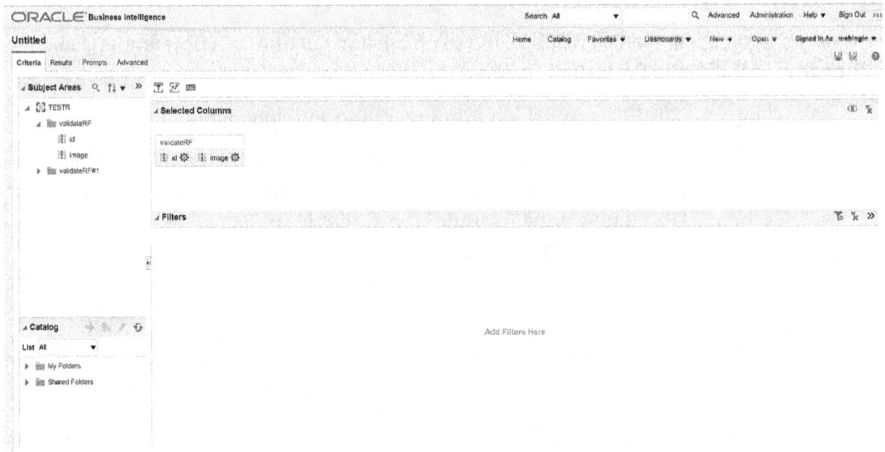

***Figure 3-33.** New analysis basd on the TESTR subject area and the validateRF table*

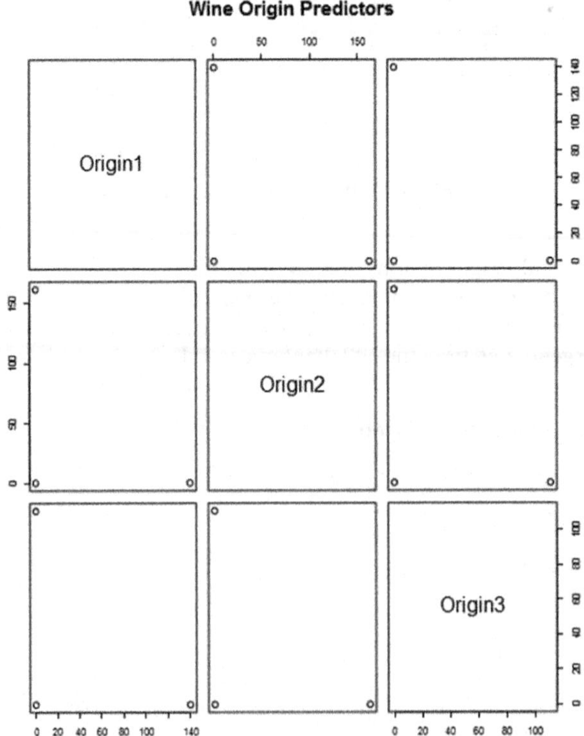

***Figure 3-34.** Pairs plot of Wine Origin Predictors*

To create a dashboard, click New ➤ Dashboard, specify TESTR Dashboard as the name, and choose a folder name where it will be saved. Choose a folder in My Folders or Shared Folders. In the Catalog section at the bottom left, choose the analysis named Pairs Plot of Wine Origin Prediction, and then drag and drop it onto the empty area to the right of the dashboard. Click Run to view the dashboard. Figure 3-35 shows the TESTR dashboard just created.

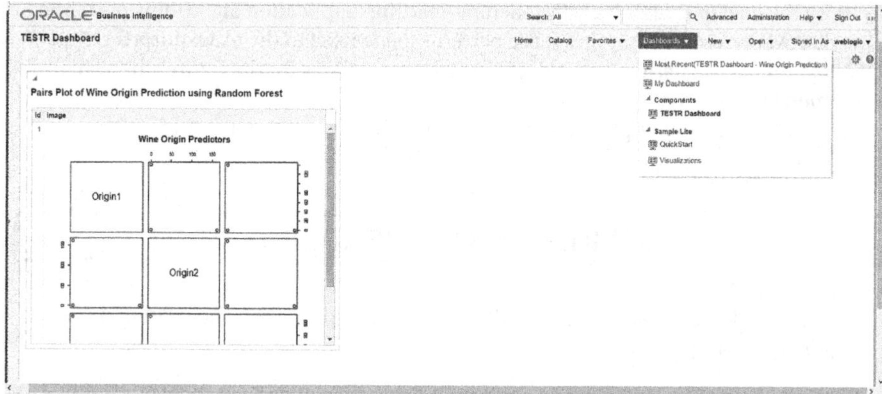

Figure 3-35. *TESTR dashboard showing the Pairs Plot of Wine Origin Prediction*

The TESTR dashboard also shows up under the Dashboards ➤ Components menu, as shown at the top-right area of the screen. The PNG image is generated via the SQL `SELECT` query that was specified in the initial physical table default initialization string and with the physical table type set to Select. This query calls the R function stored in the Oracle DB R script repository.

This completes the integration of the PNG graph output obtained from executing the ORE R script with the OBIEE12c analysis and dashboard. Additionally, multiple graphs pertaining to the same analysis can be integrated with OBIEE, based on multiple images generated from the ORE R function. Also, dynamic dashboarding can be done by defining parameterized R functions corresponding to the R scripts and defining OBIEE variables and prompts that can be interactively chosen at runtime.

Machine Learning Trending a Match for EDW

OBIEE 12 c provides five analytics alogrithms that can help in machine learning:Cluster, Outlier, Regr(ession), Trendline, and Evaluate Script. In addition, OBIEE 12 provides the TimeSeriesForecasting algorithm. Out of these, the primary one matching the requirements for an enterprise data warehouse (EDW) is TRENDLINE. This section focuses on how TRENDLINE can be used in the context of an EDW for machine-learning trending.

A multitude of algorithms have already written, and machine learning has been successfully applied to numerous applications. From the automation of tasks found in industries such as agriculture and manufacturing, we have now reached an age where new applications are being sought to automate tasks for knowledge workers.

One such area for this automation is in decision support systems (DSSs), or more specifically, in enterprise data warehouses (EDWs). Here, the power of computing and the capability to handle volumes of data are being put to the test with new applications powered by artificial intelligence. The basic goal of using an EDW is to be able to find a trend in the data that has been integrated and stored. Often, it is only in the EDW that an organization has data that is completely gathered, integrated, and further cleansed so that it can be used to provide some historical insight into the enterprise and expose trends.

With the goal of finding trends, machine-learning application algorithms pertaining to the discovery of trend lines and basic patterns lends itself to the exact purpose of an EDW, and thus is the perfect applied AI-powered technology for the future when it comes to commercial enterprises.

The following sidebar provides the OBIEE 12c documentation that defines TRENDLINE.

DEFINITION OF TRENDLINE

The `TRENDLINE` function measures data across time and shows a line chart of a metric by ordered records.

Currently, the `TRENDLINE` function can model data as linear and exponential regression.

```
TRENDLINE( <numeric_expr>, ( [<series>] ) BY ( [<partitionBy>] ),
<model_type>, <result_type>, [number_of_degrees] )
```

Where:

`numeric_expr` indicates the data to trend. This is usually a measure column. Note that this is the y-axis.

`series` indicates the x-axis. This is a list of `<valueExp> <orderByDirection>`, where `<valueExp>` is a dimension column, and `<orderByDirection>` is `ASC` or `DES`. The default is `ASC`. Note that this cannot be an arbitrary combination of numeric columns.

`partitionBy` indicates the control break for the trendline.

`model_type` indicates the type of model to use. Currently, you can specify only `LINEAR`.

`result_type` indicates the type of output. You can specify `VALUE` or `MODEL`. `VALUE` returns the regression Y values given X in the fit. `MODEL` returns the parameters in a JSON format string.

`number_of_degrees` is used in polynomial models only. This parameter is optional.

Consider the following TRENDLINE example. It defines a trendline of Full Quarter Revenue over Per Name Qtr by Order Type, meaning the result is obtained as a trendline specific to each Order Type.

```
TRENDLINE("Calculated Facts"."Full Quarter Revenue", ("Time"."Per Name Qtr")
BY ("Orders"."Order Type"), 'LINEAR', 'VALUE')
```

Figures 3-32 through 3-35 illustrate the analysis created for TRENDLINE, using the preceding function and the output obtained.Figure 3-36 shows the corresponding dashboard view.

Here are the steps required:

1. Log in to OBIEE Presentation Services and select Analysis under the SampleSales subject area.
2. Select Orders and then Order Type. Drag and drop it in the empty area on the right.
3. Select Per Name Qtr under Time. Drag and drop it to the right of Order Type field.
4. Select Full Quarter Revenue under Calculated Facts. Drag and drop it to the right of the Per Name Qtr field.

The screenshot of the analysis so far is shown in Figure 3-36.

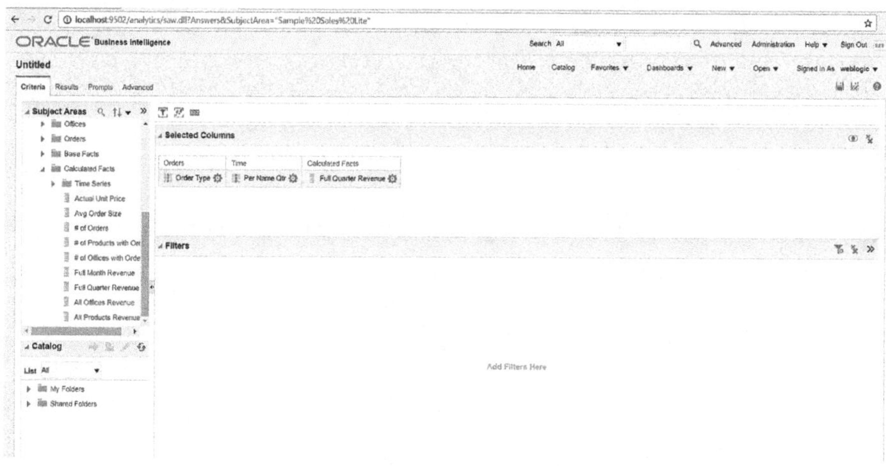

Figure 3-36. *Creating the analysis based on Order Type, Per Name Qtr, and Full Quarter Revenue*

5. Duplicate the field Full Quarter Revenue and place it to the right of the existing field.

6. Click the circular icon on it and then select and expand the Analytics node. The built-in OBIEE analytics functions appear, as shown in Figure 3-37.

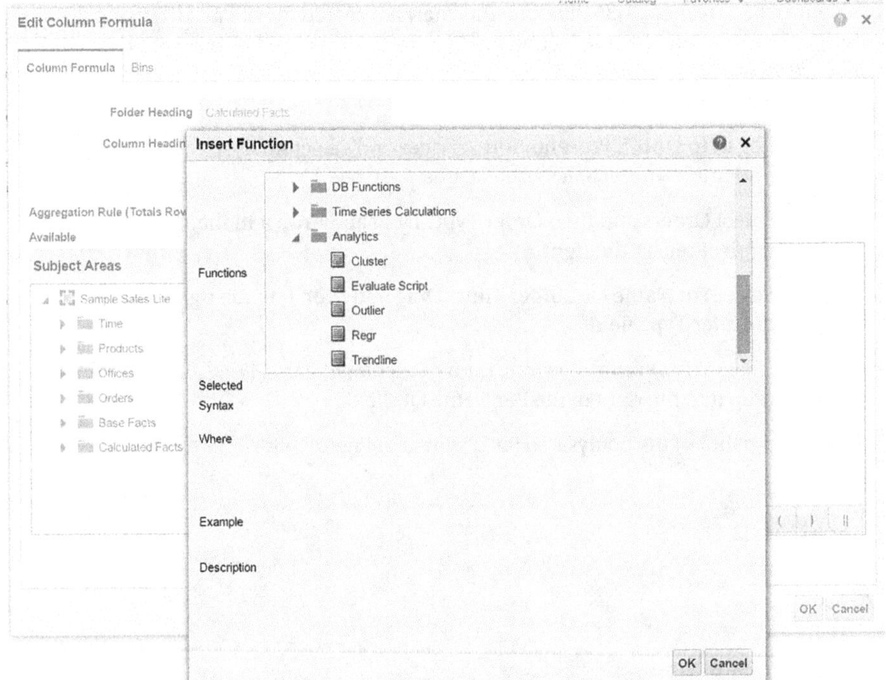

Figure 3-37. *Selecting the Trendline analytics function as part of the analysis*

7. Select the Trendline function. In the dialog box that opens, click f(...).

8. The formula for the TRENDLINE function is implicitly populated under the Column Formula area. Complete it as shown in Figure 3-38.

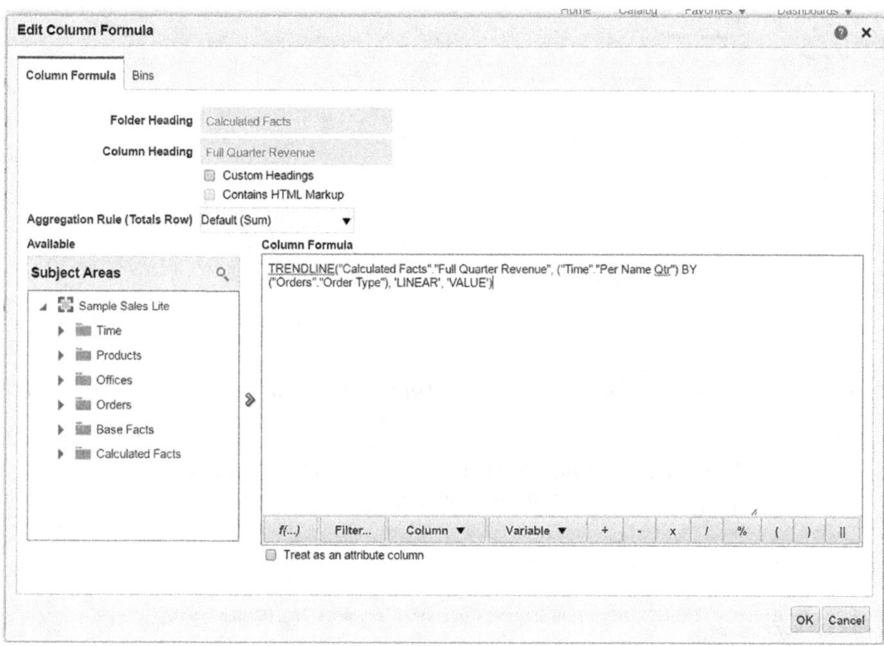

***Figure 3-38.** Specifying the TRENDLINE function formula, as shown in the Column Formula section*

9. Click OK to close the dialog box. The resulting OBIEE analysis screen is shown in Figure 3-39.

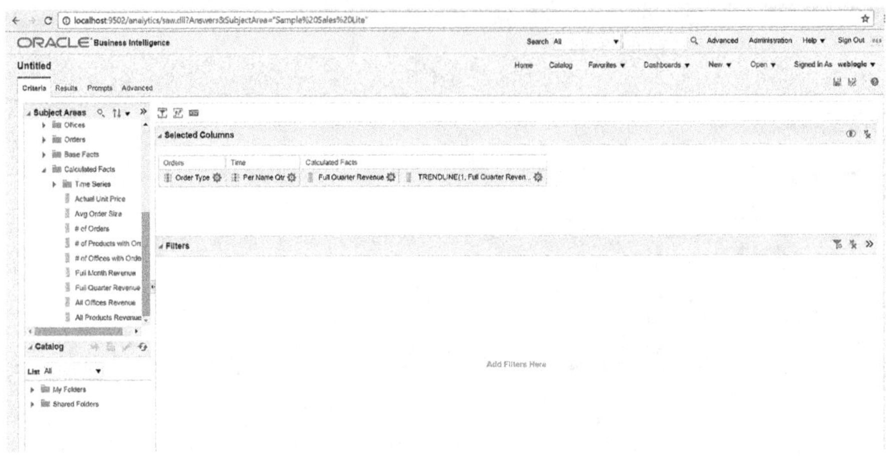

Figure 3-39. The OBIEE analysis after adding TRENDLINE to it

10. At the top left, click Results (to the right of Criteria) to display the graph of the trendline, as shown in Figure 3-40.

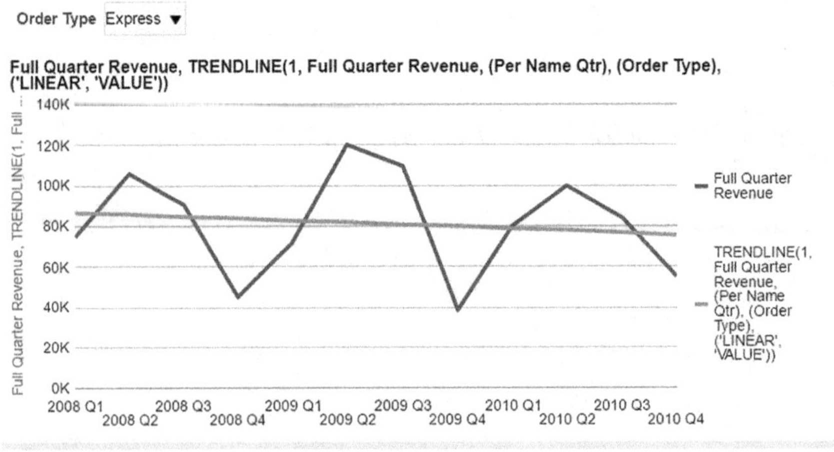

Figure 3-40. The resulting graph from the OBIEE analysis of the TRENDLINE

11. Clickthe Dashboard View icon to show how the graph appears in the OBIEE dashboard. The corresponding dashboard view is shown in Figure 3-41.

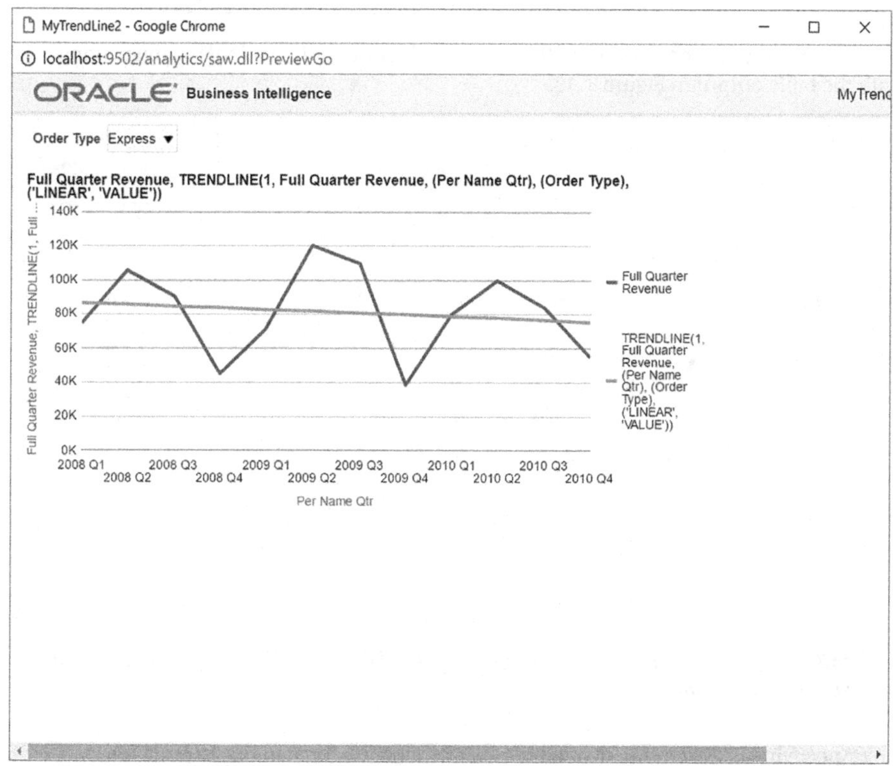

Figure 3-41. *Dashboard view of the TRENDLINE analysis from Figure 3-36*

The Analysis query issued is as follows:

```
SELECT
   0 s_0,
   "Sample Sales Lite"."Orders"."Order Type" s_1,
   "Sample Sales Lite"."Time"."Per Name Qtr" s_2,
   TRENDLINE("Sample Sales Lite"."Calculated Facts"."Full Quarter
   Revenue",("Sample Sales Lite"."Time"."Per Name Qtr") BY ("Sample Sales
   Lite"."Orders"."Order Type"),'LINEAR','VALUE') s_3
FROM "Sample Sales Lite"
ORDER BY 3 ASC NULLS LAST, 2 ASC NULLS LAST
FETCH FIRST 65001 ROWS ONLY
```

■ **Note** The x-axis has to represent a numeric or date variable for `TRENDLINE` to work. However, a string value that belongs to a Date or Time hierarchy can also be used. Here we have used `"Time"."Per Name Qtr"`.

The corresponding 3D view of the dashboard for the TRENDLINE is shown along with the table output in Figure 3-42.

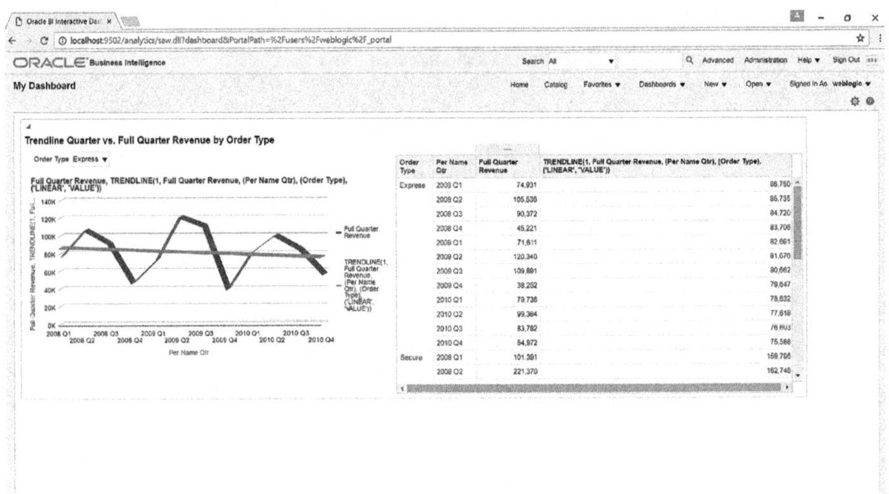

Figure 3-42. *3D view of the dashboard for the TRENDLINE in Figure 3-37 along with the corresponding table output*

Specifying `EXPONENTIAL` instead of `LINEAR` for `model_type` in the formula for `TRENDLINE` yields a different analysis, shown in Figure 3-43.

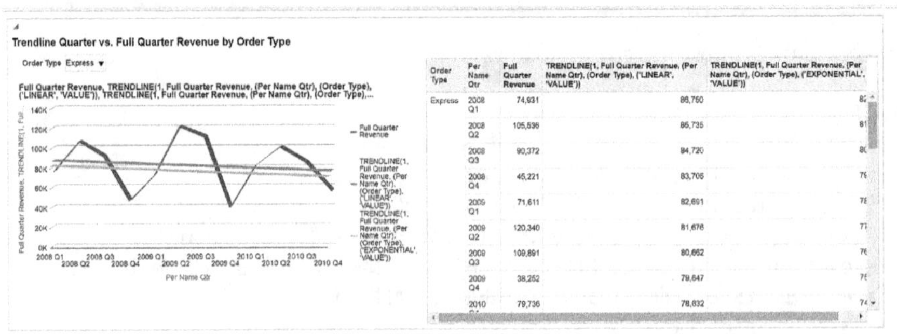

Figure 3-43. *LINEAR and EXPOENETIAL view of the 3D TRENDLINEof Figure 3-38 along with the corresponding table output*

Plotting a trellis chart for the preceding data yields the output shown in Figure 3-44.

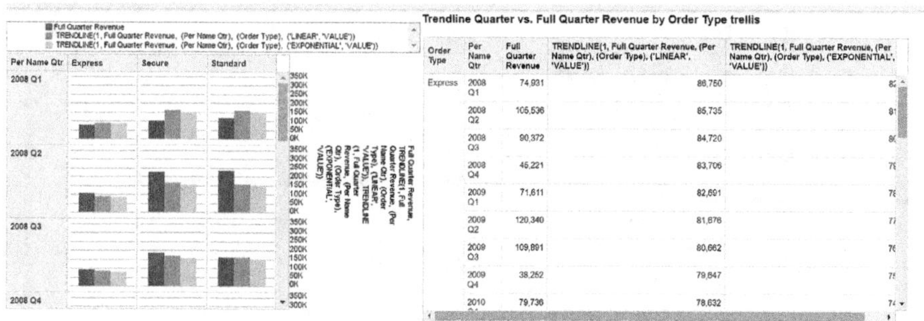

Figure 3-44. *Trellis chart for the analysis*

Creating a dashboard with the trellis chart, 3D graph, and tabular output yields the graphs shown in Figures 3-45 and 3-46.

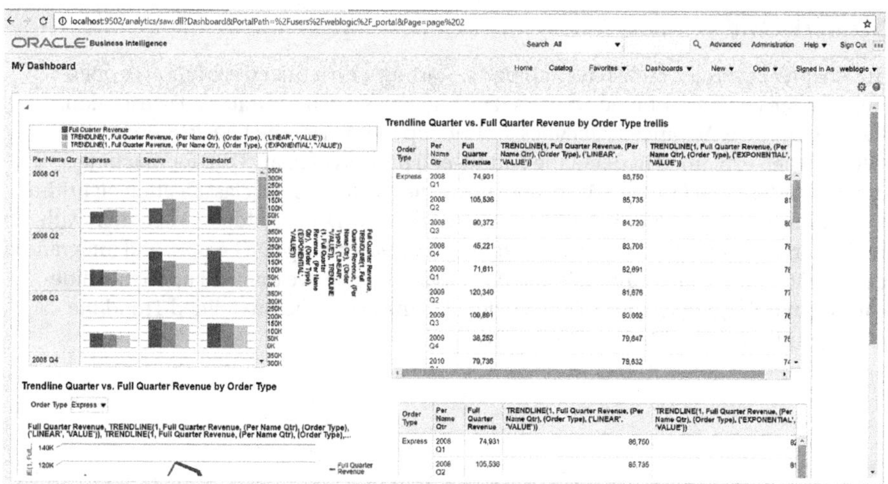

Figure 3-45. *A dashboard of the trellis chart, 3D graph, and tabular output of the TRENDLINE*

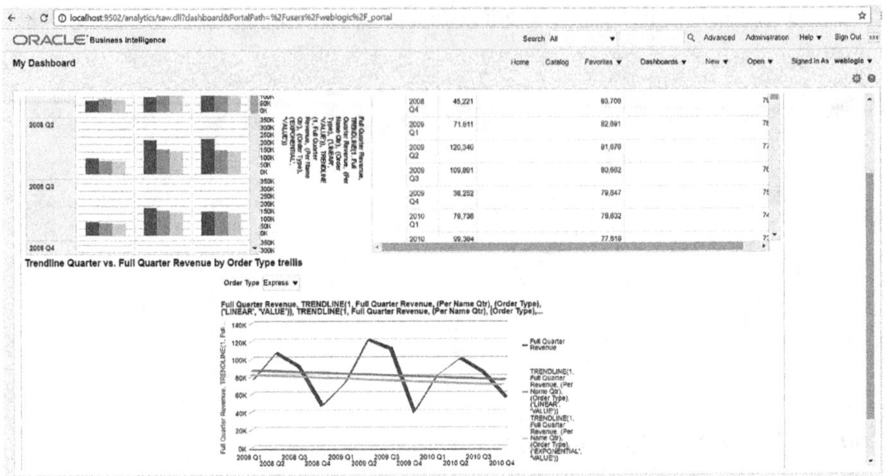

Figure 3-46. *A dashboard of trellis charts, 3D graph and tabular output of the TRENDLINE*

Summary

This chapter covered Oracle R technologies. Starting with a brief description of open source R, the chapter outlined Oracle's R technologies, such as Oracle R Distribution, ROracle, Oracle R Advanced Analytics for Hadoop (ORAAH), and Oracle R Enterprise (ORE). It then explained in detail the end-to-end process of using ORE for machine learning and BI with OBIEE. We covered using the random forest classification algorithm of machine learning in multiple ways, namely, using ORD, embedded R execution with the R interface and SQL interface, generating a corresponding PNG graph, and integrating it with OBIEE to create an analysis and dashboard. Finally, we touched upon machine-learning trending a match for EDW and detailed the use of the predefined Trendline advanced analytics function in OBIEE 12c.

CHAPTER 4

Machine Learning with OBIEE

Even from the early days of business intelligence and analytics, there have been ample promises about what this type of solution can provide for decision-makers. Because of the new technologies that have been developed in recent years, business intelligence and analytics have once again garnered a lot of attention as more functionalities appear that finally seem to be delivering on the promise.

The Marriage of Artificial Intelligence and Business Intelligence

At the turn of the century, advances in computing opened a whole new world for data warehousing. At that time, a big push for what was to become known as *business intelligence and analytics* was the priority. It was the primary focus for organizations looking to effectively use their corporate data for some kind of competitive advantage and to affect the company's bottom line. Today, almost all organizations are using some form of business intelligence and analytics, with mainstream adoption experienced during the past decade. As we look back, we can see that we rode the wave of BI adoption up to the peak of what is now referred to as the traditional data warehouse and business intelligence methods and approaches.

However, a few years ago a slowdown occurred as organizations began to ponder other methods and approaches while assessing their current environment and lessons learned. Industry changes had penetrated the data and BI landscape, warranting a second look at the effectiveness of current tools and technologies. As a result, a whole new field of vendors sprung up to brandish their new tools, ready to take on the establishment and leading vendors such as Oracle. The result is a halt to doing business—or rather, business intelligence—as usual, and allowing a second look at others. Ironically, this halt may have been beneficial to Oracle as well, as it reassessed and revamped its toolset to include new components and technologies such as artificial intelligence and big data.

R. Abellera and L. Bulusu, *Oracle Business Intelligence with Machine Learning*,
https://doi.org/10.1007/978-1-4842-3255-2_4

If we are now in the age of bigdata analytics, what does this truly mean for business intelligence? Is BI as we know it dead? Moreover, where does artificial intelligence and machine learning fit in the whole mix? There is no doubt that new methods, technologies, and tools have changed the landscape for business intelligence and data warehousing. At the heart of these changes, is what is being called *modern* data warehousing and business intelligence, which are using new approaches. They are being used to arrive at the same previous stated goal of providing "the right information to the right person at the right time." This is not a departure from what has always been the ultimate goal of data warehousing and business intelligence.

So why are vendors and industry experts claiming that BI is dead? Perhaps there is a new efficiency and effectiveness to what is now being used. Or perhaps this is just a dramatic attempt to proclaim that the status quo needs to be changed, an opportunity to usurp the industry leaders. Nevertheless, we must look at the fact that there are, indeed, new concepts that must be explored in data science. Just as the concept of big data created a buzz, Hortonworks helped to usher in a new buzz and legitimacy for the new technologies and tools with its initial public offering (IPO) in December of 2014. Big data—or at least, the promise of what big data would bring to the world of enterprise data and BI and analytics—had arrived.

A slew of software companies looking to follow suit and disrupt the industry away from the traditional data warehouse approach pushed analytical capabilities as the responsibility of front-end tools—greatly aided by artificial intelligence and machine learning. With that strategy came a new paradigm and an entirely new approach to analytics. Perhaps the perfect storm came in the form of a large volume of data coming in all sorts of formats at an incredible speed. How do we effectively handle this onslaught of big data?

Handling large amounts of data is not necessarily a new issue. Its predecessors can be clearly viewed in clickstream data warehousing and web log analysis. So what is the difference now? The difference is the prevalence of big data in our everyday lives, with social media and the number of new tools and technologies that have either evolved or been invented in order to effectively and efficiently handle big data, including machine learning. Now a new age for artificial intelligence is expected to be the game changer affecting our everyday lives. Just as BI pushed us to new technologies for utilizing and managing data for decision-making and analysis, recent advances in artificial intelligence are helping tackle old issues and have ushered in new methods, approaches, and tools to handle big data analytics and predictive analytics.

Indeed, back-end vendors have begun to offer hardware solutions to handle all the data coming into their enterprises with superb parallel processing and in-memory capabilities. Specifically, for Oracle, this includes its Exadata and Exalytics offerings. And so it seems that these advanced analytical applications and software on the front end have also evolved, to complement the capabilities on the back end.

The mid 1990s can be seen as the start of this revolution for analytical applications. At this time, new approaches and technologies began to converge with data warehousing and business intelligence. A new company and market was formed by Informatica for extract, transform, and load (ETL); new technologies from Cognos enabled new capabilities and even ushered old ways of doing analysis and statistics; and approaches and methodologies, such as Kimball's dimensional modeling for handling back-end data, provided best practices that enabled practitioners to deliver.

It was an age of enlightenment for implementing and developing BI solutions, as lessons were learned and best practices began to form for delivering world-class BI and analytical solutions—on time and under budget. As it became clear that BI and analytics was more than just a passing technological fad and that it offered the next big thing for the enterprise, successful independent BI software companies became targets of large enterprise software companies looking for strategic acquisitions that would help them provide BI and analytics offerings.

Around 2007, the top software companies began their plans for entering into the BI market. Each acquired the appropriate companies to complete their portfolio and provide the capabilities for enterprise business intelligence. For example, that year saw Oracle acquiring Hyperion, IBM acquiring Cognos, and SAP acquiring Business Objects. They all reached their goal and for a decade afterward began improving and perfecting their offerings, riding on the wave of demand for enterprise business intelligence.

So if the last decade provided a period of improvement for many vendors, it all came to a sudden halt around 2012 as new methods, tools, and technologies began to signal that business intelligence and analytic strategies had to be revamped in light of a new trend affecting business intelligence. That new trend was—and is—big data, and it posed a challenge to the status quo. With this new trend came a barrage of partnerships as companies looked to collaborate in order to offer capable offerings in the new BI and big data analytics landscape.

We are now in the age of data science, where new methods are used to provide sophisticated, meaningful analysis for decision-making. More corporations are building data science departments and hiring resources with this specific set of skills. In order to satisfy the requirements and needs of this new data science-centric environment, new advanced tools must be created. For Oracle Corporation, this comes in the form of OBIEE 12c and its Visual Analyzer.

Evolution of OBIEE to Its Current Version

Oracle is the "King of the Hill" when it comes to databases and data management tools. With the right strategic acquisitions, Oracle was also able to perfect its downstream applications for decision support and analysis with its Oracle BI Suite of tools. In the past decade, Oracle went from having almost no business intelligence products or services to becoming a major player and thought leader after 2007, when it made its strategic acquisitions. As indicated by industry analysts, Oracle then experienced a surge and enjoyed a top position for its product offerings for nearly a decade, usurping the once prominent independent vendors such as Cognos that had previously dominated the business intelligence and analytics landscape.

After Oracle acquired Siebel, Oracle released its first version of the software as Oracle Business Intelligence Enterprise Edition (OBIEE). The first major release was its 10g version. But for all the fanfare of Oracle's "new" product, OBIEE 10g was really just the Siebel product rebranded as Oracle immediately after its acquisition. It was as if the only big change to the product was that the front page replaced the Siebel logo with the Oracle logo. Under the hood, the technical components of the software were not changed or altered - even keeping naming schemes for the program files clearly evident and indicative of its Siebel roots, for instance. For all intents and purposes, OBIEE remained the same software program and package formerly known as Siebel Analytics.

In terms of its front-end and visualization aspects, it was "Siebel-esque." Although it may have been advanced in its development as a browser-based application, many users considered it cumbersome and not necessarily user-friendly or intuitive. But despite such criticism, the software package as a whole worked and offered an end-to-end BI solution. In contrast, other software vendors had to modify and transform their flagship BI products from client-server to being thin-client and browser-based. Siebel Systems, "late in the game" as a vendor in the BI industry, was able to bank on lessons learned and use best practices and the latest technologies in the development of its product.

So it was with OBIEE 10g that early practitioners gathered around Oracle's "new" BI product and rode the wave of its prominence and success into the lucrative BI and analytics market. This period allowed new practitioners and implementers "to cut their teeth" and gain experience with BI by learning it within a closed system instead of having to create one from scratch. As a result, the program became largely popular among BI offerings, and users and practitioners learned to cope with the software as it existed. We all waited with baited breath for Oracle's promise of an improved holistic program with new features and a change in the look and feel of the program.

Oracle took its first big step toward creating a new Oracle BI product based on the new foundation and suite gathered from the various software packages acquired. It came in the form of OBIEE 11g, which provided integrations of the various programs and the Google-like front end. This version was a welcome improvement for its front-end look and feel. Moreover, in 11g, improvements continued in the integration of all the components of a holistic BI suite. The menu for reports and analysis development reflected a keen distinction for different types of reporting and analysis. The new menu listed a selection for Analysis (that is, the former Answers in 10g) for ad hoc analysis primarily using OBIEE and separately called out Interactive Reporting for use with BI Publisher (that is, the former standalone product called XML Publisher).

Moreover, OBIEE 11g began to include ETL components with Oracle Data Integrator (ODI), and cube components with Essbase. For the first time, OBIEE truly began to feel and act as a single product offering. Even administration of the suite took on a whole new look and process for enterprise management. It seemed as if it was finally getting everything together for delivering business intelligence and analytics. Were we finally at the plateau? Was this all that we needed? The software package seemed to be complete, and Oracle's concentration was now on improving and enhancing the foundation. For the traditional data warehousing and business intelligence methods and approaches, Oracle with its 11g product dominated the market and enjoyed a dominant position as a top leader for business intelligence and analytics for many years.

But what happened next changed everything. The industry experienced—and still continues to experience—a huge change in the way data is handled and analyzed—dubbed as big-data analytics. Consequently, Oracle's business intelligence offering responded to that change.

In 2012, Oracle released OBIEE 12c. For many practitioners, it was the holistic BI product offering that we had been waiting for. Oracle had finally brought everything together as a cohesive BI suite for the enterprise plus included the data discovery components for big data. It was an integration of software as well as resources and staff to finally create what is truly now the Oracle Business Intelligence Suite.

The Birth and History of Machine Learning for OBIEE

It is said that it is lonely at the top. Everyone else poses as a challenger, trying to knock you off your pedestal. Oracle, a leader in databases and data management systems, was poised to remain at the top and continually provide data-centric solutions based on its RDBMS. Challenging this leading database vendor at its own game would clearly be a tough proposition, because Oracle enjoyed such dominance in the market and essentially wrote the book on database management. But then came big data. Suddenly the rules changed, and the game was no longer centered around a relational database.

Consequently, the rules were also being rewritten on how to provide solutions for business intelligence and analysis. Oracle seemed caught between a rock and a hard place, where it could, with all its resources, participate in this new market, but in doing so could also kill its own dominant position and provide for its own demise. Practitioners of Oracle BI waited with baited breath to see where the next steps would lead their champion vendor.

Upstarts and previous departmental vendors such as Tableau or Qlik were able to capitalize on the paradigm shift and the opportunity to fill in some gaps created as larger players such as Oracle were slow to acknowledge them and offer alternatives. And, finally, with OBIEE 12c, Oracle seemed to acknowledge the old notion that "if you can't beat 'em, join 'em" by providing this major release of their flagship product with big-data components incorporating such new technologies as machine learning.

Industry changes had penetrated the data and BI landscape to warrant a second look at the effectiveness of current tools and technologies. As a result, a whole new field of vendors sprung up, brandishing new tools and ready to take on the establishment and leading vendors such as Oracle. Business as usual—or rather, business intelligence—halted, allowing people to take a second look at other vendors. Ironically, although Oracle may have been targeted as the company to beat, this halt may prove beneficial for Oracle as well, as it reassesses and revamps its toolset.

If we are now in the age of big data, what does this truly mean for business intelligence? No doubt that new technologies and tools are being created, aimed at providing the right information to the right person at the right time. This is the same familiar goal of business intelligence. It has not changed. But with this push from some of the world's largest and advanced corporations, artificial intelligence and machine learning have made their way into the corporate world. Access to these tools and technologies has reached all levels of the enterprise and all rungs of the corporate ladder. No longer are artificial intelligence and machine learning reserved for only the most sophisticated statistical operations for matters of a strategic nature.

Data is now everywhere and readily available. Once very elusive, advances in technology (such as the Internet) and solutions (such as for business intelligence and analytics) enable us to access and utilize data. For decades, we struggled to efficiently and effectively use data systems, but now modern tools help us to help ourselves. With each new advancement, we have ushered in the age of self-service BI and data science. Organizations empower their people to get in on the game to allow each level of the corporate ladder to make necessary decisions that help the organization remain competitive in the marketplace.

But when we talk about self-service business intelligence, we have to acknowledge that even though the resources and data are accessible, and technology and tools have advanced, great insights and predictive analytics don't necessarily follow. The use of artificial intelligence is helping us to predict and prescribe in ways that we might not yet comprehend. For that reason, aid through artificial intelligence may be a welcome improvement to how we work.

So what is truly meant by big-data analytics? We would suggest that the elements of the solution would have to address the following:

- Access to lots of pertinent and relevant data
- Performance and processing power
- Friendly user interface
- Ability to readily add pieces of new data
- Visualization of the data to make insights

With these features, an organization could provide the necessary capabilities for data analysis in the hope that some kind of insight could be gained from data sources that would otherwise be useless or provide no advantage.

But even with these advancements in technology and tools, can a user truly utilize these systems and solutions? After all, data analysis is not merely about the data. There must be some kind of understanding of the business first, in order to form business insights from raw data. Otherwise, how would you know what kind of target or analysis is pertinent and being asked of the raw data? How would you know how to put certain pieces of data together to form some kind of useful intelligence? Even the most sophisticated system and solution created would be rather useless in those cases where an understanding of business wasn't not applied. In addition, considering the business solution *self-service* would be rather misleading; the great promise of self-service business intelligence would not be satisfied—not because of limitations of the system—but because of the limitations of the person's understanding about the business. So with a plethora of tools and technologies in today's BI landscape claiming ease of use, there are now numerous claims of platforms offering self-service BI.

Moreover, recent additions, prompted by changes and demands from the industry for self-service, have pushed OBIEE capabilities, enabling the linking of external data (such as data from a spreadsheet) to enhance the data already contained and prepared in the data warehouse. Recent advancements have allowed this to be done dynamically, on the fly. No longer does the data warehouse sit in a vacuum, dependent on a rigorous and laborious mechanism in order to be effectively used as a valuable asset for data discovery and predictive analytics. Indeed, advances like these that allow for data mashups and data visualizations have spurred more growth in BI, into the realm of advanced analytics and effective data mining under what is now generally being called data science.

For this new capability of BI and data science, effective tools are needed for the users and practitioners who warrant access to the voluminous amounts and types of data—coming in as fast as a thought. The industry needs to be able to gather, transform, and maintain this data while at the same time enabling users (or even data scientists) to easily and powerfully serve up and query the data themselves in a self-service capacity.

We proffer that the self-service BI tool that the industry has been searching for, the one that can integrate an established enterprise data warehouse with pieces of external data for data discovery, is now here.

OBIEE on the Oracle Cloud as an Optimal Platform

Self-service BI revolves around the fact that we can facilitate decision-making that's based on data by providing interactive and business-user-driven interfaces to that underlying data. Data today consists not only of structured data, but also of unstructured data. This data demands fast processing. It also requires an integrated approach to online transaction processing (OLTP) and online analytical processing (OLAP) as well as to the discovery of new information from that data coming from various unstructured sources. As a result, big data for decision-making must support new data, new analytics, and new metrics that involve past performance analytics along with predictive analytics.

The common dynamic for all of this is self-service, with such analytics depending on what is being asked for and who is being asked for in an agile nature. The changing needs of business users fit perfectly into using the Oracle Cloud as an optimal platform for accessing Oracle BI and Oracle Big Data. The platform provides real-time analytics of data, self-service analytics to all types of data, and scale-out adoption of the same. Interactive data visualization is a major component, with instant self-service access to that data.

Self-service analytics have becomes a reality made possible by such enabling technologies. Business analysis processes such as mobile device management, visual discovery, and spreadsheet analysis have become business-user driven, with no disconnect across all needed data points through Oracle Cloud.

Machine Learning in OBIEE

OBIEE covers common machine-learning functions available today. This is not an exhaustive list but presents an initial path that you could easily incorporate into your current BI solution. Common machine-learning functions include the following:

- BIN and WIDTH_BUCKET(supervised)
- Forecast (supervised)
- Cluster (unsupervised)
- Outlier (unsupervised)
- Regression (supervised)
- EVALUATE_SCRIPT

OBIEE 12c comes with four embedded R functions (Trendline, Regression, Outliers, and Clusters.) In addition, 12c allows you to create and invoke custom R scripts. This book will introduce these in further detail in later chapters.

Summary

This chapter provides a clear view of the capabilities of Oracle BI, which can easily serve standard needs for ad hoc reporting and research capabilities, and beyond into advanced analytics. In the past, there was no easy way to access data without a certain degree of technical knowledge needed to query the database. Today's tools and technologies provide AI and machine learning for the corporate world to discover and extract information and knowledge that may not have even been foreseen. Oracle BI has extended its capabilities beyond the requirement to understand the business behind the metric or measurement that you are going after. Rather, the process is now reversed, as you can find useful information from your data—sometimes even without any prior knowledge or anticipation—all through the use of artificial intelligence and machine learning.

We also touched on the concepts of big data and self-service BI. New requirements in advanced analytics as well as data discovery come into play as we step into an era where legions of data scientists, armed with their self-service tool in OBIEE, seek to include external data (or even big data) to readily enhance the established data warehouse or repository in search of answers to their queries and analysis.

CHAPTER 5

Use Case: Machine Learning in OBIEE 12c

We've covered machine learning as well as the relevance of big data and cloud computing in regards to BI. You've learned about the primary R technologies and the Oracle R Enterprise, which describe how the R-based algorithms can be used for building models in Oracle 12c. Using these algorithms in OBIEE dashboards has given you a jump start on machine learning and OBIEE. All of this, coupled with Chapter 4, which covered the "why" of machine learning in OBIEE, answers the most sought-after question in BI: why and how is machine learning a perfect solution for solving business problems, and for being used in OBIEE for actionable decision support?

This chapter starts by outlining some real-world use cases that extend the one described in Chapter 3 (predicting the origin of wine). The chapter describes one use case in detail that leverages machine learning in OBIEE to build an advanced decision-making solution. The primary focus of this chapter is in describing the real-world use chosen and how it can be used in OBIEE in combination with the one on predicting the origin of wine to build a holistic decision-making solution. The step-by-step implementation details of the preceding use case are discussed in the next chapter. Such real-world decision support solutions go a long way in providing better business outcomes and business value and raise the bar in competitive intelligence for enterprises.

Real-World Use Cases

The real-world use cases presented in this section can be broadly classified into two main categories:

- Predicting the origin of wine
- Using that origin as a base for predictive analytics, to predict the propensity to buy that wine

R. Abellera and L. Bulusu, *Oracle Business Intelligence with Machine Learning*,
https://doi.org/10.1007/978-1-4842-3255-2_5

Predicting Wine Origin: Using a Machine-Learning Classification Model

This use case predicts the origin of wine. The wines are classified as belonging to one of three origins, based on the class of each wine and other attributes. The output of the prediction is graphed as a pairs plot that is, in turn, integrated with the OBIEE dashboard.

Using Classified Wine Origin as a Base for Predictive Analytics - Extending BI using machine Learning techniques in OBIEE

By using the classified wine origin, this use case predicts the propensity to buy that particular wine. This prediction is different from predicting the wine origin; now we are predicting the probability that a consumer will buy a wine based on its source from. This means the probability always falls between the values 0 and 1, with 0 indicating that the consumer will not buy (or, to be more precise, not likely to buy) a wine based on its origin, and 1 indicating that it is highly likely that a consumer will buy a wine based on its origin. Note that in the wine origin prediction use case, the output was three distinct values: `Origin1`, `Origin2`, and `Origin3`. In contrast, this output is a numerical fractional value between 0 and 1, both inclusive.

■ **Note** Using the outputs from the Wine Origin Prediction model and the Propensity to Buy model in OBIEE analyses and dashboards, the business analyst or BI users can derive decisions that support taking proper actions that accelerate business processes. In this manner, BI can be extended to the predictive analytics domain powered by machine learning using R/ORE in Oracle 12c and OBIEE.

Using the BI Dashboard for Actionable Decision-Making

The use cases of predicting wine origin for a decision-support solution in OBIEE are multiple. The primary ones are listed here:

- Influence the propensity to buy (as described in the preceding subsection)
- Forecast the yield based on origin
- Forecast the wine's quality
- Recommend usage

You can use R-based machine-learning models integrated with OBIEE, or use OBIEE directly to as follows :

- Propensity to buy can be predicted by using the machine-learning algorithm called logistic regression or the generalized linear model (GLM). This can be done in OBIEE by using the built-in Regression analytics function or by using the R- or ORE-based logistic regression model and then using the probabilistic value to determine the outcome.
- Forecasting yield can also be done right in OBIEE by using past buying trends in combination with time series analysis or the Evaluate_Script analytics function with a SQL-based model by scoring the model. Or an R or ORE function similar to one used for predicting wine origin can be used.
- Predicting quality can be done by using the same random forest ML model based on the origin or source predictor variable.
- Recommending usage can be done by using an ML algorithm used for recommendation engines and integrating it in OBIEE dashboards.

■ **Note** Predicting the propensity to buy can aid in decision support in the following ways:

1. Demand of wine
2. Revenue and profit obtained per consumer
3. Improving quality of wine

Technical and Functional Analysis of the Use Cases

Regardless of the business use case and the machine-learning model used, using AI-based machine-learning models that can be used by OBIEE for an actionable decision-support solution can be broken down into the following steps:

1. Build an AI-based machine-learning model using R in Oracle.
2. Score the model on a business data set for graphical output or predictive analytics.

3. Integrate the preceding output with OBIEE for visualization and decision support. This can be a SQL-based script that be leveraged in OBIEE or PNG output.

   a. Interactive graphs can be dynamically driven based on user-input parameters or controls.

   b. A combination of SQL and graph-based output can be integrated with OBIEE. The former for can be used by technical users to tweak the KPI, and/or the latter can be used by technical/business users to create more detailed visualizations that feed forward-facing analytics.

Figure 5-1 shows the OBIEE dashboard visualization of the initial use case of wine origin prediction coupled with the propensity to buy use case. These might seem to be too simple, but it important to know that they are capable of driving user actions as described in the preceding steps when they are enabled as interactive or SQL-based controls.

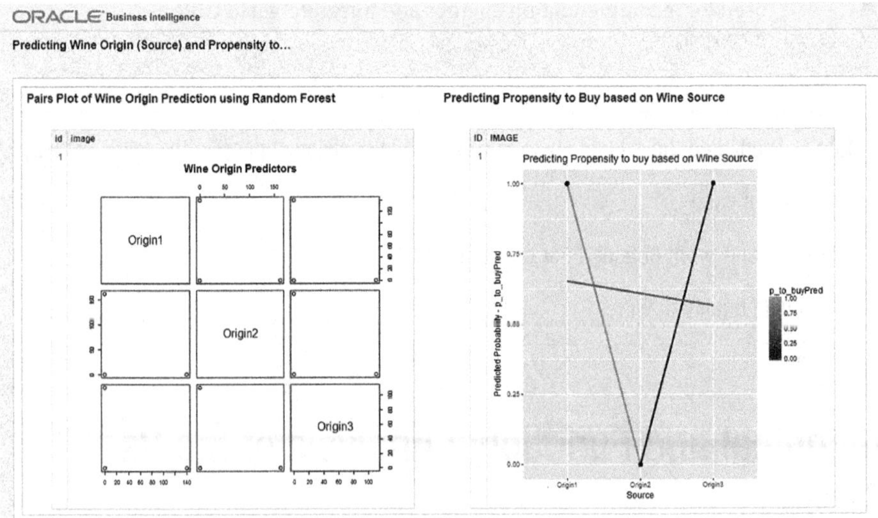

Figure 5-1. Dashboard showing the pairs plot of predicting Wine Origin and using it to predict Propensity to Buy based on Wine Origin (Source)

Analysis of Graph Output: Pairs Plot of Wine Origin Prediction Using Random Forest

The pairs plot shows the plots of `table(origin_pred, test_set$origin)`. Here's the output of `table(origin_pred, test_data$origin)`:

```
> table(origin_pred, test_data$origin)

origin_pred Origin1 Origin2 Origin3
    Origin1     140       0       0
    Origin2       0     162       0
    Origin3       0       0     111
```

And here's the call to the pairs plot in R:

```
pairs(table(origin_pred, test_set$origin), main="Wine Origin Predictors")
```

The response variables are written in a diagonal form, from top left to bottom right. These are outcomes `Origin1`, `Origin2`, and `Origin3`. Then each variable is plotted against the other. Here we have values of `origin_pred` plotted against the values of `test_data$origin` using a `table` (or matrix) output. The middle plot in the first column is an individual pairs plot of `Origin1` vs. `Origin2`—again in `table` output. This corresponds to the first row in the preceding table output.

This same plotted is replicated in the top middle row. As you can see, this corresponds to the second row in the preceding table. There's no data in the top-left corner, because it would just be a straight diagonal line plotting origin against origin, as opposed to `origin_pred` vs. `origin`.

The other individual plots can be similarly analyzed to correspond to the appropriate row(s) in the preceding table output.

Analysis of Graph Output: Predicting Propensity to Buy Based on Wine Source

The `ggplot` is a graphics visualization function belonging to the `ggplot2` R library. Using `ggplot`, a graph or plot is composed of the following:

Data + Aesthetics + Geometry

Here *Data* is an R data frame. *Aesthetics* denotes x and y variables and/or the type, color, and size of the plot elements (point, line, ribbon, bar, etc.). *Geometry* is the type of plot; examples include point, line plot, bar plot, ribbon plot, box plot, and density plot. The primary function to create a custom plot is `ggplot()`, which allows for combinations of point, line, ribbon, and so forth. The parameter group is important here. The specification of the `ggplot` call sets up the graph canvas with the response variable on the y-axis.

■ **Note** A good introduction to `ggplot` with its function call, signature, and examples, can be found at `www.r-bloggers.com/part-3a-plotting-with-ggplot2/`.

Here's the call to the ggplot() function that is used in our example use case to plot the prediction of propensity to buy based on the wine source:

```
library(ggplot2)
gg_plot <- ggplot(data=test_set, aes(x=Source, y=p_to_buyPred, group=1)) +
geom_line(aes(colour = p_to_buyPred), size = 1) + geom_point() +
stat_smooth(method="glm", family="binomial", se=FALSE) +
ggtitle("Predicting Propensity to buy based on Wine Source") +
labs(x="Source", y="Predicted Probability - p_to_buyPred")
plot(gg_plot)
```

■ **Note** geom_line and stat_smooth connect data points that belong to the same group. By specifying group=1, we are telling ggplot that all data points belong to group = 1. Hence, we get a single (V-shaped) line that connects the three data points plotted by geom_point() together. In addition, the regression line, as explained next, also appears in the plot.

The call to geom_line() includes colour=p_to_buyPred, which denotes that the line color is automatically controlled by the levels (predicted probabilities) of the p_to_buyPred variable; size = 1 indicates the line size is 1 unit. aes indicates the aesthetics of the line, as stated previously. The stat_smooth() function generates and fits a smoothed line (a regression line or the line of best fit) on the geom_line and geom_point geometry as a layer based on the transformation of the original data by the GLM model with link = "binomial". This is also called *plotting regression slope*. This is passed as an argument method = "glm", family="binomial". The argument se indicates whether to display the confidence interval to use (0.95 by default). . The method argument is the smoothing method to use (specified in this code as glm, as we used a logistic regression model), and formula is the formula to use in the smoothing function. The smoothing function helps in discerning when overplotting occurs. In Figure 5-1, this is shown as the line in the middle of the plot dissecting the V-shaped lines.

The call to geom_point() without any parameters means the default point shape (which is a dot) and color (which is black) are used. This function call plots the actual data points.

ggtitle prints the title of the plot as given in its argument. labs indicates the x-axis and y-axis labels of the plot, which are "Source" and "Predicted Probability - p_to_buyPred", respectively. The ggplot can be customized by changing the arguments that correspond to alpha, color, line type, and size.

Analysis at a More Detailed Level

At a more detailed level, the use case of propensity to buy can be further analyzed by using a ribbon graph with the geom_ribbon() geometry. We first derive test data by omitting the propensity_to_buy column from the tsetse data set obtained by sampling the original data in the Wineptobuy.csv file. We load this data into a data frame referred to as `test_set2`. Then, we use `test_set2` to derive `test_set3`. Listing 5-1 shows the full code for this analysis.

Listing 5-1. Code for Further Analyzing the Use Case of propensity_to_buy

```
library(ORE)
ore.connect("testr","orcl","localhost","testr")
library(OREmodels)
# The file Wineptobuy.csv is assumed to be in the working directory from
# where the ORE CLI is called
winedata <- read.csv("Wineptobuy.csv", header=TRUE, row.names = NULL,
sep=',') # loads input data into R data frame
head(winedata) # Displays 6 rows of data in the data frame winedata
summary(winedata) # Gives a statistical summary of the data in winedata data
# frame
sapply(winedata, sd) # Applies the standard deviation sd function to each
# variable in the data set winedata
# The below two lines display a two-way contingency table of response
# variable propensity_to_buy and the predictors
# Source and origin respectively to ensure there are not any any 0 cells in
# the winedata data set. In other words,
# xtabs function displays the frequency or count of the levels of
# categorical variables as matrix or table - a
# cross-tabulation, revealing the relationship between propensity_to_buy and
# Source; and between propensity_to_buy
# and origin.
xtabs(~propensity_to_buy +Source, data=winedata)
xtabs(~propensity_to_buy +origin, data=winedata)
label <- winedata[,23]
head(label)
library(caTools)
s <- sample.split(label, SplitRatio=3/4) # Derives a sample split s based on
# split ratio of 0.75
train_set <- winedata[s, c(2:20, 23)] # Samples the input data into train_
# set (columns 2-20, and 23) based on s
test_set <- winedata[!s, c(2:20, 23)] # Samples the data not in train_set
# into test_set
head(train_set) # Displays 6 rows of the train_set
nrow(train_set) # Displays count of rows in train set
head(test_set) # Displays 6 rows of the test set
nrow(test_set) # Displays count of rows in test set
# Loads a matrix of Source and propensity_to_buy columns in train_set into
# sp.tab
sp.tab <- table(train_set$Source, train_set$propensity_to_buy)
sp.tab # Display the above matrix
train_set$Source <- factor(train_set$Source) # This treats source as a
# categorical variable
# Builds a Logistic Regression Model in R using 'glm' Machine Learning
# algorithm with response variable as
```

```
# propensity_to_buy and predictor variable as Source using the train_set
# data set. The family function for the
# glm model is "binomial" (indicating that the model is a binomial model)
# and the link is logit), and the maximum
# iterations to be performed is 100
logitM <- glm(propensity_to_buy ~ Source, data = train_set,
family="binomial", control = glm.control(maxit=100))
# Displays a summary of the logitM model just built in terms of the function
# call for glm; the deviance residuals
# (Min, 1st Quantile, Median, 3rd Quantile, and the Max) which are a measure
# of the model fit or in other words the
# distribution of of the deviance residuals for observations used in the
# model; the table of coefficients with the
# coefficients, their standard errors, the z-statistic or the Wald
# Z-statistic, and the associated p-values
# displayed across, and the Intercept and the predictor variables displayed
# down the matrix; the fit indices which
# include the null deviance and residual deviance and the AIC (Akaike
# Information Criteria). A model with minumum
# AIC value is considered to fit without penalty for the model coefficients.
summary(logitM)
anova(logitM)
# install.packages("aod")
# The wald.test function tests for the Chi-squared test statistic based on
# the coeffieicents of the logitM model. In
# our case we can test the significance of Source predictor variable using
# this function from the aod library of R.
# The order of the model coefficients in the table of coefficients is same
# as the order of terms in the model. This
# is relevant since the wald.test function refers to their coefficients by
# their order in the model. In the below
# three wald.test calls, the argument b passes the coefficients, Sigma gives
# the variance and covariance matrix of
# the error terms, and Terms indicates which terms in the model are to be
# tested. In our use case these are the
# terms 2 and 3. Also, running the function wald.test for Terms 1 and 2; and
# 1,2 and 3 in addition to terms 2 and 3
# gives a chi-squared test statistic with degress of freedom 2, 3 and 2
# respectively and the p-value of 1.0 in all three cases thereby showing that
# Source is statistically significant.
library(aod)
wald.test(b = coef(logitM), Sigma = vcov(logitM), Terms =  1:2)
wald.test(b = coef(logitM), Sigma = vcov(logitM), Terms =  1:3)
wald.test(b = coef(logitM), Sigma = vcov(logitM), Terms =  2:3)
# The exp function below exponentiates the coefficients and analyzes them as
# odds-ratios.
exp(coef(logitM))
head(test_set) # Displays 6 rows of the test_set data set
```

```
nrow(test_set) # Displays number of rows in test_set
head(data.frame(test_set[,c(1:19)])) # Displays 6 rows of columns 1 to 19 in
# test_set
nrow(data.frame(test_set[,c(1:19)])) # Displays count of rows taking columns
# 1 to 19 in test_set
# Uses the predict() function in R to do a prediction of propensity to buy
# on a new data set which consists of
# all rows and columns 1 to 19 in test_set indicating that the values of the
# predictor variables are from this
# test_set and that the values of test_set$p_to_buyPred must be predictions
# using predict(). This is called scoring
# the model. The type of response is response and means the type of
# prediction is a predicted probability as opposed
# to an actual value.
# Note that the original column propensity_to_buy is eliminated in the new
# data set (test_set) while scoring model.
# It outputs a set of probabilities (as opposed to actual values) that fall
# in the closed interval [0,1].
# These probabilities are stored in a newly created column p_to_buyPred in
# the test_set.
test_set$p_to_buyPred <- predict(logitM,  newdata = data.frame(test_
set[,c(1:19)]), type="response")
class(test_set$p_to_buyPred) # Shows the R class of test_set$p_to_buyPred
head(test_set) # Displays 6 rows of test_set which includes the newly
# created column p_to_buyPred
test_set$p_to_buyPred <- ifelse(test_set$p_to_buyPred > 0.5,1,0)
# Quantifies probabilities into values 1 and 0
misClasificError <- mean(test_set$p_to_buyPred != test_set$propensity_to_
buy) # Displays misclassification error
print(paste('Accuracy',1-misClasificError)) # Displays the accuracy if the
# model built and scored.
# An accuracy approaching 1 is considered optimal.
# The library ROCR is used to load the R functions for plotting the Reciever
# Operating Characteristic (ROC). ROC
# summarizes the performance of the model by evaluating the cross-
# correlation between true +ve rate or sensitivity
# and false -ve rate or (1-specificity). Keeping p>0.5, ROC summarizes the
# prediction for all possible values of
# p>0.5. The area under curve (AUC) is an optimal performance metric for ROC
# and the higher value of AUC, the better
# the #prediction of the glm model.
# This package enables visualizing the performance of scoring classifiers
# using the prediction, performance and plot
# functions. Its definition can be found at http://rocr.bioinf.mpi-sb.mpg.
# de/
library(ROCR)
class(test_set$p_to_buyPred) # Displays the R class of the predicted value
# p_to_buyPred of test_set
```

```
# Used the R prediction() function of GLM to transform the input data
# containing predictions into a standard format
# Here it transforms two columns of data given by p_to_buyPred (predictions)
# and propensity_to_buy into a standard
# format and returns an object of class prediction.
pr1 <- prediction(test_set$p_to_buyPred, test_set$propensity_to_buy)
class(pr1) # This gives "prediction" as the class
# The performance function is used to do a predictor evaluation. Its
# signature is
# performance(prediction.obj, measure, x.measure). It works on a prediction
# object (pr1 in this case),
# and measure is performance measure to used for evaluation ("tpr" or the
# true positive rate in this case), and
# x.measure is a second performance measure ("fpr" or false positive rate).
# The measure is plotted in y-axis and the
# x.measure is plotted in the x-axis to result in a 2D curve. Other measures
# can also be passed such as "auc" (area
# under ROC), "acc" (accuracy), "err" (Error rate) etc.
prf1 <- performance(pr1, measure = "tpr", x.measure = "fpr")
class(prf1) # This gives "performance" as the classpdf("plot_prf1.pdf")
# This saves the plotted graph as a PDF file in the working directory
# This plots  an object of class performance, in our case, prf1. colorize
# specifies whether the curve is to be
# colorized according to cutoff.
plot(prf1, colorize = TRUE) # , text.adj = c(-0.2,1.7)
dev.off()
# This makes a different call to performance() function with the measure to
# be evaluated as "auc" or area under ROC
# curve. This returns the performance of the above prediction with "auc" as
# the evaluation measure. Auc is the area
# under ROC curve.
auc1 <- performance(pr1, measure = "auc")
auc1 <- auc1@y.values[[1]]
auc1 # "auc" closer to 1 or equaling 1 indicates a goodness of fit and a
# better prediction performance of the model
library(ROCR)
p <- predict(logitM, newdata= data.frame(test_set[,c(1:19)]),
type="response")
class(p)
pr <- prediction(p, test_set$propensity_to_buy)
class(pr)
prf <- performance(pr, measure = "tpr", x.measure = "fpr")
class(prf)
plot(prf, colorize = TRUE) # , text.adj = c(-0.2,1.7)
auc <- performance(pr, measure = "auc")
auc <- auc@y.values[[1]]
auc
test_set2 <- data.frame(test_set[,c(1:19)])
```

```
head(test_set2)
# The within R function uses the test_set3 data set as its argument and
# generates a data.frame that is used for the
# ribbon layer data. The very first line inside the within generates the
# predicted probabilities along with the
# standard errors that aid in plotting a confidence interval. The argument
# se is specified to indicate whether to
# display confidence interval to use (0.95 by default) and also enables to
# plot a confidence interval. The
# type="link" gives the estimates on the link scale.
# The remaining lines back transform both the predicted values and
# confidence intervals into probabilities.
# The cbind does a column-wise bind of the data frame test_set2 with the
# predicted outcome column scored by
# the predict function that is passed as the second argument to cbind. For
# logistic regression model, the confidence
# intervals are based on the profiled log-likelihood function. The lower and
# upper indicate the lower and upper
# confidence limits.
test_set3 <- cbind(test_set2, predict(logitM, newdata=test_set2, type =
"link", se = TRUE))
test_set3 <- within(test_set3, {
PredictedProb <- plogis(fit)
lower <- plogis(fit - (1.96 * se.fit))
upper <- plogis(fit + (1.96 * se.fit))
})
head(test_set3)
library(ggplot2)
pdf("test_set3_ribbon.pdf") # The below line sets up the graph canvas with
# response variable on y-axis
ggplot(test_set3, aes(x = Source, y = PredictedProb, group=PredictedProb)) +
geom_line(aes(colour = PredictedProb), size = 1) + geom_point() + # Plots
# the actual data points
geom_ribbon(aes(ymin = lower, ymax = upper, fill = PredictedProb), alpha =
0.25) + # alpha fades out connect lines
scale_fill_gradient(low="red", high="green") + # Defines a continuous color
# scale for the ribbon layer
ggtitle("Predicting Propensity to buy based on Wine Source") + # Title of
# the final plot
ylab("Predicted Probability - p_to_buyPred") # Specify label for y-axis.
# This also serves as the graph legend
dev.off()
```

The `scale_fill_gradient()` function is used to define a continuous color scale. In our case, high values will be filled with a green color, and low-probability values will have a red color. The plot is a ribbon plot (continuous), so adding the `scale_fill_gradient()` layer makes it a continuous scale with a colored ribbon fill—green for high, and red for low.

The following code segment from Listing 5-1 is relevant to our discussion of further analysis:

```
test_set3 <- cbind(test_set2, predict(logitM, newdata=test_set2, type =
"link", se = TRUE))
test_set3 <- within(test_set3, {
PredictedProb <- plogis(fit)
lower <- plogis(fit - (1.96 * se.fit))
upper <- plogis(fit + (1.96 * se.fit))
})
head(test_set3)
```

Here's an explanation of the code:

To see what's in `test_set2`, we run the `head(test_set2)` R command in the command line to get this output:

```
> head(test_set2)
   origin class Alcohol Malic.acid  Ash Alcanility.of.ash Magnesium
1 Origin1     1   14.22       1.70 2.30              16.3       118
2 Origin1     1   14.10       2.16 2.30              18.0       105
3 Origin1     1   14.12       1.48 2.32              16.8        95
4 Origin1     1   14.21       4.04 2.44              18.9       111
5 Origin1     1   13.05       1.73 2.04              12.4        92
6 Origin1     1   13.77       1.90 2.68              17.1       115
  Total.phenols Flavanoids Nonflavanoid.phenols Proanthocyanins Color.
  intensity
1          3.20       3.00                 0.26            2.03       6.38
2          2.95       3.32                 0.22            2.38       5.75
3          2.20       2.43                 0.26            1.57       5.00
4          2.85       2.65                 0.30            1.25       5.24
5          2.72       3.27                 0.17            2.91       7.20
6          3.00       2.79                 0.39            1.68       6.30
   Hue OD280.OD315.of.diluted.wines Proline Origin1 Origin2 Origin3  Source
1 0.94                         3.31     970   1.000   0.000       0 Origin1
2 1.25                         3.17    1510   1.000   0.000       0 Origin1
3 1.17                         2.82    1280   1.000   0.000       0 Origin1
4 0.87                         3.33    1080   0.996   0.004       0 Origin1
5 1.12                         2.91    1150   1.000   0.000       0 Origin1
6 1.13                         2.93    1375   1.000   0.000       0 Origin1
>
```

The last column, `Source`, gives the wine origin source predicted using the random forest algorithm with its output displayed as a pairs plot. We see that as the values for `Origin1` and `Origin3` equal 1 or almost approach 1, the source is predicted as `Origin1`. As the values in the `Origin2` column are either 0 or approach close to 0, the `Source` is `Origin2`.

The `within` R function uses the `test_set3` data set as its argument and generates a data frame that is used for the ribbon layer data.

The very first line in the preceding code generates the predicted probabilities along with the standard errors that aid in plotting a confidence interval. The `type="link"` gives the estimates on the link scale. The remaining lines back-transform both the predicted values and confidence intervals into probabilities.

To see the output of `test_set3`, we run the `head(test_set3)` command to get the following output:

```
> head(test_set3)
   origin class Alcohol Malic.acid  Ash Alcanility.of.ash Magnesium
1 Origin1     1   14.22       1.70 2.30              16.3       118
2 Origin1     1   14.10       2.16 2.30              18.0       105
3 Origin1     1   14.12       1.48 2.32              16.8        95
4 Origin1     1   14.21       4.04 2.44              18.9       111
5 Origin1     1   13.05       1.73 2.04              12.4        92
6 Origin1     1   13.77       1.90 2.68              17.1       115
  Total.phenols Flavanoids Nonflavanoid.phenols Proanthocyanins Color.
  intensity
1          3.20       3.00                 0.26            2.03           6.38
2          2.95       3.32                 0.22            2.38           5.75
3          2.20       2.43                 0.26            1.57           5.00
4          2.85       2.65                 0.30            1.25           5.24
5          2.72       3.27                 0.17            2.91           7.20
6          3.00       2.79                 0.39            1.68           6.30
   Hue OD280.OD315.of.diluted.wines Proline Origin1 Origin2 Origin3  Source
1 0.94                         3.31     970   1.000   0.000       0 Origin1
2 1.25                         3.17    1510   1.000   0.000       0 Origin1
3 1.17                         2.82    1280   1.000   0.000       0 Origin1
4 0.87                         3.33    1080   0.996   0.004       0 Origin1
5 1.12                         2.91    1150   1.000   0.000       0 Origin1
6 1.13                         2.93    1375   1.000   0.000       0 Origin1
       fit   se.fit residual.scale upper lower PredictedProb
1 28.56607 94471.71              1     1     0             1
2 28.56607 94471.71              1     1     0             1
3 28.56607 94471.71              1     1     0             1
4 28.56607 94471.71              1     1     0             1
5 28.56607 94471.71              1     1     0             1
6 28.56607 94471.71              1     1     0             1
```

■ **Note** The columns `fit`, `se.fit`, `residual.scale`, `upper`, `lower`, and `PredictedProb` give the fitness, standard error of fit, residual scale, predicted values along with upper and lower confidence limits, and the predicted probabilities. The confidence intervals are at a 95% level.

We then use the geom_ribbon() geometric function coupled with geom_line() and geom_point(), as shown in Listing 5-2, to arrive at the ribbon plot shown in Figure 5-2. Using ggplot in conjunction with geom_ribbon() enables you to plot a graph with predicted probabilities and 95% confidence intervals. This is evident in the call to geom_ribbon(), where the aesthetics are given using the lower and upper values of confidence limits (in the code lines in bold in Listing 5-1). This is shown in the following code segment from Listing 5-1:

```
library(ggplot2)
pdf("test_set3_ribbon.pdf")
ggplot(test_set3, aes(x = Source, y = PredictedProb, group=PredictedProb)) +
geom_line(aes(colour = PredictedProb), size = 1) + geom_point() +
geom_ribbon(aes(ymin = lower, ymax = upper, fill = PredictedProb), alpha =
0.25)  +
scale_fill_gradient(low="red", high="green") +
ggtitle("Predicting Propensity to buy based on Wine Source") +
ylab("Predicted Probability - p_to_buyPred")
dev.off()
```

The primary plot is the ggplot obtained by specifying the aesthetics as the wine Source for the x-axis, and the PredictedProb (as obtained from Listing 5-1) for the y-axis that are grouped by PredictedProb itself. This is plotted as a single line connecting two points for Origin1 and Origin 3, as these correspond to a probability of value 1. The ribbon layer itself is plotted in green, as specified by fill = PredictedProb and the call to the scale_fill_gradient() function that has low="red" and high="green". As the highest value of PredictedProb is 1, the fill color for the ribbon is green and the red color for Origin2 being masked by the layer itself. The measuring scale or legend for both geom_line() and geom_ribbon() appear alongside the ribbon and line as part of the graph. The value of alpha gives the transparency level for the ribbon plot. The scale_fill_gradient() pairs with the geom_ribbon() resulting in the compound graph in Figure 5-2. The entire plot is saved as an image file in PDF format.

```
g <- ggplot(test_set3, aes(x = Source, y = PredictedProb,
group=PredictedProb)) +
geom_line(aes(colour = PredictedProb), size = 1) + geom_point() +
geom_ribbon(aes(ymin = lower, ymax = upper, fill = PredictedProb), alpha =
0.25)  +
scale_fill_gradient(low="red", high="green") +
ggtitle("Predicting Propensity to buy based on Wine Source") +
ylab("Predicted Probability - p_to_buyPred")
```

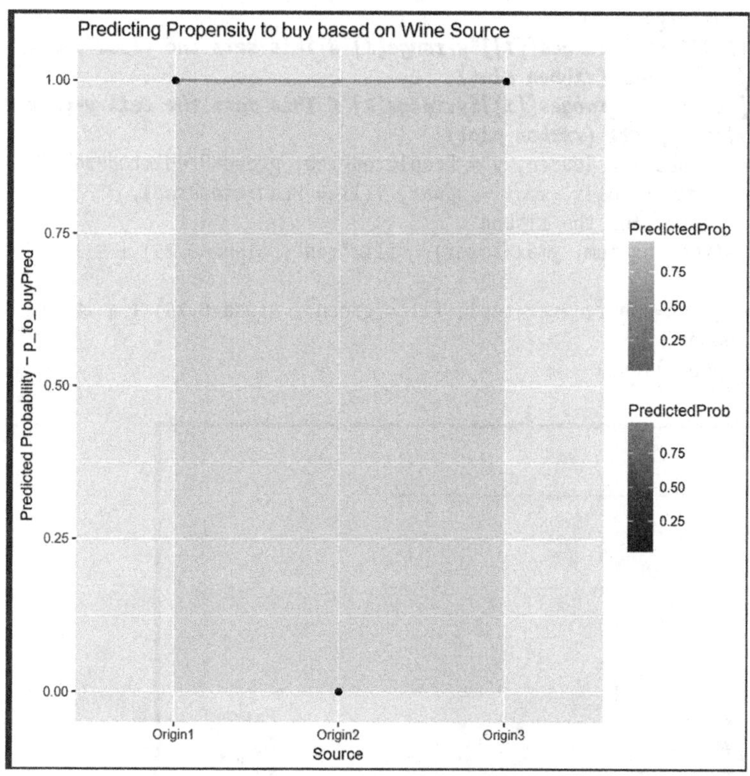

Figure 5-2. *test_set3_ribbon.pdf (ribbon plot of test_set for predicted probilities)*

Use Case(s) of Predicting Propensity to Buy

We can use multiple layers of the ribbon geometry to build a graph that depicts the way decision-making can be based on. By adding the code shown in Listing 5-2 to our code example in Listing 5-1, we can show the areas above and below the ribbon that in turn help in decision-making. The result of executing this code is shown in Figure 5-3.

Listing 5-2. Code Segment for Adding Multiple Areas Below and Above the Ribbon Layer

```
library(ggplot2)
g <- ggplot(test_set3, aes(x = Source, y = PredictedProb,
group=PredictedProb)) +
geom_line(aes(colour = PredictedProb), size = 1) + geom_point() +
geom_ribbon(aes(ymin = lower, ymax = upper, fill = PredictedProb), alpha =
0.25)
# The ggplot_build function returns a list of data frames (one for each
# layer) and a panel object with information
# about the actual x- and y- axis ranges for plot in context. In our case
# this is ribbon plot
```

```
res <- ggplot_build(g)
bottom <- res[[2]]$panel_ranges[[1]]$y.range[1] # This sets the floor y-axis
# plot range for ggplot2 (ribbon plot)
top    <- res[[2]]$panel_ranges[[1]]$y.range[2] # This sets the ceil y-axis
# plot range ffor ggplot2 (ribbon plot)
ggplot(test_set3, aes(x = Source, y = PredictedProb, group=PredictedProb)) +
geom_ribbon(aes(ymin = lower, ymax = upper, fill = PredictedProb),
alpha=0.25) + # layer for the ribbon
geom_ribbon(aes(ymin=bottom, ymax=lower), fill="red", alpha=0.25) + # layer
# below the ribbon
geom_ribbon(aes(ymin=upper, ymax=top), fill="green", alpha=0.25) + # layer
# above the ribbon
geom_point() + geom_line()
```

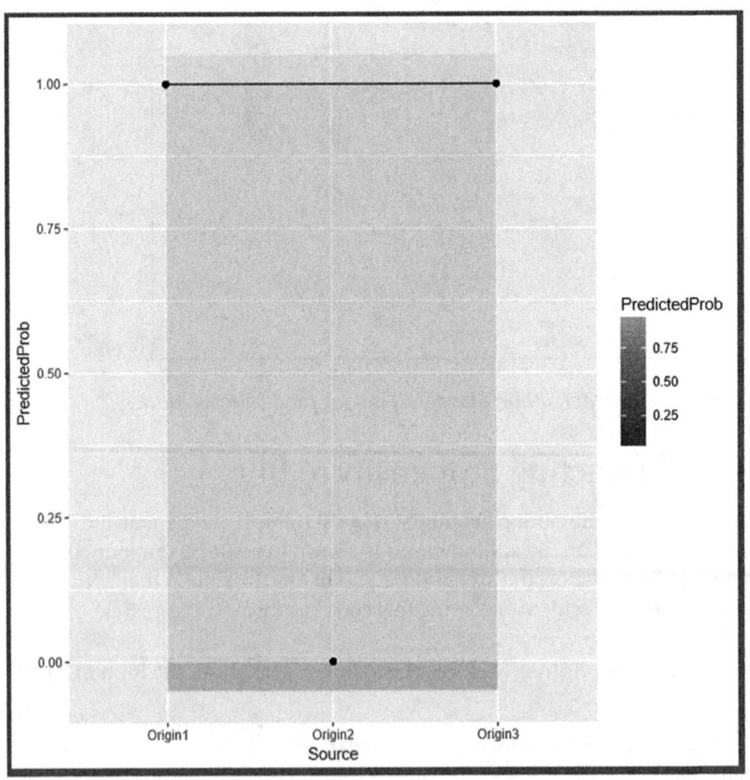

***Figure 5-3.** Graph showing areas below and above the ribbon plot (based on use case of propensity to buy)*

In the preceding graph, we can see that the area in red represents the use case for wine of Origin2, and that the demand for this wine is low. We can thereby deduce that either the quality of the wine needs improvement or the source of production needs more concentration.

However, the green area above the ribbon suggests that the demand, and hence supply, of the wine sourced from `Origin1` and `Origin3` is high. Therefore, the revenue and profit for the wine from these sources is also high.

When this output is integrated with OBIEE, the preceding conclusions can be made actionable by providing controls such as parameters and action filters that users can leverage to enable in business decision support.

Here's the output of the combination of code in Listings 5-1 and 5-2:

```
> ore.connect("testr","orcl","localhost","testr")
> library(OREmodels)
> winedata <- read.csv("Wineptobuy.csv", header=TRUE, row.names = NULL, sep=',$
> head(winedata)
  id  origin class Alcohol Malic.acid  Ash Alcanility.of.ash Magnesium
1  1 Origin1     1   14.37       1.95 2.50              16.8       113
2  2 Origin1     1   14.20       1.76 2.45              15.2       112
3  3 Origin1     1   14.06       2.15 2.61              17.6       121
4  4 Origin1     1   13.64       3.10 2.56              15.2       116
5  5 Origin1     1   14.06       1.63 2.28              16.0       126
6  6 Origin1     1   12.85       1.60 2.52              17.8        95
  Total.phenols Flavanoids Nonflavanoid.phenols Proanthocyanins Color.
  intensity
1          3.85       3.49                 0.24            2.18           7.80
2          3.27       3.39                 0.34            1.97           6.75
3          2.60       2.51                 0.31            1.25           5.05
4          2.70       3.03                 0.17            1.66           5.10
5          3.00       3.17                 0.24            2.10           5.65
6          2.48       2.37                 0.26            1.46           3.93
   Hue OD280.OD315.of.diluted.wines Proline Origin1 Origin2 Origin3  Source
1 0.86                         3.45    1480   1.000   0.000   0.000 Origin1
2 1.05                         2.85    1450   0.994   0.004   0.002 Origin1
3 1.06                         3.58    1295   1.000   0.000   0.000 Origin1
4 0.96                         3.36     845   1.000   0.000   0.000 Origin1
5 1.09                         3.71     780   1.000   0.000   0.000 Origin1
6 1.09                         3.63    1015   1.000   0.000   0.000 Origin1
  origin.1 id.1 propensity_to_buy
1  Origin1    1                 1
2  Origin1    2                 1
3  Origin1    3                 1
4  Origin1    4                 1
5  Origin1    5                 1
6  Origin1    6                 1
```

```
> summary(winedata)
       id             origin          class          Alcohol         Malic.acid
 Min.   :  1   Origin1:140   Min.   :1.00   Min.   :11.03   Min.   :0.740
 1st Qu.:104   Origin2:162   1st Qu.:1.00   1st Qu.:12.37   1st Qu.:1.530
 Median :207   Origin3:111   Median :2.00   Median :13.05   Median :1.830
 Mean   :207                 Mean   :1.93   Mean   :13.00   Mean   :2.343
 3rd Qu.:310                 3rd Qu.:3.00   3rd Qu.:13.67   3rd Qu.:3.100
 Max.   :413                 Max.   :3.00   Max.   :14.75   Max.   :5.800
      Ash          Alcanility.of.ash   Magnesium      Total.phenols
 Min.   :1.360   Min.   :10.60     Min.   : 70.00   Min.   :0.980
 1st Qu.:2.210   1st Qu.:17.00     1st Qu.: 89.00   1st Qu.:1.740
 Median :2.360   Median :19.00     Median : 97.00   Median :2.230
 Mean   :2.366   Mean   :19.43     Mean   : 99.58   Mean   :2.276
 3rd Qu.:2.580   3rd Qu.:21.50     3rd Qu.:107.00   3rd Qu.:2.800
 Max.   :3.230   Max.   :30.00     Max.   :162.00   Max.   :3.880
   Flavanoids    Nonflavanoid.phenols Proanthocyanins Color.intensity
 Min.   :0.340   Min.   :0.1300      Min.   :0.410   Min.   : 1.280
 1st Qu.:1.200   1st Qu.:0.2700      1st Qu.:1.140   1st Qu.: 3.300
 Median :2.140   Median :0.3400      Median :1.460   Median : 4.600
 Mean   :2.011   Mean   :0.3658      Mean   :1.538   Mean   : 4.934
 3rd Qu.:2.780   3rd Qu.:0.4500      3rd Qu.:1.870   3rd Qu.: 5.850
 Max.   :5.080   Max.   :0.6600      Max.   :3.580   Max.   :13.000
      Hue          OD280.OD315.of.diluted.wines    Proline
 Min.   :0.5400   Min.   :1.270               Min.   : 278.0
 1st Qu.:0.7600   1st Qu.:1.830               1st Qu.: 510.0
 Median :0.9600   Median :2.780               Median : 678.0
 Mean   :0.9618   Mean   :2.587               Mean   : 749.5
 3rd Qu.:1.1300   3rd Qu.:3.140               3rd Qu.: 985.0
 Max.   :1.7100   Max.   :4.000               Max.   :1680.0
    Origin1          Origin2          Origin3           Source        origin.1
 Min.   :0.0000  Min.   :0.0000  Min.   :0.0000   Origin1:140   Origin1:140
 1st Qu.:0.0000  1st Qu.:0.0000  1st Qu.:0.0000   Origin2:162   Origin2:162
 Median :0.0000  Median :0.0020  Median :0.0000   Origin3:111   Origin3:111
 Mean   :0.3395   Mean   :0.3922   Mean   :0.2683
 3rd Qu.:1.0000   3rd Qu.:1.0000   3rd Qu.:0.9760
 Max.   :1.0000   Max.   :1.0000   Max.   :1.0000
      id.1      propensity_to_buy
 Min.   :  1   Min.   :0.0000
 1st Qu.:104   1st Qu.:0.0000
 Median :207   Median :1.0000
 Mean   :207   Mean   :0.6077
 3rd Qu.:310   3rd Qu.:1.0000
 Max.   :413   Max.   :1.0000
> sapply(winedata, sd)
```

```
                     id                         origin
            119.3670809                      0.7773550
                  class                        Alcohol
              0.7773550                      0.7667311
             Malic.acid                            Ash
              1.1720914                      0.2931987
      Alcanility.of.ash                      Magnesium
              3.4096871                     14.2594176
          Total.phenols                     Flavanoids
              0.6270436                      0.9700433
   Nonflavanoid.phenols                Proanthocyanins
              0.1293551                      0.5520653
        Color.intensity                            Hue
              2.1460253                      0.2289449
OD280.OD315.of.diluted.wines                   Proline
              0.7162199                    311.4138632
                Origin1                        Origin2
              0.4731436                      0.4869368
                Origin3                         Source
              0.4421105                      0.7773550
               origin.1                           id.1
              0.7773550                    119.3670809
      propensity_to_buy
              0.4888445
> xtabs(~propensity_to_buy +Source, data=winedata)
                 Source
propensity_to_buy Origin1 Origin2 Origin3
                0       0     162       0
                1     140       0     111
> xtabs(~propensity_to_buy +origin, data=winedata)
                 origin
propensity_to_buy Origin1 Origin2 Origin3
                0       0     162       0
                1     140       0     111
> label <- winedata[,23]
> head(label)
[1] 1 1 1 1 1 1
> library(caTools)
Warning message:
package 'caTools' was built under R version 3.2.5
> s <- sample.split(label, SplitRatio=3/4)
> train_set <- winedata[s, c(2:20, 23)]
> test_set <- winedata[!s, c(2:20, 23)]
> head(train_set)
```

```
   origin class Alcohol Malic.acid  Ash Alcanility.of.ash Magnesium
1 Origin1     1   14.37       1.95 2.50              16.8       113
3 Origin1     1   14.06       2.15 2.61              17.6       121
4 Origin1     1   13.64       3.10 2.56              15.2       116
6 Origin1     1   12.85       1.60 2.52              17.8        95
7 Origin1     1   13.87       1.90 2.80              19.4       107
9 Origin1     1   13.51       1.80 2.65              19.0       110
  Total.phenols Flavanoids Nonflavanoid.phenols Proanthocyanins Color.intensity
1          3.85       3.49                 0.24            2.18            7.80
3          2.60       2.51                 0.31            1.25            5.05
4          2.70       3.03                 0.17            1.66            5.10
6          2.48       2.37                 0.26            1.46            3.93
7          2.95       2.97                 0.37            1.76            4.50
9          2.35       2.53                 0.29            1.54            4.20
   Hue OD280.OD315.of.diluted.wines Proline Origin1 Origin2 Origin3  Source
1 0.86                         3.45    1480   1.000   0.000       0 Origin1
3 1.06                         3.58    1295   1.000   0.000       0 Origin1
4 0.96                         3.36     845   1.000   0.000       0 Origin1
6 1.09                         3.63    1015   1.000   0.000       0 Origin1
7 1.25                         3.40     915   0.996   0.004       0 Origin1
9 1.10                         2.87    1095   1.000   0.000       0 Origin1
  propensity_to_buy
1                 1
3                 1
4                 1
6                 1
7                 1
9                 1
> nrow(train_set)
[1] 310
> head(test_set)
    origin class Alcohol Malic.acid  Ash Alcanility.of.ash Magnesium
2  Origin1     1   14.20       1.76 2.45              15.2       112
5  Origin1     1   14.06       1.63 2.28              16.0       126
8  Origin1     1   13.73       1.50 2.70              22.5       101
10 Origin1     1   13.05       1.65 2.55              18.0        98
11 Origin1     1   13.88       1.89 2.59              15.0       101
18 Origin1     1   13.74       1.67 2.25              16.4       118
   Total.phenols Flavanoids Nonflavanoid.phenols Proanthocyanins
2           3.27       3.39                 0.34            1.97
5           3.00       3.17                 0.24            2.10
8           3.00       3.25                 0.29            2.38
10          2.45       2.43                 0.29            1.44
11          3.25       3.56                 0.17            1.70
18          2.60       2.90                 0.21            1.62
```

```
   Color.intensity  Hue OD280.OD315.of.diluted.wines Proline Origin1 Origin2
2             6.75 1.05                           2.85    1450   0.994   0.004
5             5.65 1.09                           3.71     780   1.000   0.000
8             5.70 1.19                           2.71    1285   0.998   0.002
10            4.25 1.12                           2.51    1105   1.000   0.000
11            5.43 0.88                           3.56    1095   0.996   0.002
18            5.85 0.92                           3.20    1060   1.000   0.000
   Origin3  Source propensity_to_buy
2    0.002 Origin1                 1
5    0.000 Origin1                 1
8    0.000 Origin1                 1
10   0.000 Origin1                 1
11   0.002 Origin1                 1
18   0.000 Origin1                 1
> nrow(test_set)
[1] 103
> sp.tab <- table(train_set$Source, train_set$propensity_to_buy)
> sp.tab

           0   1
  Origin1   0  98
  Origin2 122   0
  Origin3   0  90
> train_set$Source <- factor(train_set$Source)
> logitM <- glm(propensity_to_buy ~ Source, data = train_set,
family="binomial$
> summary(logitM)

Call:
glm(formula = propensity_to_buy ~ Source, family = "binomial",
    data = train_set, control = glm.control(maxit = 100))

Deviance Residuals:
       Min           1Q      Median           3Q          Max
-8.861e-07  -8.861e-07  8.861e-07   8.861e-07   8.861e-07

Coefficients:
                Estimate Std. Error z value Pr(>|z|)
(Intercept)    2.857e+01  9.779e+04       0        1
SourceOrigin2 -5.713e+01  1.313e+05       0        1
SourceOrigin3  1.838e-05  1.413e+05       0        1

(Dispersion parameter for binomial family taken to be 1)

    Null deviance: 4.1559e+02  on 309  degrees of freedom
Residual deviance: 2.4340e-10  on 307  degrees of freedom
AIC: 6
```

```
Number of Fisher Scoring iterations: 27

> anova(logitM)
Analysis of Deviance Table

Model: binomial, link: logit

Response: propensity_to_buy

Terms added sequentially (first to last)

       Df Deviance Resid. Df Resid. Dev
NULL                     309     415.59
Source  2   415.59       307       0.00
> # install.packages("aod")
> library(aod)
Warning message:
package 'aod' was built under R version 3.2.5
> wald.test(b = coef(logitM), Sigma = vcov(logitM), Terms =  1:2)
Wald test:
----------

Chi-squared test:
X2 = 1.9e-07, df = 2, P(> X2) = 1.0
> wald.test(b = coef(logitM), Sigma = vcov(logitM), Terms =  1:3)
Wald test:
----------

Chi-squared test:
X2 = 2.7e-07, df = 3, P(> X2) = 1.0
> wald.test(b = coef(logitM), Sigma = vcov(logitM), Terms =  2:3)
Wald test:
----------

Chi-squared test:
X2 = 2.6e-07, df = 2, P(> X2) = 1.0
> exp(coef(logitM))
  (Intercept) SourceOrigin2 SourceOrigin3
 2.547343e+12  1.541085e-25  1.000018e+00
> head(test_set)
    origin class Alcohol Malic.acid  Ash Alcanility.of.ash Magnesium
2  Origin1     1   14.20       1.76 2.45              15.2       112
5  Origin1     1   14.06       1.63 2.28              16.0       126
8  Origin1     1   13.73       1.50 2.70              22.5       101
10 Origin1     1   13.05       1.65 2.55              18.0        98
11 Origin1     1   13.88       1.89 2.59              15.0       101
18 Origin1     1   13.74       1.67 2.25              16.4       118
   Total.phenols Flavanoids Nonflavanoid.phenols Proanthocyanins
```

```
2           3.27      3.39                0.34            1.97
5           3.00      3.17                0.24            2.10
8           3.00      3.25                0.29            2.38
10          2.45      2.43                0.29            1.44
11          3.25      3.56                0.17            1.70
18          2.60      2.90                0.21            1.62
   Color.intensity  Hue OD280.OD315.of.diluted.wines Proline Origin1 Origin2
2             6.75 1.05                          2.85    1450   0.994   0.004
5             5.65 1.09                          3.71     780   1.000   0.000
8             5.70 1.19                          2.71    1285   0.998   0.002
10            4.25 1.12                          2.51    1105   1.000   0.000
11            5.43 0.88                          3.56    1095   0.996   0.002
18            5.85 0.92                          3.20    1060   1.000   0.000
   Origin3  Source propensity_to_buy
2    0.002 Origin1                 1
5    0.000 Origin1                 1
8    0.000 Origin1                 1
10   0.000 Origin1                 1
11   0.002 Origin1                 1
18   0.000 Origin1                 1
> nrow(test_set)
[1] 103
> head(data.frame(test_set[,c(1:19)]))
   origin class Alcohol Malic.acid  Ash Alcanility.of.ash Magnesium
1 Origin1     1   14.20       1.76 2.45              15.2       112
2 Origin1     1   14.06       1.63 2.28              16.0       126
3 Origin1     1   13.73       1.50 2.70              22.5       101
4 Origin1     1   13.05       1.65 2.55              18.0        98
5 Origin1     1   13.88       1.89 2.59              15.0       101
6 Origin1     1   13.74       1.67 2.25              16.4       118
  Total.phenols Flavanoids Nonflavanoid.phenols Proanthocyanins Color.
  intensity
1          3.27       3.39                 0.34            1.97         6.75
2          3.00       3.17                 0.24            2.10         5.65
3          3.00       3.25                 0.29            2.38         5.70
4          2.45       2.43                 0.29            1.44         4.25
5          3.25       3.56                 0.17            1.70         5.43
6          2.60       2.90                 0.21            1.62         5.85
   Hue OD280.OD315.of.diluted.wines Proline Origin1 Origin2 Origin3  Source
1 1.05                         2.85    1450   0.994   0.004   0.002 Origin1
2 1.09                         3.71     780   1.000   0.000   0.000 Origin1
3 1.19                         2.71    1285   0.998   0.002   0.000 Origin1
4 1.12                         2.51    1105   1.000   0.000   0.000 Origin1
5 0.88                         3.56    1095   0.996   0.002   0.002 Origin1
6 0.92                         3.20    1060   1.000   0.000   0.000 Origin1
> nrow(data.frame(test_set[,c(1:19)]))
[1] 103
```

```
> test_set$p_to_buyPred <- predict(logitM,  newdata = data.frame(test_
set[,c(1$
> class(test_set$p_to_buyPred)
[1] "numeric"
> head(test_set)
    origin class Alcohol Malic.acid  Ash Alcanility.of.ash Magnesium
2  Origin1     1   14.20       1.76 2.45              15.2       112
5  Origin1     1   14.06       1.63 2.28              16.0       126
8  Origin1     1   13.73       1.50 2.70              22.5       101
10 Origin1     1   13.05       1.65 2.55              18.0        98
11 Origin1     1   13.88       1.89 2.59              15.0       101
18 Origin1     1   13.74       1.67 2.25              16.4       118
   Total.phenols Flavanoids Nonflavanoid.phenols Proanthocyanins
2           3.27       3.39                 0.34            1.97
5           3.00       3.17                 0.24            2.10
8           3.00       3.25                 0.29            2.38
10          2.45       2.43                 0.29            1.44
11          3.25       3.56                 0.17            1.70
18          2.60       2.90                 0.21            1.62
   Color.intensity  Hue OD280.OD315.of.diluted.wines Proline Origin1 Origin2
2             6.75 1.05                         2.85    1450   0.994   0.004
5             5.65 1.09                         3.71     780   1.000   0.000
8             5.70 1.19                         2.71    1285   0.998   0.002
10            4.25 1.12                         2.51    1105   1.000   0.000
11            5.43 0.88                         3.56    1095   0.996   0.002
18            5.85 0.92                         3.20    1060   1.000   0.000
   Origin3  Source propensity_to_buy p_to_buyPred
2    0.002 Origin1                 1            1
5    0.000 Origin1                 1            1
8    0.000 Origin1                 1            1
10   0.000 Origin1                 1            1
11   0.002 Origin1                 1            1
18   0.000 Origin1                 1            1
> test_set$p_to_buyPred <- ifelse(test_set$p_to_buyPred > 0.5,1,0)
> misClasificError <- mean(test_set$p_to_buyPred != test_set$propensity_to_buy)
> print(paste('Accuracy',1-misClasificError))
[1] "Accuracy 1"
> ####
> library(ROCR)
Loading required package: gplots

Attaching package: 'gplots'

The following object is masked from 'package:stats':

    lowess
```

```
Warning messages:
1: package 'ROCR' was built under R version 3.2.5
2: package 'gplots' was built under R version 3.2.5
> # p1 <- predict(logitM, newdata= data.frame(test_set[,c(1:19)]),
type="respo$
> class(test_set$p_to_buyPred)
[1] "numeric"
> pr1 <- prediction(test_set$p_to_buyPred, test_set$propensity_to_buy)
> class(pr1)
[1] "prediction"
attr(,"package")
[1] "ROCR"
> prf1 <- performance(pr1, measure = "tpr", x.measure = "fpr")
> class(prf1)
[1] "performance"
attr(,"package")
[1] "ROCR"
> pdf("plot_prf1.pdf")
> plot(prf1, colorize = TRUE) # , text.adj = c(-0.2,1.7)
> dev.off()
null device
          1
> auc1 <- performance(pr1, measure = "auc")
> auc1 <- auc1@y.values[[1]]
> auc1
[1] 1
> ####
> library(ROCR)
> p <- predict(logitM, newdata= data.frame(test_set[,c(1:19)]),
type="response$
> class(p)
[1] "numeric"
> pr <- prediction(p, test_set$propensity_to_buy)
> class(pr)
[1] "prediction"
attr(,"package")
[1] "ROCR"
> prf <- performance(pr, measure = "tpr", x.measure = "fpr")
> class(prf)
[1] "performance"
attr(,"package")
[1] "ROCR"
> # plot(prf, colorize = TRUE) # , text.adj = c(-0.2,1.7)
> auc <- performance(pr, measure = "auc")
> auc <- auc@y.values[[1]]
> auc
[1] 1
> test_set2 <- data.frame(test_set[,c(1:19)])
```

```
> head(test_set2)
   origin class Alcohol Malic.acid  Ash Alcanility.of.ash Magnesium
1 Origin1     1   14.20       1.76 2.45              15.2       112
2 Origin1     1   14.06       1.63 2.28              16.0       126
3 Origin1     1   13.73       1.50 2.70              22.5       101
4 Origin1     1   13.05       1.65 2.55              18.0        98
5 Origin1     1   13.88       1.89 2.59              15.0       101
6 Origin1     1   13.74       1.67 2.25              16.4       118
  Total.phenols Flavanoids Nonflavanoid.phenols Proanthocyanins
  Color.intensity
1          3.27       3.39                 0.34            1.97            6.75
2          3.00       3.17                 0.24            2.10            5.65
3          3.00       3.25                 0.29            2.38            5.70
4          2.45       2.43                 0.29            1.44            4.25
5          3.25       3.56                 0.17            1.70            5.43
6          2.60       2.90                 0.21            1.62            5.85
   Hue OD280.OD315.of.diluted.wines Proline Origin1 Origin2 Origin3  Source
1 1.05                         2.85    1450   0.994   0.004   0.002 Origin1
2 1.09                         3.71     780   1.000   0.000   0.000 Origin1
3 1.19                         2.71    1285   0.998   0.002   0.000 Origin1
4 1.12                         2.51    1105   1.000   0.000   0.000 Origin1
5 0.88                         3.56    1095   0.996   0.002   0.002 Origin1
6 0.92                         3.20    1060   1.000   0.000   0.000 Origin1
> test_set3 <- cbind(test_set2, predict(logitM, newdata=test_set2, type = "lin$
> test_set3 <- within(test_set3, {
+ PredictedProb <- plogis(fit)
+ lower <- plogis(fit - (1.96 * se.fit))
+ upper <- plogis(fit + (1.96 * se.fit))
+ })
> head(test_set3)
   origin class Alcohol Malic.acid  Ash Alcanility.of.ash Magnesium
1 Origin1     1   14.20       1.76 2.45              15.2       112
2 Origin1     1   14.06       1.63 2.28              16.0       126
3 Origin1     1   13.73       1.50 2.70              22.5       101
4 Origin1     1   13.05       1.65 2.55              18.0        98
5 Origin1     1   13.88       1.89 2.59              15.0       101
6 Origin1     1   13.74       1.67 2.25              16.4       118
  Total.phenols Flavanoids Nonflavanoid.phenols Proanthocyanins Color.intensity
1          3.27       3.39                 0.34            1.97            6.75
2          3.00       3.17                 0.24            2.10            5.65
3          3.00       3.25                 0.29            2.38            5.70
4          2.45       2.43                 0.29            1.44            4.25
5          3.25       3.56                 0.17            1.70            5.43
6          2.60       2.90                 0.21            1.62            5.85
   Hue OD280.OD315.of.diluted.wines Proline Origin1 Origin2 Origin3  Source
```

```
1 1.05                          2.85    1450   0.994   0.004    0.002 Origin1
2 1.09                          3.71     780   1.000   0.000    0.000 Origin1
3 1.19                          2.71    1285   0.998   0.002    0.000 Origin1
4 1.12                          2.51    1105   1.000   0.000    0.000 Origin1
5 0.88                          3.56    1095   0.996   0.002    0.002 Origin1
6 0.92                          3.20    1060   1.000   0.000    0.000 Origin1
       fit    se.fit residual.scale upper lower PredictedProb
1 28.56607 97787.51              1     1     0             1
2 28.56607 97787.51              1     1     0             1
3 28.56607 97787.51              1     1     0             1
4 28.56607 97787.51              1     1     0             1
5 28.56607 97787.51              1     1     0             1
6 28.56607 97787.51              1     1     0             1
> library(ggplot2)
Warning message:
package 'ggplot2' was built under R version 3.2.5
> g <- ggplot(test_set3, aes(x = Source, y = PredictedProb, group=PredictedPro$
+ geom_line(aes(colour = PredictedProb), size = 1) + geom_point() +
+ geom_ribbon(aes(ymin = lower, ymax = upper, fill = PredictedProb), alpha = 0$
> res <- ggplot_build(g)
> bottom <- res[[2]]$panel_ranges[[1]]$y.range[1]
> top    <- res[[2]]$panel_ranges[[1]]$y.range[2]
> ggplot(test_set3, aes(x = Source, y = PredictedProb, group=PredictedProb)) +
+ geom_ribbon(aes(ymin = lower, ymax = upper, fill = PredictedProb),
alpha=0.2$
+ geom_ribbon(aes(ymin=bottom, ymax=lower), fill="red", alpha=0.25) +
+ geom_ribbon(aes(ymin=upper, ymax=top), fill="green", alpha=0.25) +
+ geom_point() + geom_line()
```

Summary

This chapter briefly discussed the primary use case of predicting wine origin as well as its extension to predict analytics by way of predicting the propensity to buy a particular wine based on its origin. It explained multiple options for plotting the output in both cases; we created pairs plots as well as compound plots involving lines, points, and ribbons. You also saw how a regression line can be fit into the resulting graph.

CHAPTER 6

Implementing Machine Learning in OBIEE 12c

Chapter 3 highlighted the use of a machine-learning model, namely, the `randomForest` algorithm, taking a business use case of predicting wine origin and integrating its results with OBIEE 12c. It explained how this is implemented using R and Oracle R Enterprise (ORE) and then its graphical output integrated with OBIEE dashboards for BI purposes. Chapter 5 discussed additional business use cases for leveraging machine learning in OBIEE that helps build a decision support solution. One of them extended the Wine Origin Prediction use case to predict propensity to buy based on the origin of the wine. Such real-world decision support solutions go a long way in providing better business outcomes and business value and raise the bar in competitive intelligence for enterprises.

This chapter focuses on implementing the preceding business case by using R- and ORE-based algorithms in Oracle 12c for building and scoring the model and then incorporating the output in OBIEE 12c visually or otherwise. Finally, it describes the steps for building interactive dashboards based on the machine-learning output by way of dynamic user-based input.

Business Use Case Problem Description and Solution

The Wine Origin Prediction use case classifies the origin of wines into `Origin1`, `Origin2`, or `Origin3` based on the class of each wine and other attributes. Depending on the origin, the problem at hand is to predict the propensity to buy a particular wine. The latter was presented as one of four example use cases that are real-world business problems as outcomes associated with wine origin. This was highlighted in Chapter 5, as well as the methods to solve each of them using machine learning and/or OBIEE-based functionality.

R. Abellera and L. Bulusu, *Oracle Business Intelligence with Machine Learning*,
https://doi.org/10.1007/978-1-4842-3255-2_6

Technically Speaking

Analyzing the preceding business use case from a data science perspective, the problem of predicting the propensity to buy has a binary outcome of 1 or 0. An outcome of 1 denotes the customer will buy the wine from that source, and 0 denotes the customer will not buy that wine. Though this sounds like a classification problem, it is in fact more meaningful to treat this as prediction of probability that a customer will buy a particular wine or not based on from where it is sourced.

Solutions to solving this problem exist using both R and ORE, and this chapter discusses them in depth. Before we delve into the programming and graphics part of it, we will discuss the foundation behind the machine-learning algorithm used to solve this kind of prediction—that is, one that involves a binary outcome of probabilities. This requires some explanation of mathematical concepts behind the model to be built as well as scoring the model for predicted output.

■ **Note** From the plethora of machine-learning algorithms available, the closest one that can be applied to predicting probabilities (binary outcomes) is the *generalized linear model*, also called *logistic regression*. It outputs a probability value that is bounded between 0 and 1 and hence is accurate in terms of prediction. Using a linear model such as linear regression for this problem can result in the predicted probabilities being below 0 or above 1. In contrast, the logistic regression outcomes are confined to the bounded set [0,1], which is not the actual values but the probabilistic values, and hence can be directly interpreted as such.

First Part of Solution

The wine Source variable in our use case is called the *categorical variable*, and the propensity to buy is called the *response variable*. Our machine-learning model using logistic regression predicts a probability between 0 and 1, which can be converted into a binary response by using a certain threshold. For example, if p >= 0.5, then the probability is 1; otherwise, it is 0, where p is the predicted probability value.

Listing 6-1 shows the code for predicting a wine source (similar to Listing in Chapter 3). It uses the ore.randomForest machine-learning algorithm to predict wine origin and assigns the column name Source to the predicted origin column.

Listing 6-1. Using ore.randomForest to Predict Wine Origin

```
library(ORE)
ore.connect("testr","orcl","localhost","testr")
library(OREmodels)
winedata <- read.csv("winedata.csv", header=TRUE, row.names = NULL, sep=',')
head(winedata)
winedata$origin <- ifelse(winedata$class == 1, 'Origin1',
```

```
ifelse(winedata$class == 2, 'Origin2',
ifelse(winedata$class == 3, 'Origin3', '')))
class(winedata$origin)
winedata$origin <- as.factor(winedata$origin)
class(winedata$origin)
head(winedata$origin)
table(winedata$origin)
set.seed(123)
sample_size <- 0.70 * nrow(winedata)
sampledata <-sample(seq_len(nrow(winedata)), sample_size)
training_data <- winedata[sampledata, ]
class(training_data)
TRAINING_DATA <- ore.push(training_data)
class(TRAINING_DATA)
test_data <- winedata[-sampledata, ]
TEST_DATA <- ore.push(test_data)
class(TEST_DATA)
head(TRAINING_DATA)
head(TEST_DATA)
wine.rf <- ore.randomForest(origin ~ . - class, TRAINING_DATA)
class(wine.rf)
tree15 = grabTree(wine.rf, k = 15, labelVar = TRUE)
origin_pred <- predict(wine.rf, TEST_DATA, type = "all", supplemental.
cols="origin")
res <- table(origin_pred$origin, origin_pred$prediction)
library(AppliedPredictiveModeling)
transparentTheme(trans = .4)
pairs(table(origin_pred$origin, origin_pred$prediction), main="Wine Origin
Predictors")
test_data$id <- seq_len(nrow(test_data))
row.names(test_data) <- test_data$id
head(test_data[,c(16,1,15)])
origin_pred2 <- ore.pull(origin_pred)
origin_pred2$id <- seq_len(nrow(origin_pred2))
head(origin_pred2)
row.names(origin_pred2) <- origin_pred2$id
head(test_data)
head(origin_pred2)
head(origin_pred2[,c(6,5,4)])
df1 <- test_data[,c(16,15,1:14)]
df2 <- origin_pred2[, c(1:6)]
class(df1)
df1_new <- df1[order(df1$origin),]
head(df1_new)
df2_new <- df2[order(df2$origin),]
head(df2_new)
nrow(df1_new)
nrow(df2_new)
```

```
data_set <- data.frame(df1_new, df2_new)
nrow(data_set)
head(data_set)
colnames(data_set)[20] <- "Source"
head(data_set)
data_set$propensity_to_buy <- ifelse((data_set$Source == 'Origin1'), 1,
ifelse((data_set$Source == 'Origin2'), 0,
ifelse((data_set$Source == 'Origin3'), 1, '')))
class(data_set)
nrow(data_set)
head(data_set)
write.csv(data_set, "Wineptobuy.csv", row.names=FALSE)
```

The output of Listing 6-1 is shown here, with comments inserted to explain the code:

```
> library(ORE)  # load the ORE library, which is the primary library for
# Oracle R Enterprise execution
Loading required package: OREbase
Loading required package: OREcommon

Attaching package: 'OREbase'

The following objects are masked from 'package:base':

    cbind, data.frame, eval, interaction, order, paste, pmax, pmin,
    rbind, table

Loading required package: OREembed
Loading required package: OREstats
Loading required package: MASS
Loading required package: OREgraphics
Loading required package: OREeda
Loading required package: OREmodels
Loading required package: OREdm
Loading required package: lattice
Loading required package: OREpredict
Loading required package: ORExml
> ore.connect("testr","orcl","localhost","testr") # connect to DB by calling
# ore.connect
> library(OREmodels) # load the OREmodels library for calling ORE machine
# learning model(s)
> winedata <- read.csv("winedata.csv", header=TRUE, row.names = NULL,
sep=',') # Read input data from .csv file into a data.frame R object
> head(winedata) # Display 6 rows in the input data frame. This displays the
# various columns which includes predictor variable(s), attributes
  class Alcohol Malic.acid  Ash Alcanility.of.ash Magnesium Total.phenols
```

```
1     1   14.23         1.71 2.43                    15.6        127            2.80
2     1   13.20         1.78 2.14                    11.2        100            2.65
3     1   13.16         2.36 2.67                    18.6        101            2.80
4     1   14.37         1.95 2.50                    16.8        113            3.85
5     1   13.24         2.59 2.87                    21.0        118            2.80
6     1   14.20         1.76 2.45                    15.2        112            3.27
  Flavanoids Nonflavanoid.phenols Proanthocyanins Color.intensity   Hue
1       3.06                 0.28            2.29            5.64  1.04
2       2.76                 0.26            1.28            4.38  1.05
3       3.24                 0.30            2.81            5.68  1.03
4       3.49                 0.24            2.18            7.80  0.86
5       2.69                 0.39            1.82            4.32  1.04
6       3.39                 0.34            1.97            6.75  1.05
  OD280.OD315.of.diluted.wines Proline
1                         3.92    1065
2                         3.40    1050
3                         3.17    1185
4                         3.45    1480
5                         2.93     735
6                         2.85    1450
> winedata$origin <- ifelse(winedata$class == 1, 'Origin1', # Create a
# origin column in the winedata data frame based on 'class' predictor
+ ifelse(winedata$class == 2, 'Origin2',
+ ifelse(winedata$class == 3, 'Origin3', '')))
> class(winedata$origin) # Display the R class of the newly created 'origin'
# column
[1] "character"
> winedata$origin <- as.factor(winedata$origin) # Convert 'origin' into a
# categorical variable by applying the factor() R function
> class(winedata$origin) # Display the R class of the converted 'origin'
# column
[1] "factor"
> head(winedata$origin) # Displays number of distinct classes for 'origin'
# as levels of the 'origin' predictor
[1] Origin1 Origin1 Origin1 Origin1 Origin1 Origin1
Levels: Origin1 Origin2 Origin3
> table(winedata$origin) # Display count of each distinct 'origin' value

Origin1 Origin2 Origin3
    489     549     336
> set.seed(123) # set the seed for sampling the input winedata data set
> sample_size <- 0.70 * nrow(winedata) # set the sample size for sampling
# the winedata data set. Here we use a sample size of 70%
> sampledata <-sample(seq_len(nrow(winedata)), sample_size) # Randomly
# sample the winedata based on the sample size set above
> training_data <- winedata[sampledata, ] # Split the winedata data set into
# training_data containing 70% of the samples
> class(training_data) # Display the R class for training_data
```

```
[1] "data.frame"
> TRAINING_DATA <- ore.push(training_data) # Store the training_data in the
# DB in an ore.frame object callexd TRAINING_DATA
> class(TRAINING_DATA)
[1] "ore.frame"
attr(,"package")
[1] "OREbase"
> test_data <- winedata[-sampledata, ] # Create a test_data set in R that
# contains the reamining data in the same set
> TEST_DATA <- ore.push(test_data) # Store the test_data in the DB in an
# ore.frame object called TEST_DATA
> class(TEST_DATA)
[1] "ore.frame"
attr(,"package")
[1] "OREbase"
> head(TRAINING_DATA) # Display 6 rows of the TRAINING_DATA data set. Notice
# that it contains an additional 'origin' column
     class Alcohol Malic.acid  Ash Alcanility.of.ash Magnesium Total.phenols
396      3   12.60       2.46 2.20              18.5        94          1.62
1083     3   13.45       3.70 2.60              23.0       111          1.70
562      2   11.82       1.72 1.88              19.5        86          2.50
1211     2   11.82       1.47 1.99              20.8        86          1.98
1289     3   12.70       3.55 2.36              21.5       106          1.70
63       2   13.67       1.25 1.92              18.0        94          2.10
     Flavanoids Nonflavanoid.phenols Proanthocyanins Color.intensity  Hue
396        0.66                 0.63            0.94            7.10 0.73
1083       0.92                 0.43            1.46           10.68 0.85
562        1.64                 0.37            1.42            2.06 0.94
1211       1.60                 0.30            1.53            1.95 0.95
1289       1.20                 0.17            0.84            5.00 0.78
63         1.79                 0.32            0.73            3.80 1.23
     OD280.OD315.of.diluted.wines Proline  origin
396                          1.58     695 Origin3
1083                         1.56     695 Origin3
562                          2.44     415 Origin2
1211                         3.33     495 Origin2
1289                         1.29     600 Origin3
63                           2.46     630 Origin2 # This too contains an
# additional column 'origin'
> head(TEST_DATA) # Display 6 rows of the TEST_DATA data set
   class Alcohol Malic.acid  Ash Alcanility.of.ash Magnesium Total.phenols
4      1   14.37       1.95 2.50              16.8       113          3.85
6      1   14.20       1.76 2.45              15.2       112          3.27
8      1   14.06       2.15 2.61              17.6       121          2.60
20     1   13.64       3.10 2.56              15.2       116          2.70
21     1   14.06       1.63 2.28              16.0       126          3.00
24     1   12.85       1.60 2.52              17.8        95          2.48
   Flavanoids Nonflavanoid.phenols Proanthocyanins Color.intensity  Hue
```

```
4        3.49                0.24            2.18            7.80 0.86
6        3.39                0.34            1.97            6.75 1.05
8        2.51                0.31            1.25            5.05 1.06
20       3.03                0.17            1.66            5.10 0.96
21       3.17                0.24            2.10            5.65 1.09
24       2.37                0.26            1.46            3.93 1.09
   OD280.OD315.of.diluted.wines Proline  origin
4                          3.45    1480 Origin1
6                          2.85    1450 Origin1
8                          3.58    1295 Origin1
20                         3.36     845 Origin1
21                         3.71     780 Origin1
24                         3.63    1015 Origin1
```

The next part of the output shows building the random forest model by calling the `ore.randomForest()` function using `class` as predictor variable and `origin` as the response variable and working on the TRAINING_DATA data set. It grows a specific number of decision trees and averages the output from them and uses this information. to arrive at the classification.

```
> wine.rf <- ore.randomForest(origin ~ . - class, TRAINING_DATA)
> class(wine.rf) # Display the class of the object returned by the build
# model. It is of class "ore.model"
[1] "ore.randomForest" "ore.model"
# grabTree() extracts a particular decision tree and k represents which tree
# to use. labelVar set to TRUE means the 'split var' and
# 'prediction' columns in the output frame are assigned meaningful labels.
> tree15 = grabTree(wine.rf, k = 15, labelVar = TRUE)
# Score the built model on TEST_DATA by calling predict(). type="all"
# specifies that both predicted values and matrix of vote counts are
# returned in the output. supplemental.cols="origin" specifies that the
# 'origin' column from the TEST_DATA data set must be included in the
# predicted results
> origin_pred <- predict(wine.rf, TEST_DATA, type = "all", supplemental.
cols="$
# Outputs a table of counts for 'origin' levels, namely, Origin1, Origin2,
# Origin3 and the actual response prediction, and stores it in
# a 'res' object

> res <- table(origin_pred$origin, origin_pred$prediction
> library(AppliedPredictiveModeling)
Warning message:
package 'AppliedPredictiveModeling' was built under R version 3.2.5
> transparentTheme(trans = .4)
# Plots a pairs plot of the above table with heading 'Wine Origin
# Predictors'
```

```
> pairs(table(origin_pred$origin, origin_pred$prediction), main="Wine Origin
P$
# Create a new column id and assign it to each row of the test_data data
# set. Seq_len() creates a sequence upto count of rows in test_data
> test_data$id <- seq_len(nrow(test_data))
> row.names(test_data) <- test_data$id # Assigns the id column for each row
# with the corresponding value of the sequence created for id
> head(test_data[,c(16,1,15)]) # Display the 16th, 1st, and 15th columns for
# 6 rows in test_data with ids 1 to 6
  id class  origin
1  1     1 Origin1
2  2     1 Origin1
3  3     1 Origin1
4  4     1 Origin1
5  5     1 Origin1
6  6     1 Origin1
> origin_pred2 <- ore.pull(origin_pred) # Retrieve the origin_pred result
# scored from DB to an R object
Warning message:
ORE object has no unique key - using random order
> origin_pred2$id <- seq_len(nrow(origin_pred2)) # Create a unique index for
# the rows in origin_pred2 and assign it to a new column 'id'
> head(origin_pred2) # Display 6 rows of the origin_pred2 data for ids 1 to 6
  Origin1 Origin2 Origin3 prediction  origin id
1   1.000   0.000   0.000    Origin1 Origin1  1
2   0.994   0.004   0.002    Origin1 Origin1  2
3   1.000   0.000   0.000    Origin1 Origin1  3
4   1.000   0.000   0.000    Origin1 Origin1  4
5   1.000   0.000   0.000    Origin1 Origin1  5
6   1.000   0.000   0.000    Origin1 Origin1  6
> row.names(origin_pred2) <- origin_pred2$id  # Assigns the id column for
# each row to corresponding value of the sequence created for id
> head(test_data) # Display 6 rows of test_data after adding 'origin' and
# 'id' columns.
  class Alcohol Malic.acid  Ash Alcanility.of.ash Magnesium Total.phenols
1     1   14.37       1.95 2.50              16.8       113          3.85
2     1   14.20       1.76 2.45              15.2       112          3.27
3     1   14.06       2.15 2.61              17.6       121          2.60
4     1   13.64       3.10 2.56              15.2       116          2.70
5     1   14.06       1.63 2.28              16.0       126          3.00
6     1   12.85       1.60 2.52              17.8        95          2.48
  Flavanoids Nonflavanoid.phenols Proanthocyanins Color.intensity   Hue
1       3.49                 0.24            2.18            7.80  0.86
2       3.39                 0.34            1.97            6.75  1.05
3       2.51                 0.31            1.25            5.05  1.06
4       3.03                 0.17            1.66            5.10  0.96
5       3.17                 0.24            2.10            5.65  1.09
6       2.37                 0.26            1.46            3.93  1.09
```

```
  OD280.OD315.of.diluted.wines Proline  origin id
1                         3.45    1480 Origin1  1
2                         2.85    1450 Origin1  2
3                         3.58    1295 Origin1  3
4                         3.36     845 Origin1  4
5                         3.71     780 Origin1  5
6                         3.63    1015 Origin1  6
> head(origin_pred2) # Display 6 rows of origin_pred2 along with id column
  Origin1 Origin2 Origin3 prediction  origin id
1   1.000   0.000   0.000    Origin1 Origin1  1
2   0.994   0.004   0.002    Origin1 Origin1  2
3   1.000   0.000   0.000    Origin1 Origin1  3
4   1.000   0.000   0.000    Origin1 Origin1  4
5   1.000   0.000   0.000    Origin1 Origin1  5
6   1.000   0.000   0.000    Origin1 Origin1  6
> head(origin_pred2[,c(6,5,4)]) # Display 6 rows of origin_pred2 containg
# only the 6th, 5th, and 4th columns
  id  origin prediction
1  1 Origin1    Origin1
2  2 Origin1    Origin1
3  3 Origin1    Origin1
4  4 Origin1    Origin1
5  5 Origin1    Origin1
6  6 Origin1    Origin1
> df1 <- test_data[,c(16,15,1:14)] # Assign a data frame called df1 for the
# subset of test_data with 16th, 15th, and 1 to 14th, columns
> df2 <- origin_pred2[, c(1:6)] # Assign a data frame called df2 for the
# subset of origin_pred2 with columns 1st to 6th.
> class(df1)
[1] "data.frame"
> df1_new <- df1[order(df1$origin),] # Sort the df1 data frame on the origin
# column and assign the sorted data to the df1_new data frame
> head(df1_new) # Display 6 rows of sorted data in df1_new
  id  origin class Alcohol Malic.acid  Ash Alcanility.of.ash Magnesium
1  1 Origin1     1   14.37       1.95 2.50              16.8       113
2  2 Origin1     1   14.20       1.76 2.45              15.2       112
3  3 Origin1     1   14.06       2.15 2.61              17.6       121
4  4 Origin1     1   13.64       3.10 2.56              15.2       116
5  5 Origin1     1   14.06       1.63 2.28              16.0       126
6  6 Origin1     1   12.85       1.60 2.52              17.8        95
  Total.phenols Flavanoids Nonflavanoid.phenols Proanthocyanins Color.
  intensity
1          3.85       3.49                 0.24            2.18         7.80
2          3.27       3.39                 0.34            1.97         6.75
3          2.60       2.51                 0.31            1.25         5.05
4          2.70       3.03                 0.17            1.66         5.10
5          3.00       3.17                 0.24            2.10         5.65
6          2.48       2.37                 0.26            1.46         3.93
```

```
   Hue OD280.OD315.of.diluted.wines Proline
1 0.86                         3.45    1480
2 1.05                         2.85    1450
3 1.06                         3.58    1295
4 0.96                         3.36     845
5 1.09                         3.71     780
6 1.09                         3.63    1015
> df2_new <- df2[order(df2$origin),] # Sort the df2 data frame on the origin
# column and assign the sorted data to the df2_new data frame
> head(df2_new) # Display 6 rows of the df2_new sorted data frame
  Origin1 Origin2 Origin3 prediction  origin id
1   1.000   0.000   0.000    Origin1 Origin1  1
2   0.994   0.004   0.002    Origin1 Origin1  2
3   1.000   0.000   0.000    Origin1 Origin1  3
4   1.000   0.000   0.000    Origin1 Origin1  4
5   1.000   0.000   0.000    Origin1 Origin1  5
6   1.000   0.000   0.000    Origin1 Origin1  6
> nrow(df1_new) # Display count of rows in df1_new
[1] 413
> nrow(df2_new) # Display count of rows in df2_new
[1] 413
> data_set <- data.frame(df1_new, df2_new) # Create a combined data frame of
# df1_new and df2_new and store it in data_set data frame
> nrow(data_set) # Display count of rows in data_set
[1] 413
> head(data_set) # Display 6 rows of data_set
  id  origin class Alcohol Malic.acid  Ash Alcanility.of.ash Magnesium
1  1 Origin1     1   14.37       1.95 2.50              16.8       113
2  2 Origin1     1   14.20       1.76 2.45              15.2       112
3  3 Origin1     1   14.06       2.15 2.61              17.6       121
4  4 Origin1     1   13.64       3.10 2.56              15.2       116
5  5 Origin1     1   14.06       1.63 2.28              16.0       126
6  6 Origin1     1   12.85       1.60 2.52              17.8        95
  Total.phenols Flavanoids Nonflavanoid.phenols Proanthocyanins
  Color.intensity
1          3.85       3.49                 0.24            2.18            7.80
2          3.27       3.39                 0.34            1.97            6.75
3          2.60       2.51                 0.31            1.25            5.05
4          2.70       3.03                 0.17            1.66            5.10
5          3.00       3.17                 0.24            2.10            5.65
6          2.48       2.37                 0.26            1.46            3.93
   Hue OD280.OD315.of.diluted.wines Proline Origin1 Origin2 Origin3
   prediction
```

```
1 0.86                          3.45    1480   1.000   0.000   0.000    Origin1
2 1.05                          2.85    1450   0.994   0.004   0.002    Origin1
3 1.06                          3.58    1295   1.000   0.000   0.000    Origin1
4 0.96                          3.36     845   1.000   0.000   0.000    Origin1
5 1.09                          3.71     780   1.000   0.000   0.000    Origin1
6 1.09                          3.63    1015   1.000   0.000   0.000    Origin1
  origin.1 id.1
1  Origin1    1
2  Origin1    2
3  Origin1    3
4  Origin1    4
5  Origin1    5
6  Origin1    6
> colnames(data_set)[20] <- "Source"  # Assign the label "Source" to the
# 20th column in the data_set data frame
> head(data_set)
  id  origin class Alcohol Malic.acid  Ash Alcanility.of.ash Magnesium
1  1 Origin1     1   14.37       1.95 2.50              16.8       113
2  2 Origin1     1   14.20       1.76 2.45              15.2       112
3  3 Origin1     1   14.06       2.15 2.61              17.6       121
4  4 Origin1     1   13.64       3.10 2.56              15.2       116
5  5 Origin1     1   14.06       1.63 2.28              16.0       126
6  6 Origin1     1   12.85       1.60 2.52              17.8        95
  Total.phenols Flavanoids Nonflavanoid.phenols Proanthocyanins
  Color.intensity
1          3.85       3.49                 0.24            2.18            7.80
2          3.27       3.39                 0.34            1.97            6.75
3          2.60       2.51                 0.31            1.25            5.05
4          2.70       3.03                 0.17            1.66            5.10
5          3.00       3.17                 0.24            2.10            5.65
6          2.48       2.37                 0.26            1.46            3.93
   Hue OD280.OD315.of.diluted.wines Proline Origin1 Origin2 Origin3  Source
1 0.86                         3.45    1480   1.000   0.000   0.000 Origin1
2 1.05                         2.85    1450   0.994   0.004   0.002 Origin1
3 1.06                         3.58    1295   1.000   0.000   0.000 Origin1
4 0.96                         3.36     845   1.000   0.000   0.000 Origin1
5 1.09                         3.71     780   1.000   0.000   0.000 Origin1
6 1.09                         3.63    1015   1.000   0.000   0.000 Origin1
  origin.1 id.1
1  Origin1    1
2  Origin1    2
3  Origin1    3
4  Origin1    4
5  Origin1    5
6  Origin1    6
> data_set$propensity_to_buy <- ifelse((data_set$Source == 'Origin1'), 1,
# create a new column propensity_to_buy based on 'Source' column
+ ifelse((data_set$Source == 'Origin2'), 0,
```

```
+ ifelse((data_set$Source == 'Origin3'), 1, '')))
> class(data_set) # Display class of final data_set
[1] "data.frame"
> nrow(data_set) # Display count of rows in final data_set
[1] 413
> head(data_set) # Display 6 rows in final data_set
  id  origin class Alcohol Malic.acid  Ash Alcanility.of.ash Magnesium
1  1 Origin1     1   14.37       1.95 2.50              16.8       113
2  2 Origin1     1   14.20       1.76 2.45              15.2       112
3  3 Origin1     1   14.06       2.15 2.61              17.6       121
4  4 Origin1     1   13.64       3.10 2.56              15.2       116
5  5 Origin1     1   14.06       1.63 2.28              16.0       126
6  6 Origin1     1   12.85       1.60 2.52              17.8        95
  Total.phenols Flavanoids Nonflavanoid.phenols Proanthocyanins Color.
  intensity
1          3.85       3.49                 0.24            2.18            7.80
2          3.27       3.39                 0.34            1.97            6.75
3          2.60       2.51                 0.31            1.25            5.05
4          2.70       3.03                 0.17            1.66            5.10
5          3.00       3.17                 0.24            2.10            5.65
6          2.48       2.37                 0.26            1.46            3.93
   Hue OD280.OD315.of.diluted.wines Proline Origin1 Origin2 Origin3  Source
1 0.86                         3.45    1480   1.000   0.000   0.000 Origin1
2 1.05                         2.85    1450   0.994   0.004   0.002 Origin1
3 1.06                         3.58    1295   1.000   0.000   0.000 Origin1
4 0.96                         3.36     845   1.000   0.000   0.000 Origin1
5 1.09                         3.71     780   1.000   0.000   0.000 Origin1
6 1.09                         3.63    1015   1.000   0.000   0.000 Origin1
  origin.1 id.1 propensity_to_buy
1  Origin1    1                 1
2  Origin1    2                 1
3  Origin1    3                 1
4  Origin1    4                 1
5  Origin1    5                 1
6  Origin1    6                 1
> write.csv(data_set, "Wineptobuy.csv", row.names=FALSE) # Write the data
# contained in data_set to a new .csv file in working directory
>
```

Second Part of Solution

Now that we have the wine origin predicted and a new data set created with the column Source, we need to use this to predict the propensity to buy. As stated at the beginning of this section, we will use the logistic regression machine-learning algorithm that fits the data by applying a generalized linear model. The predictor variable used is Source, and response variable is propensity_to_buy. Listing 6-2 shows the code.

Listing 6-2. Using Logistic Regression to Determine the Propensity to Buy Based on the Wine Source

```
library(ORE)
ore.connect("testr","orcl","localhost","testr")
library(OREmodels)
winedata <- read.csv("Wineptobuy.csv", header=TRUE, row.names = NULL,
sep=',')
head(winedata)
summary(winedata)
sapply(winedata, sd)
xtabs(~propensity_to_buy +Source, data=winedata)
xtabs(~propensity_to_buy +origin, data=winedata)
label <- winedata[,23]
head(label)
library(caTools)
s <- sample.split(label, SplitRatio=3/4)
train_set <- winedata[s, c(2:20, 23)]
test_set <- winedata[!s, c(2:20, 23)]
head(train_set)
nrow(train_set)
head(test_set)
nrow(test_set)
sp.tab <- table(train_set$Source, train_set$propensity_to_buy)
sp.tab
train_set$Source <- factor(train_set$Source)
logitM <- glm(propensity_to_buy ~ Source, data = train_set,
family="binomial", control = glm.control(maxit=100))
summary(logitM)
anova(logitM)
# install.packages("aod")
library(aod)
wald.test(b = coef(logitM), Sigma = vcov(logitM), Terms =  1:2)
wald.test(b = coef(logitM), Sigma = vcov(logitM), Terms =  1:3)
wald.test(b = coef(logitM), Sigma = vcov(logitM), Terms =  2:3)
exp(coef(logitM))
head(test_set)
nrow(test_set)
head(data.frame(test_set[,c(1:19)]))
```

```
nrow(data.frame(test_set[,c(1:19)]))
test_set$p_to_buyPred <- predict(logitM,  newdata = data.frame(test_
set[,c(1:19)]), type="response")
class(test_set$p_to_buyPred)
head(test_set)
test_set$p_to_buyPred <- ifelse(test_set$p_to_buyPred > 0.5,1,0)
misClasificError <- mean(test_set$p_to_buyPred != test_set$propensity_to_
buy)
print(paste('Accuracy',1-misClasificError))
####
library(ROCR)
class(test_set$p_to_buyPred)
pr1 <- prediction(test_set$p_to_buyPred, test_set$propensity_to_buy)
class(pr1)
prf1 <- performance(pr1, measure = "tpr", x.measure = "fpr")
class(prf1)
pdf("plot_prf1.pdf")
plot(prf1, colorize = TRUE) # , text.adj = c(-0.2,1.7)
dev.off()
auc1 <- performance(pr1, measure = "auc")
auc1 <- auc1@y.values[[1]]
auc1
####
library(ROCR)
p <- predict(logitM, newdata= data.frame(test_set[,c(1:19)]),
type="response")
class(p)
pr <- prediction(p, test_set$propensity_to_buy)
class(pr)
prf <- performance(pr, measure = "tpr", x.measure = "fpr")
class(prf)
plot(prf, colorize = TRUE) # , text.adj = c(-0.2,1.7)
auc <- performance(pr, measure = "auc")
auc <- auc@y.values[[1]]
auc
test_set2 <- data.frame(test_set[,c(1:19)])
test_set3 <- cbind(test_set2, predict(logitM, newdata=test_set2, type =
"link", se = TRUE))
test_set3 <- within(test_set3, {
PredictedProb <- plogis(fit)
LL <- plogis(fit - (1.96 * se.fit))
UL <- plogis(fit + (1.96 * se.fit))
})
head(test_set3)
```

The next part shows the ggplot2 function. A description of ggplot is given in Chapter 5 in the section "Analysis of Graph Output: Predicting Propensity to Buy Based on Wine Source."

```
library(ggplot2)
pdf("test_set3_ribbon.pdf")
ggplot(test_set3, aes(x = Source, y = PredictedProb, group=PredictedProb)) +
geom_line(aes(colour = PredictedProb), size = 1) + geom_point() +
geom_ribbon(aes(ymin = LL, ymax = UL, fill = PredictedProb), alpha =
0.25)  +
scale_fill_gradient(low="red", high="green") +
ggtitle("Predicting Propensity to buy based on Wine Source") +
ylab("Predicted Probability - p_to_buyPred")
dev.off()
fillc_train <- train_set$Source # c("Origin1", "Origin2", "Origin3")
train_set <- cbind(train_set, fillc_train)
library(ggplot2)
pdf("WineOriginTrainingDataGLMPlot_test_bar.pdf")
ggplot(data=train_set, aes(x=Source, y=propensity_to_buy, fill = Source)) +
geom_bar(stat="identity", width=0.25) +
scale_fill_manual("legend", values = c("Origin1" = "green", "Origin2" =
"orange", "Origin3" = "blue"))
dev.off()
fillc_test <- test_set$Source
test_set <- cbind(test_set, fillc_test)
library(ggplot2)
pdf("WineOriginTestDataGLMPlot_test_bar.pdf")
ggplot(data=test_set, aes(x=Source, y=p_to_buyPred, fill = Source)) +
geom_bar(stat="identity", width=0.25)  +
scale_fill_manual("legend", values = c("Origin1" = "green", "Origin2" =
"orange", "Origin3" = "blue"))
dev.off()
library(ggplot2)
pdf("WineOriginTrainingDataGLMPlot_test_lineNpoint.pdf")
ggplot(data=train_set, aes(x=Source, y=propensity_to_buy, group=1)) +
geom_line(aes(colour = propensity_to_buy), size = 1) + geom_point() +
stat_smooth(method="glm", family="binomial", se=FALSE)
dev.off()
library(ggplot2)
pdf("WineOriginTestDataGLMPlot_test_lineNpoint.pdf")
ggplot(data=test_set, aes(x=Source, y=p_to_buyPred, group=1)) +
geom_line(aes(colour = p_to_buyPred), size = 1) + geom_point() +
stat_smooth(method="glm", family="binomial", se=FALSE)
dev.off()
```

Here's the output from executing the code in Listing 6-2:

```
> library(ORE) # load the ORE library which is the primary library for
# Oracle R Enterprise execution
Loading required package: OREbase
Loading required package: OREcommon

Attaching package: 'OREbase'

The following objects are masked from 'package:base':

    cbind, data.frame, eval, interaction, order, paste, pmax, pmin,
    rbind, table

Loading required package: OREembed
Loading required package: OREstats
Loading required package: MASS
Loading required package: OREgraphics
Loading required package: OREeda
Loading required package: OREmodels
Loading required package: OREdm
Loading required package: lattice
Loading required package: OREpredict
Loading required package: OREXml
> ore.connect("testr","orcl","localhost","testr") # Using ORE requires
# connecting to the Oracle DB
> library(OREmodels) # load the OREmodels library for calling ORE machine
# learning model(s)
# The file Wineptobuy.csv is assumed to be in the working directory from
# where the ORE CLI is called
> winedata <- read.csv("Wineptobuy.csv", header=TRUE, row.names =$ # Loads
# input data in .csv file into an R data frame called winedata
> head(winedata) # Displays 6 rows of data in the data frame winedata
  id  origin class Alcohol Malic.acid  Ash Alcanility.of.ash Magnesium
1  1 Origin1     1   14.37       1.95 2.50              16.8       113
2  2 Origin1     1   14.20       1.76 2.45              15.2       112
3  3 Origin1     1   14.06       2.15 2.61              17.6       121
4  4 Origin1     1   13.64       3.10 2.56              15.2       116
5  5 Origin1     1   14.06       1.63 2.28              16.0       126
6  6 Origin1     1   12.85       1.60 2.52              17.8        95
  Total.phenols Flavanoids Nonflavanoid.phenols Proanthocyanins
  Color.intensity
1          3.85       3.49                 0.24            2.18            7.80
2          3.27       3.39                 0.34            1.97            6.75
3          2.60       2.51                 0.31            1.25            5.05
4          2.70       3.03                 0.17            1.66            5.10
5          3.00       3.17                 0.24            2.10            5.65
6          2.48       2.37                 0.26            1.46            3.93
```

```
   Hue OD280.OD315.of.diluted.wines Proline Origin1 Origin2 Origin3  Source
1 0.86                         3.45    1480   1.000   0.000   0.000 Origin1
2 1.05                         2.85    1450   0.994   0.004   0.002 Origin1
3 1.06                         3.58    1295   1.000   0.000   0.000 Origin1
4 0.96                         3.36     845   1.000   0.000   0.000 Origin1
5 1.09                         3.71     780   1.000   0.000   0.000 Origin1
6 1.09                         3.63    1015   1.000   0.000   0.000 Origin1
  origin.1 id.1 propensity_to_buy
1  Origin1    1                 1
2  Origin1    2                 1
3  Origin1    3                 1
4  Origin1    4                 1
5  Origin1    5                 1
6  Origin1    6                 1
> summary(winedata) # Gives a statistical summary of the data in winedata
# data frame as shown below for each variable/attribute
       id             origin         class          Alcohol         Malic.acid
 Min.   :  1    Origin1:140   Min.   :1.00   Min.   :11.03   Min.   :0.740
 1st Qu.:104    Origin2:162   1st Qu.:1.00   1st Qu.:12.37   1st Qu.:1.530
 Median :207    Origin3:111   Median :2.00   Median :13.05   Median :1.830
 Mean   :207                  Mean   :1.93   Mean   :13.00   Mean   :2.343
 3rd Qu.:310                  3rd Qu.:3.00   3rd Qu.:13.67   3rd Qu.:3.100
 Max.   :413                  Max.   :3.00   Max.   :14.75   Max.   :5.800
      Ash         Alcanility.of.ash   Magnesium       Total.phenols
 Min.   :1.360   Min.   :10.60     Min.   : 70.00   Min.   :0.980
 1st Qu.:2.210   1st Qu.:17.00     1st Qu.: 89.00   1st Qu.:1.740
 Median :2.360   Median :19.00     Median : 97.00   Median :2.230
 Mean   :2.366   Mean   :19.43     Mean   : 99.58   Mean   :2.276
 3rd Qu.:2.580   3rd Qu.:21.50     3rd Qu.:107.00   3rd Qu.:2.800
 Max.   :3.230   Max.   :30.00     Max.   :162.00   Max.   :3.880
   Flavanoids    Nonflavanoid.phenols Proanthocyanins Color.intensity
 Min.   :0.340   Min.   :0.1300       Min.   :0.410   Min.   : 1.280
 1st Qu.:1.200   1st Qu.:0.2700       1st Qu.:1.140   1st Qu.: 3.300
 Median :2.140   Median :0.3400       Median :1.460   Median : 4.600
 Mean   :2.011   Mean   :0.3658       Mean   :1.538   Mean   : 4.934
 3rd Qu.:2.780   3rd Qu.:0.4500       3rd Qu.:1.870   3rd Qu.: 5.850
 Max.   :5.080   Max.   :0.6600       Max.   :3.580   Max.   :13.000
      Hue         OD280.OD315.of.diluted.wines    Proline
 Min.   :0.5400   Min.   :1.270                Min.   : 278.0
 1st Qu.:0.7600   1st Qu.:1.830                1st Qu.: 510.0
 Median :0.9600   Median :2.780                Median : 678.0
 Mean   :0.9618   Mean   :2.587                Mean   : 749.5
 3rd Qu.:1.1300   3rd Qu.:3.140                3rd Qu.: 985.0
 Max.   :1.7100   Max.   :4.000                Max.   :1680.0
    Origin1           Origin2           Origin3            Source         origin.1
 Min.   :0.0000   Min.   :0.0000   Min.   :0.0000   Origin1:140   Origin1:140
```

```
 1st Qu.:0.0000   1st Qu.:0.0000   1st
Qu.:0.0000   Origin2:162   Origin2:162
 Median :0.0000   Median :0.0020  Median :0.0000   Origin3:111   Origin3:111
 Mean   :0.3395   Mean   :0.3922   Mean   :0.2683
 3rd Qu.:1.0000   3rd Qu.:1.0000   3rd Qu.:0.9760
 Max.   :1.0000   Max.   :1.0000   Max.   :1.0000
      id.1       propensity_to_buy
 Min.   :  1    Min.   :0.0000
 1st Qu.:104    1st Qu.:0.0000
 Median :207    Median :1.0000
 Mean   :207    Mean   :0.6077
 3rd Qu.:310    3rd Qu.:1.0000
 Max.   :413    Max.   :1.0000
> sapply(winedata, sd) # Applies the standard deviation sd function to each
# variable in the data set winedata
                          id                       origin
                 119.3670809                    0.7773550
                       class                      Alcohol
                   0.7773550                    0.7667311
                  Malic.acid                          Ash
                   1.1720914                    0.2931987
            Alcanility.of.ash                    Magnesium
                   3.4096871                   14.2594176
               Total.phenols                   Flavanoids
                   0.6270436                    0.9700433
        Nonflavanoid.phenols              Proanthocyanins
                   0.1293551                    0.5520653
             Color.intensity                          Hue
                   2.1460253                    0.2289449
OD280.OD315.of.diluted.wines                      Proline
                   0.7162199                  311.4138632
                     Origin1                      Origin2
                   0.4731436                    0.4869368
                     Origin3                       Source
                   0.4421105                    0.7773550
                    origin.1                         id.1
                   0.7773550                  119.3670809
           propensity_to_buy
                   0.4888445
```

The following two lines display a two-way contingency table of the response variable propensity_to_buy and the predictors Source and origin, respectively, to ensure that there are no 0 cells in the winedata data set. In other words, the xtabs function displays the frequency, or count, of the levels of categorical variables as a matrix or table—a cross-tabulation, revealing the relationship between propensity_to_buy and Source, and between propensity_to_buy and origin.

```
> xtabs(~propensity_to_buy +Source, data=winedata)
                 Source
propensity_to_buy Origin1 Origin2 Origin3
                0       0     162       0
                1     140       0     111
> xtabs(~propensity_to_buy +origin, data=winedata)
                 origin
propensity_to_buy Origin1 Origin2 Origin3
                0       0     162       0
                1     140       0     111
> label <- winedata[,23]
> head(label)
[1] 1 1 1 1 1 1
> library(caTools)
Warning message:
package 'caTools' was built under R version 3.2.5
> s <- sample.split(label, SplitRatio=3/4) # Derives a sample split s based
# on split ratio of 0.75
> train_set <- winedata[s, c(2:20, 23)] # Samples the input data into train_
# set (columns 2-20, and 23) based on s
> test_set <- winedata[!s, c(2:20, 23)] # Samples the data not in train_set
# into test_set
> head(train_set) # Displays 6 rows in the train_set
   origin class Alcohol Malic.acid  Ash Alcanility.of.ash Magnesium
1 Origin1     1   14.37       1.95 2.50              16.8       113
3 Origin1     1   14.06       2.15 2.61              17.6       121
4 Origin1     1   13.64       3.10 2.56              15.2       116
5 Origin1     1   14.06       1.63 2.28              16.0       126
6 Origin1     1   12.85       1.60 2.52              17.8        95
7 Origin1     1   13.87       1.90 2.80              19.4       107
  Total.phenols Flavanoids Nonflavanoid.phenols Proanthocyanins Color.
intensity
1          3.85       3.49                 0.24            2.18            7.80
3          2.60       2.51                 0.31            1.25            5.05
4          2.70       3.03                 0.17            1.66            5.10
5          3.00       3.17                 0.24            2.10            5.65
6          2.48       2.37                 0.26            1.46            3.93
7          2.95       2.97                 0.37            1.76            4.50
   Hue OD280.OD315.of.diluted.wines Proline Origin1 Origin2 Origin3  Source
1 0.86                         3.45    1480   1.000   0.000       0 Origin1
3 1.06                         3.58    1295   1.000   0.000       0 Origin1
4 0.96                         3.36     845   1.000   0.000       0 Origin1
5 1.09                         3.71     780   1.000   0.000       0 Origin1
6 1.09                         3.63    1015   1.000   0.000       0 Origin1
7 1.25                         3.40     915   0.996   0.004       0 Origin1
  propensity_to_buy
```

```
1                 1
3                 1
4                 1
5                 1
6                 1
7                 1
> nrow(train_set) # Displays count of rows in train set
[1] 310
> head(test_set) # Displays 6 rows in the test_set
   origin class Alcohol Malic.acid  Ash Alcanility.of.ash Magnesium
2  Origin1     1   14.20       1.76 2.45              15.2       112
9  Origin1     1   13.51       1.80 2.65              19.0       110
10 Origin1     1   13.05       1.65 2.55              18.0        98
11 Origin1     1   13.88       1.89 2.59              15.0       101
13 Origin1     1   14.38       3.59 2.28              16.0       102
17 Origin1     1   13.83       1.65 2.60              17.2        94
   Total.phenols Flavanoids Nonflavanoid.phenols Proanthocyanins
2           3.27       3.39                 0.34            1.97
9           2.35       2.53                 0.29            1.54
10          2.45       2.43                 0.29            1.44
11          3.25       3.56                 0.17            1.70
13          3.25       3.17                 0.27            2.19
17          2.45       2.99                 0.22            2.29
   Color.intensity  Hue OD280.OD315.of.diluted.wines Proline Origin1 Origin2
2             6.75 1.05                         2.85    1450   0.994   0.004
9             4.20 1.10                         2.87    1095   1.000   0.000
10            4.25 1.12                         2.51    1105   1.000   0.000
11            5.43 0.88                         3.56    1095   0.996   0.002
13            4.90 1.04                         3.44    1065   1.000   0.000
17            5.60 1.24                         3.37    1265   1.000   0.000
   Origin3  Source propensity_to_buy
2    0.002 Origin1                 1
9    0.000 Origin1                 1
10   0.000 Origin1                 1
11   0.002 Origin1                 1
13   0.000 Origin1                 1
17   0.000 Origin1                 1
> nrow(test_set) # Displays count of rows in test set
[1] 103
# Loads a matrix of Source and propensity_to_buy columns in train_set into
# sp.tab
> sp.tab <- table(train_set$Source, train_set$propensity_to_buy)
> sp.tab # Display the above matrix
```

```
           0   1
  Origin1   0 104
  Origin2 122   0
  Origin3   0  84
> train_set$Source <- factor(train_set$Source) # This treats source as a
# categorical variable
```

We build a logistic regression model in R by using the `glm` machine-learning algorithm with the response variable as `propensity_to_buy` and the predictor variable as `Source`, using the `train_set` data set. The family function for the glm model is `"binomial"` (indicating that the model is a binomial model), the link is `logit`, and the maximum iterations to be performed is 100:

```
> logitM <- glm(propensity_to_buy ~ Source, data = train_set,
family="binomial$
```

We display a summary of the `logitM` model just built in terms of the function call for `glm`: the deviance residuals (the minimum, first quantile, median, third quantile, and the maximum), which are a measure of the model fit or, in other words, the distribution of the deviance residuals for observations used in the model; the table of coefficients, with the coefficients, their standard errors, the z-statistic or the Wald Z-statistic, and the associated p-values displayed across, and the intercept and the predictor variables displayed down the matrix; the fit indices, which include the null deviance and residual deviance and the Akaike information criterion (AIC). A model with a minimum AIC value is considered to fit without penalty for the model coefficients.

```
> summary(logitM)

Call:
glm(formula = propensity_to_buy ~ Source, family = "binomial",
    data = train_set, control = glm.control(maxit = 100))

Deviance Residuals:
       Min          1Q      Median          3Q         Max
-8.861e-07  -8.861e-07   8.861e-07   8.861e-07   8.861e-07

Coefficients:
                Estimate Std. Error z value Pr(>|z|)
(Intercept)    2.857e+01  9.493e+04       0        1
SourceOrigin2 -5.713e+01  1.292e+05       0        1
SourceOrigin3 -1.927e-05  1.420e+05       0        1

(Dispersion parameter for binomial family taken to be 1)

    Null deviance: 4.1559e+02  on 309  degrees of freedom
Residual deviance: 2.4340e-10  on 307  degrees of freedom
AIC: 6
```

```
Number of Fisher Scoring iterations: 27

> anova(logitM)
Analysis of Deviance Table

Model: binomial, link: logit

Response: propensity_to_buy

Terms added sequentially (first to last)

       Df Deviance Resid. Df Resid. Dev
NULL                     309     415.59
Source  2   415.59       307       0.00
> # install.packages("aod")
```

The wald.test function tests for the chi-squared test statistic based on the coefficients of the logitM model. In our case, we can test the significance of the Source predictor variable by using this function from the aod library of R. The order of the model coefficients in the table of coefficients is the same as the order of terms in the model. This is relevant because the wald.test function refers to its coefficients by their order in the model. In the following three wald.test calls, the argument b passes the coefficients, Sigma gives the variance and covariance matrix of the error terms, and Terms indicates which terms in the model are to be tested. In our use case, these are the terms 2 and 3. Also, running the function wald.test for terms 1 and 2, and for 1, 2, and 3 in addition to terms 2 and 3, gives a chi-squared test statistic with degrees of freedom 2, 3, and 2, respectively, and the p-value of 1.0 in all three cases, thereby showing that Source is statistically significant.

```
> library(aod)
Warning message:
package 'aod' was built under R version 3.2.5
> wald.test(b = coef(logitM), Sigma = vcov(logitM), Terms =  1:2)
Wald test:
----------

Chi-squared test:
X2 = 2e-07, df = 2, P(> X2) = 1.0
> wald.test(b = coef(logitM), Sigma = vcov(logitM), Terms =  1:3)
Wald test:
----------

Chi-squared test:
X2 = 2.7e-07, df = 3, P(> X2) = 1.0
> wald.test(b = coef(logitM), Sigma = vcov(logitM), Terms =  2:3)
Wald test:
----------
```

```
Chi-squared test:
X2 = 2.6e-07, df = 2, P(> X2) = 1.0
> exp(coef(logitM)) # The exp function exponentiates the coefficients and
# analyzes them as odds-ratios.
  (Intercept) SourceOrigin2 SourceOrigin3
 2.547392e+12  1.541056e-25  9.999807e-01
> head(test_set) # Displays 6 rows of the test_set data set
    origin class Alcohol Malic.acid  Ash Alcanility.of.ash Magnesium
2  Origin1     1   14.20       1.76 2.45              15.2       112
9  Origin1     1   13.51       1.80 2.65              19.0       110
10 Origin1     1   13.05       1.65 2.55              18.0        98
11 Origin1     1   13.88       1.89 2.59              15.0       101
13 Origin1     1   14.38       3.59 2.28              16.0       102
17 Origin1     1   13.83       1.65 2.60              17.2        94
   Total.phenols Flavanoids Nonflavanoid.phenols Proanthocyanins
2           3.27       3.39                 0.34            1.97
9           2.35       2.53                 0.29            1.54
10          2.45       2.43                 0.29            1.44
11          3.25       3.56                 0.17            1.70
13          3.25       3.17                 0.27            2.19
17          2.45       2.99                 0.22            2.29
   Color.intensity  Hue OD280.OD315.of.diluted.wines Proline Origin1 Origin2
2             6.75 1.05                         2.85    1450   0.994   0.004
9             4.20 1.10                         2.87    1095   1.000   0.000
10            4.25 1.12                         2.51    1105   1.000   0.000
11            5.43 0.88                         3.56    1095   0.996   0.002
13            4.90 1.04                         3.44    1065   1.000   0.000
17            5.60 1.24                         3.37    1265   1.000   0.000
   Origin3  Source propensity_to_buy
2    0.002 Origin1                 1
9    0.000 Origin1                 1
10   0.000 Origin1                 1
11   0.002 Origin1                 1
13   0.000 Origin1                 1
17   0.000 Origin1                 1
> nrow(test_set) # Displays number of rows in test_set
[1] 103
> head(data.frame(test_set[,c(1:19)])) # Displays 6 rows of columns 1 to 19
# in test_set
   origin class Alcohol Malic.acid  Ash Alcanility.of.ash Magnesium
1 Origin1     1   14.20       1.76 2.45              15.2       112
2 Origin1     1   13.51       1.80 2.65              19.0       110
3 Origin1     1   13.05       1.65 2.55              18.0        98
4 Origin1     1   13.88       1.89 2.59              15.0       101
5 Origin1     1   14.38       3.59 2.28              16.0       102
6 Origin1     1   13.83       1.65 2.60              17.2        94
  Total.phenols Flavanoids Nonflavanoid.phenols Proanthocyanins Color.
  intensity
```

```
1        3.27       3.39              0.34              1.97              6.75
2        2.35       2.53              0.29              1.54              4.20
3        2.45       2.43              0.29              1.44              4.25
4        3.25       3.56              0.17              1.70              5.43
5        3.25       3.17              0.27              2.19              4.90
6        2.45       2.99              0.22              2.29              5.60
   Hue OD280.OD315.of.diluted.wines Proline Origin1 Origin2 Origin3  Source
1 1.05                         2.85    1450   0.994   0.004   0.002 Origin1
2 1.10                         2.87    1095   1.000   0.000   0.000 Origin1
3 1.12                         2.51    1105   1.000   0.000   0.000 Origin1
4 0.88                         3.56    1095   0.996   0.002   0.002 Origin1
5 1.04                         3.44    1065   1.000   0.000   0.000 Origin1
6 1.24                         3.37    1265   1.000   0.000   0.000 Origin1
> nrow(data.frame(test_set[,c(1:19)])) # Displays count of rows taking
# columns 1 to 19 in test_set
[1] 103
```

We use the predict() function in R to predict the propensity to buy on a new data set that consists of all rows and of columns 1 to 19 in test_set, indicating that the values of the predictor variables are from this test_set and that the values of test_set$p_to_buyPred must be predictions using predict(). **This is called *scoring the model*.** The type of response is response and means the type of prediction is a predicted probability as opposed to an actual value. Note that the original column propensity_to_buy is eliminated in the new data set (test_set) while scoring the model. It outputs a set of probabilities (as opposed to actual values) that fall in the closed interval [0,1]. These probabilities are stored in a newly created column p_to_buyPred in test_set.

```
> test_set$p_to_buyPred <- predict(logitM,  newdata = data.frame(test_set[,c(1$
> class(test_set$p_to_buyPred) # Shows the R class of test_set$p_to_buyPred
[1] "numeric"
> head(test_set) # Displays 6 rows of test_set which includes the newly
# created column p_to_buyPred
    origin class Alcohol Malic.acid  Ash Alcanility.of.ash Magnesium
2  Origin1     1   14.20       1.76 2.45              15.2       112
9  Origin1     1   13.51       1.80 2.65              19.0       110
10 Origin1     1   13.05       1.65 2.55              18.0        98
11 Origin1     1   13.88       1.89 2.59              15.0       101
13 Origin1     1   14.38       3.59 2.28              16.0       102
17 Origin1     1   13.83       1.65 2.60              17.2        94
   Total.phenols Flavanoids Nonflavanoid.phenols Proanthocyanins
2           3.27       3.39                 0.34            1.97
9           2.35       2.53                 0.29            1.54
10          2.45       2.43                 0.29            1.44
11          3.25       3.56                 0.17            1.70
13          3.25       3.17                 0.27            2.19
17          2.45       2.99                 0.22            2.29
   Color.intensity  Hue OD280.OD315.of.diluted.wines Proline Origin1 Origin2
```

```
2              6.75 1.05                          2.85    1450   0.994   0.004
9              4.20 1.10                          2.87    1095   1.000   0.000
10             4.25 1.12                          2.51    1105   1.000   0.000
11             5.43 0.88                          3.56    1095   0.996   0.002
13             4.90 1.04                          3.44    1065   1.000   0.000
17             5.60 1.24                          3.37    1265   1.000   0.000
   Origin3  Source propensity_to_buy p_to_buyPred
2    0.002 Origin1                 1            1
9    0.000 Origin1                 1            1
10   0.000 Origin1                 1            1
11   0.002 Origin1                 1            1
13   0.000 Origin1                 1            1
17   0.000 Origin1                 1            1
> test_set$p_to_buyPred <- ifelse(test_set$p_to_buyPred > 0.5,1,0)
# Quantifies probabilities into values 1 and 0
> misClasificError <- mean(test_set$p_to_buyPred != test_set$propensity_to_
buy) # Displays misclassification error
> print(paste('Accuracy',1-misClasificError)) # Displays the accuracy of the
# model built and scored.
[1] "Accuracy 1"
> ####
```

An accuracy approaching 1 is considered optimal. The library ROCR is used to load the R functions for plotting the receiver operating characteristic (ROC). ROC summarizes the performance of the model by evaluating the cross-correlation between true +ve rate (or sensitivity) and false -ve rate (or 1-specificity). Keeping p > 0.5, ROC summarizes the prediction for all possible values of p > 0.5. The area under the curve (AUC) is an optimal performance metric for ROC; the higher the value of AUC, the better the prediction of the `glm` model. This package enables visualizing the performance of scoring classifiers by using the **`prediction, performance, and plot`** `functions`. Its definition can be found at `http://rocr.bioinf.mpi-sb.mpg.de/`.

```
> library(ROCR)
Loading required package: gplots

Attaching package: 'gplots'

The following object is masked from 'package:stats':

    lowess

Warning messages:
1: package 'ROCR' was built under R version 3.2.5
2: package 'gplots' was built under R version 3.2.5
> class(test_set$p_to_buyPred) # Displays the R class of the predicted value
# p_to_buyPred of test_set
[1] "numeric"
```

We use the R prediction() function of GLM to transform the input data containing predictions into a standard format. Here it transforms two columns of data given by p_to_buyPred (predictions) and propensity_to_buy into a standard format and returns an object of class prediction.

```
> pr1 <- prediction(test_set$p_to_buyPred, test_set$propensity_to_buy)
> class(pr1) # This gives "prediction" as the class
[1] "prediction"
attr(,"package")
[1] "ROCR"
```

The performance function is used to do a predictor evaluation. Its signature is performance(prediction.obj, measure, x.measure). It works on a prediction object (pr1 in this case), measure is the performance measure used for evaluation ("tpr", or the true positive rate in this case), and x.measure is a second performance measure ("fpr", or false positive rate). The measure is plotted on the y-axis, and the x.measure is plotted on the x-axis, to result in a 2D curve. Other measures can also be passed, such as "auc" (area under ROC), "acc" (accuracy), and "err" (error rate).

```
> prf1 <- performance(pr1, measure = "tpr", x.measure = "fpr")
> class(prf1) # This gives "performance" as the class
[1] "performance"
attr(,"package")
[1] "ROCR"
> pdf("plot_prf1.pdf") # This saves the plotted graph as a PDF file in the
# working directory
```

The following plots an object of class performance, in our case, prf1. colorize specifies whether the curve is to be colorized according to the cut-off.

```
> plot(prf1, colorize = TRUE) # , text.adj = c(-0.2,1.7)
> dev.off()
null device
          1
```

This makes a different call to the performance() function, with the measure to be evaluated as "auc", or area under the ROC curve. This returns the performance of the preceding prediction with "auc" as the evaluation measure, the area under ROC curve.

```
> auc1 <- performance(pr1, measure = "auc")
> auc1 <- auc1@y.values[[1]]
> auc1 # "auc" closer to 1 or equaling 1 indicates a goodness of fit and a
# better prediction performance of the model
[1] 1
> ####
> library(ROCR)
> p <- predict(logitM, newdata= data.frame(test_set[,c(1:19)]),
type="response$
```

```
> class(p)
[1] "numeric"
> pr <- prediction(p, test_set$propensity_to_buy)
> class(pr)
[1] "prediction"
attr(,"package")
[1] "ROCR"
> prf <- performance(pr, measure = "tpr", x.measure = "fpr")
> class(prf)
[1] "performance"
attr(,"package")
[1] "ROCR"
> plot(prf, colorize = TRUE) # , text.adj = c(-0.2,1.7)
> auc <- performance(pr, measure = "auc")
> auc <- auc@y.values[[1]]
> auc
[1] 1
> test_set2 <- data.frame(test_set[,c(1:19)])
> # test_set2$p_to_buyPred <- predict(logitM, newdata=test_set2, type =
"link"$
```

The within R function uses the test_set3 data set as its argument and generates a data.frame that is used for the ribbon layer data. The very first line inside within generates the predicted probabilities along with the standard errors that aid in plotting a confidence interval. The argument se is specified to indicate whether to display a confidence interval to use (0.95 by default) and also enables us to plot a confidence interval. The type="link" gives the estimates on the link scale. The remaining lines back-transform both the predicted values and confidence intervals into probabilities. The cbind does a column-wise bind of the data frame test_set2 with the predicted outcome column scored by the predict function that is passed as the second argument to cbind. For the logistic regression model, the confidence intervals are based on the profiled log-likelihood function. The lower and upper indicate the lower and upper confidence limits, respectively.

```
> test_set3 <- cbind(test_set2, predict(logitM, newdata=test_set2, type =
"lin$
> test_set3 <- within(test_set3, {
+ PredictedProb <- plogis(fit)
+ lower <- plogis(fit - (1.96 * se.fit))
+ upper <- plogis(fit + (1.96 * se.fit))
+ })
> head(test_set3)
   origin class Alcohol Malic.acid  Ash Alcanility.of.ash Magnesium
1 Origin1     1   14.20       1.76 2.45              15.2       112
2 Origin1     1   13.51       1.80 2.65              19.0       110
3 Origin1     1   13.05       1.65 2.55              18.0        98
4 Origin1     1   13.88       1.89 2.59              15.0       101
5 Origin1     1   14.38       3.59 2.28              16.0       102
```

```
6 Origin1     1   13.83        1.65 2.60                 17.2         94
  Total.phenols Flavanoids Nonflavanoid.phenols Proanthocyanins Color.
  intensity
1          3.27       3.39                 0.34            1.97            6.75
2          2.35       2.53                 0.29            1.54            4.20
3          2.45       2.43                 0.29            1.44            4.25
4          3.25       3.56                 0.17            1.70            5.43
5          3.25       3.17                 0.27            2.19            4.90
6          2.45       2.99                 0.22            2.29            5.60
   Hue OD280.OD315.of.diluted.wines Proline Origin1 Origin2 Origin3  Source
1 1.05                         2.85    1450   0.994   0.004   0.002 Origin1
2 1.10                         2.87    1095   1.000   0.000   0.000 Origin1
3 1.12                         2.51    1105   1.000   0.000   0.000 Origin1
4 0.88                         3.56    1095   0.996   0.002   0.002 Origin1
5 1.04                         3.44    1065   1.000   0.000   0.000 Origin1
6 1.24                         3.37    1265   1.000   0.000   0.000 Origin1
       fit   se.fit residual.scale upper lower PredictedProb
1 28.56609 94925.73              1     1     0             1
2 28.56609 94925.73              1     1     0             1
3 28.56609 94925.73              1     1     0             1
4 28.56609 94925.73              1     1     0             1
5 28.56609 94925.73              1     1     0             1
6 28.56609 94925.73              1     1     0             1
> library(ggplot2)
> pdf("test_set3_ribbon.pdf") # The following line sets up the graph canvas
# with response variable on y-axis
> ggplot(test_set3, aes(x = Source, y = PredictedProb, group=PredictedProb))
+
+ geom_line(aes(colour = PredictedProb), size = 1) + geom_point() + # Plots
# the actual data points
+ geom_ribbon(aes(ymin = LL, ymax = UL, fill = PredictedProb), alpha =
0.25)  + # alpha fades out connection lines
+ scale_fill_gradient(low="red", high="green") + # Defines a continuous
# color scale for the ribbon layer
+ ggtitle("Predicting Propensity to buy based on Wine Source") + # Title of
# the final plot
+ ylab("Predicted Probability - p_to_buyPred") # Specify label for y-axis.
# This also serves as the graph legend
> dev.off()
windows
      2
>  fillc_train <- train_set$Source # c("Origin1", "Origin2", "Origin3")
>  train_set <- cbind(train_set, fillc_train)
>  library(ggplot2)
```

This plots a bar graph with heights of the bars from `train_set` data, where the y values are in `propensity_to_buy` (when `stat="identity"` is specified). `scale_fill_manual()` adds a manual scale as opposed to hue in the legend of the bar graph color.

Here, Origin1 is filled in green, Origin2 is filled in orange, and Origin3 is filled in blue. The width of each bar is 0.25 units. The final graph is saved in a PDF file.

```
> pdf("WineOriginTrainingDataGLMPlot_test_bar.pdf")
> ggplot(data=train_set, aes(x=Source, y=propensity_to_buy, fill = Source))
+
+ geom_bar(stat="identity", width=0.25) +
+ scale_fill_manual("legend", values = c("Origin1" = "green", "Origin2" =
"or$
> dev.off()
null device
          1
> fillc_test <- test_set$Source
> test_set <- cbind(test_set, fillc_test)
> library(ggplot2)
> pdf("WineOriginTestDataGLMPlot_test_bar.pdf") # This plots a bar graph
# with values of p_to_buyPred along the y-axis using data in test_set.
> ggplot(data=test_set, aes(x=Source, y=p_to_buyPred, fill = Source)) +
+ geom_bar(stat="identity", width=0.25) +
+ scale_fill_manual("legend", values = c("Origin1" = "green", "Origin2" =
"or$
> dev.off()
null device
          1
> library(ggplot2)
> pdf("WineOriginTrainingDataGLMPlot_test_lineNpoint.pdf")
```

This plots a connected line graph using train_set with data points for the same group to which Source and propensity_to_buy belong. Here, this group is #, specified as 1. This tells ggplot to plot all data points in group 1. We get a single V-spaged line that connects Origin1, Origin2, #, and Origin3. The measuring scale, or legend, for geom_line() appears alongside the line as part of the graph. The color argument in geom_line() is specified as propensity_to_buy, which means it is autocontrolled by the levels of this variable. The stat_smooth() function generates and fits a smoothed line (a regression line or the line of best fit) on the geom_line and geom_point geometry as a layer based on the transformation of the original data as done by the glm model with link="binomial". This is also called *plotting regression slope*. This is passed as an argument method="glm", family="binomial". The argument se is specified to indicate whether to display a confidence interval to use (0.95 by default). The method argument is the smoothing method to use (specified in this code as glm, as we used a logistic regression model), and formula is the formula to use in the smoothing function. The smoothing function helps in discerning when overplotting occurs.

```
> ggplot(data=train_set, aes(x=Source, y=propensity_to_buy, group=1)) +
+ geom_line(aes(colour = propensity_to_buy), size = 1) + geom_point() +
+ stat_smooth(method="glm", family="binomial", se=FALSE)
Warning: Ignoring unknown parameters: family
> dev.off()
```

```
null device
          1
> library(ggplot2)
> pdf("WineOriginTestDataGLMPlot_test_lineNpoint.pdf") # This is similar to
# the plot above but works on test_set.
> ggplot(data=test_set, aes(x=Source, y=p_to_buyPred, group=1)) +
+ geom_line(aes(colour = p_to_buyPred), size = 1) + geom_point() +
+ stat_smooth(method="glm", family="binomial", se=FALSE)
Warning: Ignoring unknown parameters: family
> dev.off()
null device
          1
>
```

The AUC plot and the GLM plots (based on source vs. propensity to buy) are shown in Figures 6-1 to 6-6.

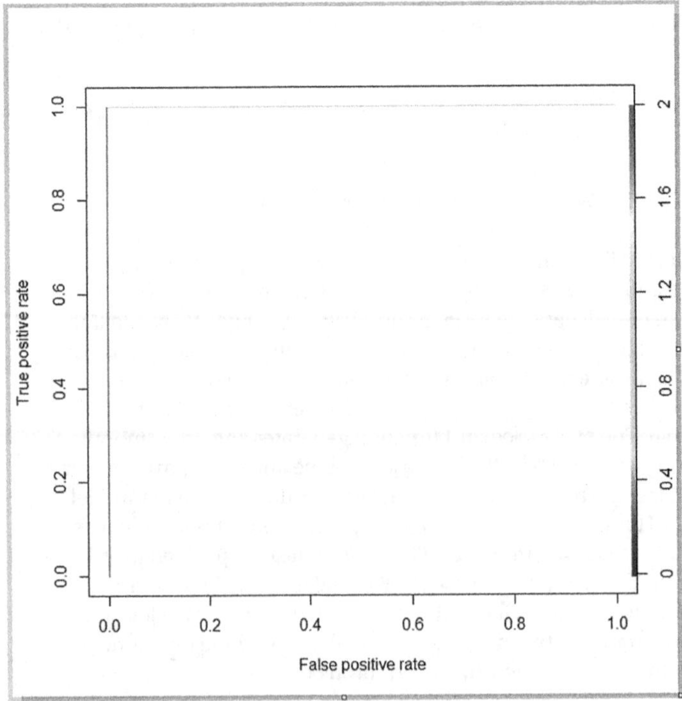

***Figure 6-1.** AUC plot for the executed GLM model*

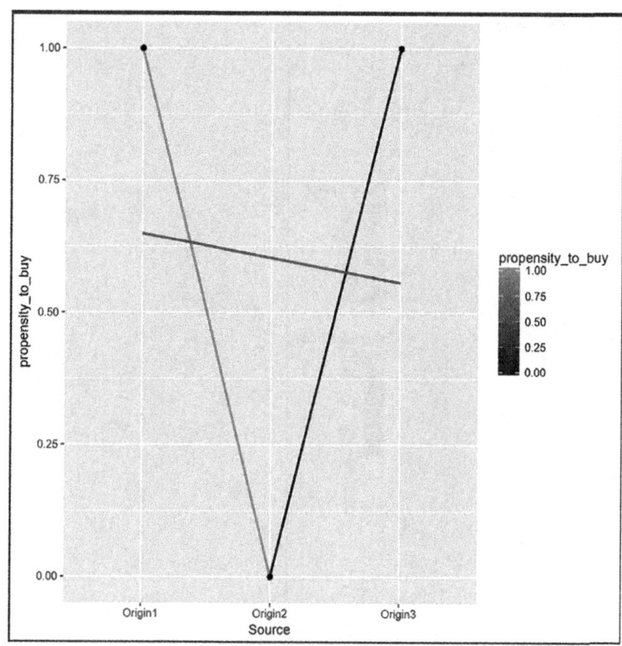

Figure 6-2. *WineOriginTrainingDataGLMPlot_test_lineNpoint.pdf*

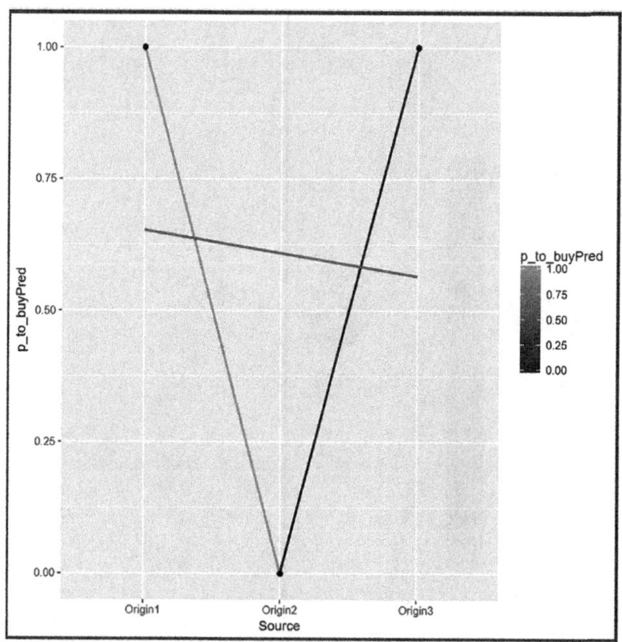

Figure 6-3. *WineOriginTestDataGLMPlot_test_lineNpoint.pdf*

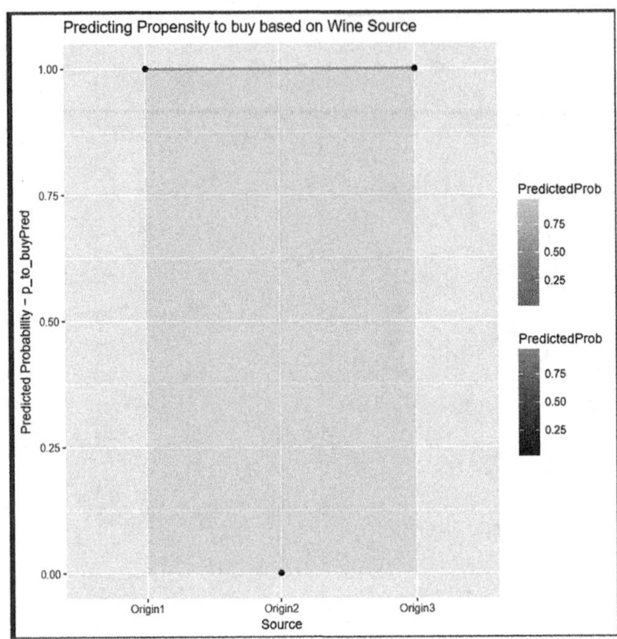

Figure 6-4. *test_set3_ribbon.pdf (ribbon plot of test_set for predicted probilities)*

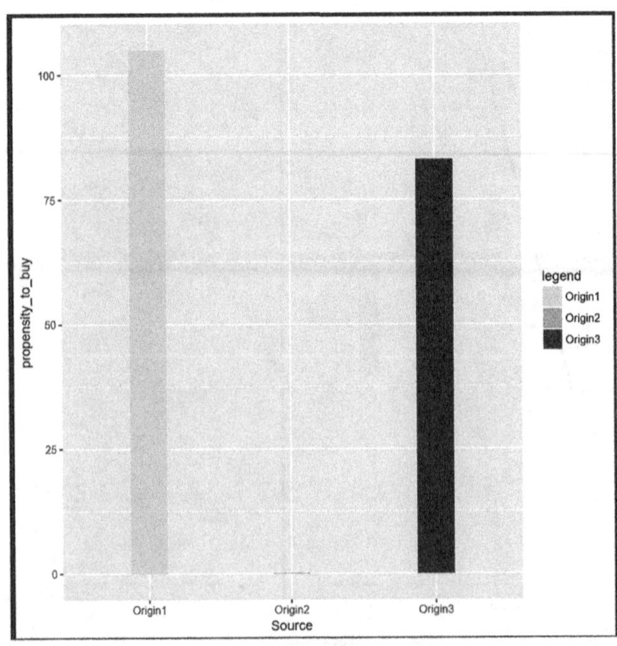

Figure 6-5. *WineOriginTrainingDataGLMPlot_test_bar.pdf*

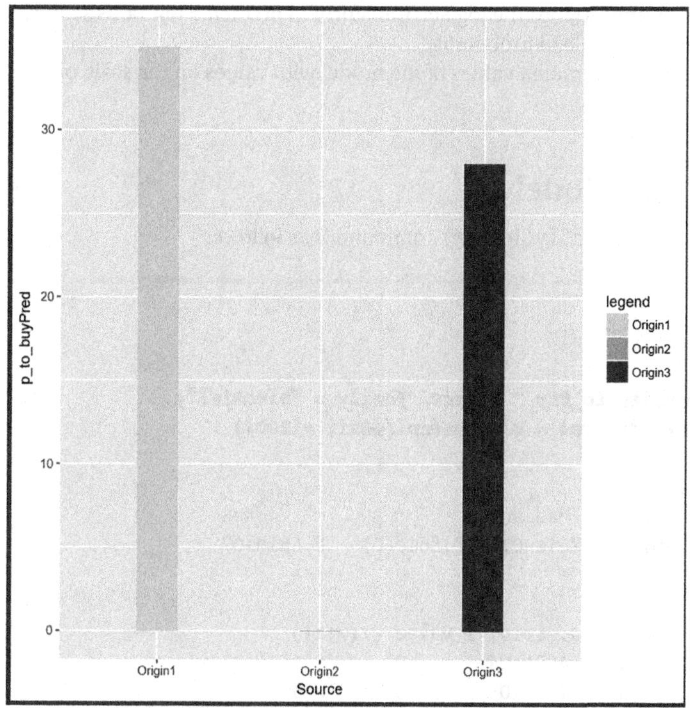

Figure 6-6. *WineOriginTestDataGLMPlot_test_bar.pdf*

Let's look at the matrix (or table) of source vs. propensity to buy in both `train_set` and `test_set`:

```
> table(train_set$Source, train_set$propensity_to_buy)

          0   1
  Origin1   0  99
  Origin2 122   0
  Origin3   0  89
> table(test_set$Source, test_set$p_to_buyPred)

         0  1
  Origin1  0 34
  Origin2 40  0
  Origin3  0 29
>
```

These table outputs indicate that there are some cells in both tables that have 0 as values. This might result in significant codes not being displayed in the summary of the `glm` model, as shown below.

`type='response'` simply applies the logistic transform to predicted log-odds scores, so the predictions are on the scale of probability.

The coefficients are the estimated values of the model with values on the scale of the log odds.

Summary of Logit Model

The output of the preceding `summary(logitM)` command is as follows:

```
> summary(logitM)

Call:
glm(formula = propensity_to_buy ~ Source, family = "binomial",
    data = train_set, control = glm.control(maxit = 100))

Deviance Residuals:
       Min          1Q      Median          3Q         Max
-8.861e-07  -8.861e-07   8.861e-07   8.861e-07   8.861e-07

Coefficients:
               Estimate Std. Error z value Pr(>|z|)
(Intercept)    2.857e+01  9.493e+04       0        1
SourceOrigin2 -5.713e+01  1.292e+05       0        1
SourceOrigin3 -1.927e-05  1.420e+05       0        1

(Dispersion parameter for binomial family taken to be 1)

    Null deviance: 4.1559e+02  on 309  degrees of freedom
Residual deviance: 2.4340e-10  on 307  degrees of freedom
AIC: 6

Number of Fisher Scoring iterations: 27
```

This summary gives information about and the convergence of the model. An analysis of our GLM model's output can be done as follows:

- `summary(logitM)`
    - Model information and model convergence status
        - Call
        - Dispersion parameter
        - Number of Fisher scoring iterations

- Table of coefficients
    - Coefficients
    - Significant codes
- Testing individual parameters
    - Wald chi-squared statistics
- Confidence intervals of individual parameters
- Overall goodness-of-fit
    - Null deviance
    - Residual deviance
    - Akaike information criterion (AIC)

- `anova(logitM)`
    - Analysis of deviance table

Out of these metrics, AIC, null deviance, and residual deviance, along with the confusion matrix and ROC curve, give the performance of the `glm` model. These are outlined here:

AIC, as noted previously, stands for Akaike information criterion and represents the measure of fit that costs the model for the number of coefficients involved in the model. A model with a lower AIC value is recommended. In our example use case, an AIC of 6, as shown in the output of `summary(logitM)`, indicates that the model is a good fit.

Null deviance represents the response predicted by a model with only an intercept. The lower the value, the better the model.

Residual deviance represents predicted by a model with the use of independent variables. The lower the value, the better the model.

A *confusion matrix* defines a table of actual vs. predicted values. This is useful for determining the accuracy of the model and helps in avoiding overfitting. The actual and predicted values are presented as Good and Bad, and the cell values are represented by true positive, true negative, false positive, and false negative values. It looks like Table 6-1.

Table 6-1. *Sample Confusion Matrix in Regard to Logistic Regression*

		Predicted	
		Good	***Bad***
Actual	*Good*	*True +ve (d)*	*False -ve (c)*
	Bad	*False +ve (b)*	*True -ve (a)*

(Source: `www.analyticsvidhya.com`)

The details about the ROC curve are presented in a later subsection.

The lines in bold give information about the data set being used as the training data set (that is, `train_set`), the labels of response and predictor variables (`propensity_to_buy` and `Source`, respectively), and the type of logistic regression algorithm used for fitting (`glm`, or generalized linear model, of the `binary(logit)` family). It also gives the type of scoring model for parameter estimation.

Here the model is using the Fisher scoring algorithm for maximum likelihood estimation. The `maxit` parameter to the `glm` model gives the number of iterations to fit the model, which enables us to determine the maximum likelihood estimates.

■ **Note** *Fisher scoring* is an ascending steps algorithm for getting results; it maximizes the likelihood by getting successively closer and closer to the maximum (top) by taking a subsequent step (also called an *iteration*). It is aware of the fact that it has reached the top, and taking a subsequent step does not increase the likelihood. It is known to be an efficient procedure—not many iterations are usually needed—and generally converges to an answer. If the number of Fisher scoring iterations is large, it means the `glm` model is not optimal in terms of convergence. This might happen if the sample data set is small or the correlation between predictor variables is not collinear. This is a numerical analysis algorithm that is an alternative to the Newton-Raphson method.

In the `glm` model, the binomial link uses the logit link. This indicates that we are fitting a logit model, and the response variable is log odds, mathematically denoted as follows:

logit(p) = log(p/(1-p))

`logit(p)` takes values in the closed interval `[0,1]` and outputs real values on the y-axis. The inverse-logit function data points on x-axis and outputs values in the closed interval `[0,1]` on the y-axis. When the data involved is discrete, overdispersion can occur if there are discrepancies between the observed responses and their predicted values, and these values are larger than what the `binomial(link=logit)` model would predict.

■ **Note** You can refer to the mathematics behind the `glm` algorithm, as detailed in `https://onlinecourses.science.psu.edu/stat504/node/225`. Other web sites also explain the concepts behind the logistic regression model, such as `https://datascienceplus.com/perform-logistic-regression-in-r/` and `www.r-bloggers.com/how-to-perform-a-logistic-regression-in-r/` etc.

A dissection of the summary output of the `glm` model is given here:

```
=>Model information and model convergence status
->Call:
```

The two lines under call provide information about the data set being used as the training data (that is, `train_set`), the labels of response and predictor variables (`propensity_to_buy` and `Source`, respectively), and the type of logistic regression algorithm used for fitting (`glm`, or generalized linear model of the `binary(logit)` family). The `maxit` parameter to the `glm` model gives the number of iterations to fit the model, which enables us to determine the maximum likelihood estimates.

```
->Deviance residuals
```

The deviance residuals output is a description of the distribution of calculated deviance associated with each data point used in the `glm` model. This is output in a nonparametric form. The deviance residuals are the standard residuals that the `glm` model outputs.

```
->Dispersion parameter for the binomial family is assumed to be 1.
```

The dispersion parameter is printed by default with GLMs, but adds more value with count models. This simply means that the dispersion parameter for the binomial family is assumed to be 1.

```
-> Number of Fisher scoring iterations
```

It gives the type of scoring model for parameter estimation, how the model was estimated. A linear model is usually estimated with equations that are solvable with output in closed form, but GLMs are estimated using an iterative approach. The Newton-Raphson method is used by default. Here, the model uses the Fisher scoring algorithm for maximum likelihood estimation.

■ **Note** In numerical analysis, *Newton's method* (also known as the *Newton–Raphson method*, named after Isaac Newton and Joseph Raphson) is a method for finding successively better approximations to the roots (or zeros) of a real-valued function. It is one example of a root-finding algorithm. It is an alternative to the Fisher scoring method previously described. Further discussion of this method can be found at `www.math.ubc.ca/~anstee/math104/104newtonmethod.pdf`.

=>Table of coefficients

The coefficients and Signif. codes give details about the covariates.

->Coefficients

```
Coefficients:
                   Estimate Std. Error z value Pr(>|z|)
(Intercept)       2.857e+01  9.493e+04       0        1
SourceOrigin2 -5.713e+01  1.292e+05       0        1
SourceOrigin3 -1.927e-05  1.420e+05       0        1

    Null deviance: 4.1559e+02  on 309  degrees of freedom
Residual deviance: 2.4340e-10  on 307  degrees of freedom
AIC: 6
```

Our model has one predictor, the `Source`, and the intercept, called the *constant*. The following outlines how the output can be analyzed:

Under the `Estimate` column in the second row, the value gives the coefficient associated with the variable listed to the left. It is the estimated amount by which the log odds of `propensity_to_buy` would increase if the `Source` were one unit higher (`Source` with value `Origin2`). Similarly, the third row with `Source` having `Origin3` as value.

The log odds of `propensity_to_buy` when `Source` is 00 is given in the first row (above the second row). Log odds is an interpretation of simple predictions to odds ratios in the `glm` model.

The next column, `Std. Error`, gives the standard error associated with these estimates (as outlined in the second row). It is an estimate of how much, on average, these estimates would spread around if the model were rerun identically, but with new data, over and over. Dividing the estimate by the standard error, the quotient obtained is assumed to be normally distributed with large enough estimates. This value is listed in the column `z value`. The final column, `Pr(>|z|)`, lists the two-tailed p-values that correspond to those z-values in a standard normal distribution.

->Significant codes

Additional significant codes information appears as stars to the right of the last column. This information follows the key that appears directly below the coefficients table. In our case, we don't see these stars, as there are zeros as values in the tables `table(train_set$Source, train_set$propensity_to_buy`, and `table(test_set$Source, test_set$p_to_buyPred)`.

=> Testing individual parameters
->Wald chi-squared statistics

```
> library(aod)
Warning message:
package 'aod' was built under R version 3.2.5
> wald.test(b = coef(logitM), Sigma = vcov(logitM), Terms =  1:2)
```

```
Wald test:
----------

Chi-squared test:
X2 = 2e-07, df = 2, P(> X2) = 1.0
> wald.test(b = coef(logitM), Sigma = vcov(logitM), Terms =  1:3)
Wald test:
----------

Chi-squared test:
X2 = 2.7e-07, df = 3, P(> X2) = 1.0
> wald.test(b = coef(logitM), Sigma = vcov(logitM), Terms =  2:3)
Wald test:
----------

Chi-squared test:
X2 = 2.6e-07, df = 2, P(> X2) = 1.0
```

=> Confidence intervals of individual parameters
->Overall goodness-of-fit

The overall goodness-of-fit is governed by three metrics: the null deviance, residual deviance, and AIC.

Null deviance measures the response predicted by the model having only an intercept (a reduced model with no predictors). This is the case of a reduced model.

Residual deviance is the response predicted by a model with the predictor variables included. In other words, these two give the lack of fit of the `glm` model; the lower the value, the better the model. In this manner, it is a metric for goodness-of-fit.

The difference in degrees of freedom associated with these two is only 2. In our case, we had one predictor, `Source`; but with two estimated values for its values Origin2 and Origin3, so two additional degrees of freedom were used.

-> AIC

AIC is another metric for goodness-of-fit that measures how well the model fits the data. In other words, this tells how costly the model is, based on the number of coefficients it has to estimate. A recommended model is one with a lower AIC value. In our case, this value is 6 and can be treated as a properly fitting model.

AUC Curve

This pertains to the ROC of the GLM model. It provides a performance characteristic of the model by evaluating the true positive rate (also called sensitivity) and false negative rate (also derived as 1- specificity). Considering p > 0.5, a plot of ROC gives a best-fit scenario of the success rate by giving a prediction of all possible values of p > 0.5. The area under the curve, also called AUC, is a performance metric for the ROC curve. AOC gives the index of accuracy, or concordance index.

■ **Note** The higher the AOC, the better the prediction capability of the model.

Figure 6-1 depicts the AUC curve of our logistic regression model to predict the propensity to buy. Given our data values for `Source` and the corresponding propensity to buy, we see that AUC is a perfect, flipped, L-shaped, right-angled curve that starts with 0 on the x-axis and extends to 1 on the y-axis, and then curves in a right-angled fashion to the right, ending at an x = 1 value.

This is because the data we started from has the value 1 for `Origin1` and `Origin3`, and 0 for `Origin2`, and the corresponding values in the `propensity_to_buy` column are 1 and 0. And the predicted probabilities are also 1 and 0 for the respective `Source` values.

=> anova(logitM)
-> Analysis of deviance table

The anova function in R enables us to test the effects of factors by analyzing the `pf` deviance table. In our logistic regression model, there was one explanatory variable and the corresponding factor, `Source`. The `glm` model fit the intercept-only model, outputting the same statistics as shown against the NULL deviance (below the coefficients): deviance = 415.59. This is shown by the anova output here:

```
Analysis of Deviance Table

Model: binomial, link: logit

Response: propensity_to_buy

Terms added sequentially (first to last)

       Df Deviance Resid. Df Resid. Dev
NULL                     309     415.59

Source  2   415.59       307       0.00
```

Implementing the Solution Using the ORE SQL Interface

Now that we have the initial solution, we implement it by using the ORE SQL interface for integration with OBIEE 12c. The steps for implementing this are as follows:

1. Create an R function as a script in the R script repository by using `sys.rqScriptCreate` to creates an input table in the Oracle DB to hold Wine Source data along with a column `propensity_to_buy` based on the `Source` column. The code is shown in Listing 6-3.

Listing 6-3. R Script That Creates an Oracle Table Based on the input .csv File

```
begin
sys.rqScriptDrop('CreateInputTable');
sys.rqScriptCreate('CreateInputTable',
'function(dat) {
    library(ORE)
    ore.connect("testr","orcl","localhost","testr")
    setwd("F:/testr")
    dat <- read.csv("Wineptobuy.csv")
    ore.drop(table="WINE_SOURCE_DATA")
    ore.create(dat, table="WINE_SOURCE_DATA")
  }');
end;
/
```

2. Execute the preceding code to create the `WINE_SOURCE_DATA` table in the `testr` schema. This is done using the following `select` statement:

```
select * from table (rqEval(NULL, 'XML', 'CreateInputTable'));
```

Here's the output of executing this `select` statement:

```
---------------------------------------------------------------------
SQL> select * from table (rqEval(NULL, 'XML', 'CreateInputTable'));

NAME
---------------------------------------------------------------------
VALUE
---------------------------------------------------------------------

<root><ANY_obj><ROW-ANY_obj><value></value></ROW-ANY_obj></ANY_obj></root>

SQL>
```

3. Create an R function that builds the logistic regression model for predicting the propensity to buy based on the wine source and then scores the model on test data. The machine-learning algorithm of the GLM is used for this. This function is associated with an R script to be saved in the R script repository of ORE. Listing 6-4 shows the code.

Listing 6-4. GLM-Based Logistic Regression Model to Build and Score the Propensity to Buy Based on the Wine Source

```
begin
   sys.rqscriptDrop('BuildandScoreptobuy');
   sys.rqScriptcreate('BuildandScoreptobuy',
'function(table_name) {
ore.sync(table=table_name)
ore.attach()
winedata <- ore.pull(ore.get(table_name))
winedata$ID <- 1:nrow(winedata)
sapply(winedata, sd)
xtabs(~propensity_to_buy +Source, data=winedata)
xtabs(~propensity_to_buy +origin, data=winedata)
label <- winedata[,23]
library(caTools)
s <- sample.split(label, SplitRatio=3/4)
train_set <- winedata[s, c(2:20, 23)]
test_set <- winedata[!s, c(2:20, 23)]
sp.tab <- table(train_set$Source, train_set$propensity_to_buy)
train_set$Source <- factor(train_set$Source)
logitM <- glm(propensity_to_buy ~ Source, data = train_set,
family="binomial", control = glm.control(maxit=100))
library(aod)
head(data.frame(test_set[,c(1:19)]))
p_to_buyPred <- predict(logitM,  newdata = data.frame(test_set[,c(1:19)]),
type="response")
p_to_buyPred <- ifelse(p_to_buyPred > 0.5,1,0)
misClasificError <- mean(p_to_buyPred != test_set$propensity_to_buy)
p_to_buyPred[as.integer(rownames(p_to_buyPred))] <- p_to_buyPred
res <- cbind(data.frame(test_set[,c(1:19)]), PRED = p_to_buyPred)
res1.df <- data.frame(res[,c(1,2,19,20)])
library(ggplot2)
gg_plot <- ggplot(data=test_set, aes(x=Source, y=p_to_buyPred, group=1)) +
geom_line(aes(colour = p_to_buyPred), size = 1) + geom_point() +
stat_smooth(method="glm", family="binomial", se=FALSE) +
ggtitle("Predicting Propensity to buy based on Wine Source") +
labs(x="Source", y="Predicted Probability - p_to_buyPred")
plot(gg_plot)
res1.df
}');
end;
/
```

4. Create an R function that calls the preceding `BuildandScoreptobuy` function to execute it inside the ORE engine spawned by Listing Oracle 12c DB to output the predicted probability of the propensity to buy based on the wine source. Listing 6-5 shows the code.

Listing 6-5. R Function That Calls the BuildandScoreptobuy Function to Output Predicted Probability of Propensity to Buy Based on the Source

```
begin
sys.rqScriptDrop('CallPtoBuy');
sys.rqScriptCreate('CallPtoBuy',
'function(dat, input_table_name) {
    input_table_name <- "WINE_SOURCE_DATA"
    ore.scriptLoad(name = "BuildandScoreptobuy")
    res1 <- BuildandScoreptobuy(input_table_name)
    res1.df <- data.frame(res1)
    res1.df
  }');
end;
/
```

The code in Listing 6-5 can be executed in multiple ways by using the ORE SQL interface, to output XML, individual columns, or a PNG image graph. The following `SELECT` statements show this can be done:

a. Outputting XML:

The initial SQL `SELECT` for the getting the XML output for the integrated graph is as follows:

```
select * from table(rqTableEval(cursor(select *
from WINE_SOURCE_DATA),

cursor(select 1 as "ore.connect", 'WINE_SOURCE_
DATA' as "input_table_name" from dual),
'XML',
'CallPtoBuy'));
```

The output can be improvised so that it is visible as XML when opened from Internet Explorer or other XML display software. The following query does the trick to achieve this:

```
select xmltype(a.value).getClobVal() as "XML Output with image included"
from table(rqTableEval(cursor(select * from WINE_SOURCE_DATA),
cursor(select 1 as "ore.connect", 'WINE_SOURCE_DATA' as "input_table_name"
from dual),
'XML',
'CallPtoBuy')) a;
```

```
  <?xml version="1.0"?>
- <root>
  - <R-data>
    - <frame_obj>
      - <ROW-frame_obj>
          <origin>Origin1</origin>
          <class>1</class>
          <Source>Origin1</Source>
          <PRED>1</PRED>
        </ROW-frame_obj>
      - <ROW-frame_obj>
          <origin>Origin1</origin>
          <class>1</class>
          <Source>Origin1</Source>
          <PRED>1</PRED>
        </ROW-frame_obj>
      - <ROW-frame_obj>
          <origin>Origin1</origin>
          <class>1</class>
          <Source>Origin1</Source>
          <PRED>1</PRED>
        </ROW-frame_obj>
      - <ROW-frame_obj>
          <origin>Origin1</origin>
          <class>1</class>
          <Source>Origin1</Source>
          <PRED>1</PRED>
        </ROW-frame_obj>
      - <ROW-frame_obj>
          <origin>Origin1</origin>
          <class>1</class>
          <Source>Origin1</Source>
          <PRED>1</PRED>
        </ROW-frame_obj>
      - <ROW-frame_obj>
          <origin>Origin1</origin>
          <class>1</class>
          <Source>Origin1</Source>
          <PRED>1</PRED>
        </ROW-frame_obj>
```

```
- <ROW-frame_obj>
      <origin>Origin2</origin>
      <class>2</class>
      <Source>Origin2</Source>
      <PRED>0</PRED>
  </ROW-frame_obj>
- <ROW-frame_obj>
      <origin>Origin2</origin>
      <class>2</class>
      <Source>Origin2</Source>
      <PRED>0</PRED>
  </ROW-frame_obj>
- <ROW-frame_obj>
      <origin>Origin2</origin>
      <class>2</class>
      <Source>Origin2</Source>
      <PRED>0</PRED>
  </ROW-frame_obj>
- <ROW-frame_obj>
      <origin>Origin2</origin>
      <class>2</class>
      <Source>Origin2</Source>
      <PRED>0</PRED>
  </ROW-frame_obj>
- <ROW-frame_obj>
      <origin>Origin2</origin>
      <class>2</class>
      <Source>Origin2</Source>
      <PRED>0</PRED>
  </ROW-frame_obj>
- <ROW-frame_obj>
      <origin>Origin2</origin>
      <class>2</class>
      <Source>Origin2</Source>
      <PRED>0</PRED>
  </ROW-frame_obj>

- <ROW-frame_obj>
      <origin>Origin3</origin>
      <class>3</class>
      <Source>Origin3</Source>
      <PRED>1</PRED>
  </ROW-frame_obj>
- <ROW-frame_obj>
      <origin>Origin3</origin>
      <class>3</class>
      <Source>Origin3</Source>
      <PRED>1</PRED>
  </ROW-frame_obj>
- <ROW-frame_obj>
      <origin>Origin3</origin>
      <class>3</class>
      <Source>Origin3</Source>
      <PRED>1</PRED>
  </ROW-frame_obj>
- <ROW-frame_obj>
      <origin>Origin3</origin>
      <class>3</class>
      <Source>Origin3</Source>
      <PRED>1</PRED>
  </ROW-frame_obj>
```

```
    </R-data>
  - <images>
    - <image>
      - <img src="data:image/pngbase64">
        - <![CDATA[
            iVBORw0KGgoAAAANSUhEUgAAAeAAAAHgCAYAAAB91L6VAAAgAElEQVR4nOzdaX
          ]]>
        </img>
      </image>
    </images>
</root>
```


b. Outputting individual columns:

```
SQL> select * from table(rqTableEval(cursor(select * from WINE_SOURCE_DATA),
  2  cursor(select 1 as "ore.connect", 'WINE_SOURCE_DATA' as "input_table_
name" from dual),
  3  'select "origin", "class","Source", 1 "PRED" from WINE_SOURCE_DATA a',
  4  'CallPtoBuy'));

origin
------------------------------------------------------------------------------
     class
----------
Source
------------------------------------------------------------------------------
      PRED
----------
Origin1
         1
Origin1
         1

Origin1
         1
Origin1
         1

Origin1
         1
Origin1
         1

Origin1
         1
Origin1
         1

Origin1
         1
Origin1
```

```
              1

Origin1
              1
Origin1
              1

Origin1
              1
Origin1
              1

Origin1
              1
Origin1
              1

Origin1
              1
Origin1
              1

Origin1
              1
Origin1
              1

Origin1
              1
Origin1
              1

Origin1
              1
Origin1
              1

Origin1
              1
Origin1
              1

Origin1
              1
Origin1
              1
```

```
Origin1
         1
Origin1
         1

Origin1
         1
Origin1
         1

Origin2
         2
Origin2
         0

Origin2
         2
Origin2
         0

......

103 rows selected.
```

c. Outputting a PNG graph:

```
SQL>select id, image from table(rqTableEval(cursor(select * from WINE_
SOURCE_DATA),
   cursor(select 1 as "ore.connect", 'WINE SOURCE_DATA' as "input_table_
   name" from dual),
    'PNG',
    'CallPtoBuy'));

SQL> select id, image from table(rqTableEval(cursor(select * from WINE_
SOURCE_DATA),
        cursor(select 1 as "ore.connect", 'WINE_SOURCE_DATA' as "input_
        table_name" from dual),
         'PNG',
         'CallPtoBuy'));

        ID
----------
IMAGE
--------------------------------------------------------------------------
         1



         .
```

89504E470D0A1A0A0000000D49484452000001E0000001E008060000007DD4BE950000200049444154789CECDD6B701BE79A27F67F032078274851574A962C8B775D6C89B22D03E3736AB333734269C5
28991AED566EAA64CBD4EC4C2AD497A3DA0FA7E6A476BDB5159F9A1D22134FAD349BA9782A959495
AA73142922D7D94A65667C08D19628DBBA5014015D2D93922551BCDF00F49B0F4D800DB0890B8946
77A3FFBF2A9648400D3CB8F583F7F6BC92104280888888F2CA61740044444476C4044C4444640026
6022222033001EB2C140A191D42C158CF73C9D78188CCC6D209589224CD9FDEDEDE9CDE4F6F6F2F
24494AB8DF4C4EE83E9F0F57AE5CC9FAB8B5C8D773914FEAE72BF9B9CCC67A8E8DC591AFE7D14CAF
59F2FB5E4FA74F9FC6E9D3A735EFDFEFF7275CEEF7FBE1F3F900E8FB998AC5A5FE3C25C748B41E96
4EC000D0D3D3032144FCA7A7A707478F1ED5F5432984407D7D7DDE8ECB9411CF859EF47EBEC83C5A
5B5B71FBF6ED84CB2E5EBC88CECE4E0C0E0E265C7EE1C2059C3C791280BEEF9158B2557FA66EDFBE
CD244CB9232C0C80E8E9E95971B9D7EB15DDDDDD09BF0310004430188C5F1EBBCCEBF56ADE76EC27
76BCFABAD8ED048341CDDB51DF7E6767E78AE362B1ABEF27765D2631E4EBB9D08A53EB3EB2395EFD
38D5F1245F17FB3BF9B98CFDA8757777AFB82C3936F5F5E95EFFE4C7901CA7D6638C893D5E214456
B166725FEAF75BEC477DDFA99ECF4C1E7736EFB974B797C97B3CF97125DFB6D6E5C99FA36C3E53D9
BEEEC9C7AB5FDB6C9E83D58ED7FA4CAE764E59CB6320732BD8041CBBDCEBF5AE7893AA939210CA49
2B3979AAAF4F3E116A7DE8B58ED3BA1DF571EADBECECEC4C882176021422F1A4ABC773A14E065A71
A8EF37F9A49CEEB94CF538934F46C97F277F4988DDCF6A2741ADC7AF1563BAC79C2CDD7390EA249B
6DACD9DE576767E7AAF7B5DAC95E7DDBD9BCEF9365FBDE49F73CAB9F97D8172FADCB537D1653DD5F
BAC79FEEF165F27FB49E8374093855D24E774E49F718C8DC0A2E01C7DEE05A276EF5F5C9621F72AD
EB574B0CABDD96FA365325E05427EDE40FD55A5AC0E99E0BADD645F26D69DD6EECB274CF65268F33
DD635A2D76F5EDAEF638D4F1247F9949F59833B92ED573A4F57EC934D674F7952CD3E73317EF7BB5
B5BC77D2BDDE9D9D9D095FB262BF77777727FCAE4E78D97CA6D2BD57B5A85BD3C99FC95C3C07999E
9FD6F318C8BC2C3F067CF4E8D1844912478F1E4530184C18176A6C6C8CFF3E3C3C0C60E5A4A54020
80E1E1610C0F0FC3EBF526DC47434383E67D6BFDDF5C181E1EC6BE7DFB122E533F86D564FB5C0483
41CDF8BD5E6FFC7902563EFED8F5E99ECB74DADBDBE1F57AD73461ACB3B313172F5E04005CB97205
9D9D9D191D97E9634EB6DA73A047AC99DC97FA358E49F57CE6F27D0FACFD794CE5C48913F1F1DE8B
172FC6DFABC78E1DC3850B1700008383833871E244D6B7BDD6F7AA508DFF060281848958B97A0E92
CF4FAB9D53D6FB7923F3B17C024E9E7824329894E1F57A571C2384405757579EA2D6C75A9E8BF55A
EF73D9D7D70721043A3B3BE35F20329934F6F39FFF1CE7CF9F07A04CCA59CB49395F72196BECA4DB
DDDD1D9F68A796EAF934FBFBBEA1A121FE3C9D3F7F1EEDEDED0080FAFA7A04020100C0EDDBB7537E
314865BD8F5F0881603088F3E7CF1B36B1D1ECAF2165C7F209385B8D8D8DF10F73A6D70783C135DD
D65A353636AE9811AAC737DC868606CDF80381C08A96B2D6F5B97CFCE7CE9D8310025EAF37A32543
F5F5F5F07ABDF0FBFD080402F193753A993EE664AB3D0799C836D6D5EEABB7B7377E024E77C24D7E
3E73F9BE07D6FE3CA6127B9E628F53ADB3B333BE1C692D5F2AB37DAFAEB6042B76DFC1605097E720
559C7A9D6FC8403A756DE705528C8DC5688D8F244F7CD01A2B4D1E67523F555865DC29797C6AAD63
C0AB1D9BEAE55ACF73B19E8934E99ECB548F33F931C7C6D4B466B8263F1F422C8F8B673251269793
B0B49E03AD19D66B8935D57DADF67CC59EA774CFE77ADFF7C9D63B01494BEC36B45E6BADCBB3FD4C
A57AFC5A8F2FDD5C8C74CF41BAF786D66732DD39259BC740E666CB041CBB3C7682D17A03ABAFCF74
1952BA936E36278BD8FF51C7902E49E4E2B9D09A91199B69AB757DF2F1C9CF65BAC7A9BEEDE4FFAB
BE2DAD04167BEED33D6EAD63533DE664B1FB48F5FF931F43F26B9969ACE9EE2BF9F9521FA375BDD6
17AEB5BEEFB5A47BEF649B8063FF2739EED59EBF6C3F53E91E7FB2E4E733DDFB3FDBF786D66732D5
39652D8F81CC4B12420890E9F5F6F6E2E38F3F465F5F5F5EEF579224F4F4F464DCC59B4FA150080D
0D0DB0C25BD84AB112517ED86E0CD80A62E34FEA891E1F7FFC71BCFA0F29AE5CB982EEEE6EA3C3C8
88956225A2FC70191D00ADD4DEDE8EEEEEEE84D99EDDDDDD9CE9B824D69AF47ABD79EF11C8969562
25A2FC62173411119101D8054D444464002660222222033001131111198009988888C8004CC04444
440660022622223280025D701CBB28CD7AF5F1B1D46DE6DD8B001737373989B9B333A144A525D5D8D
70388C999919A343A124555555104260 6A6ACAE850F2AEB6B6D6E81028054B266000B62DE92796B6
1F2373E26B635E7C6DC86CD8054D444464002660222222033001131111198009988888C8004CC044

```
444406600226222232001330111191019880898888OCC0044C444464002660222222033001131111
198009988888C8004CC0444444066002262222324O5E12F0E5CB97313030A079DDD9B367D1D1D181
4F3FFD34E5......
```


When the preceding SELECT statement is run and its output is viewed in Oracle SQL Developer, we get the graph shown in Figure 6-7. This graph is based on the ggplot graph that plots source vs. predicted probability (`p_to_buyPred`).

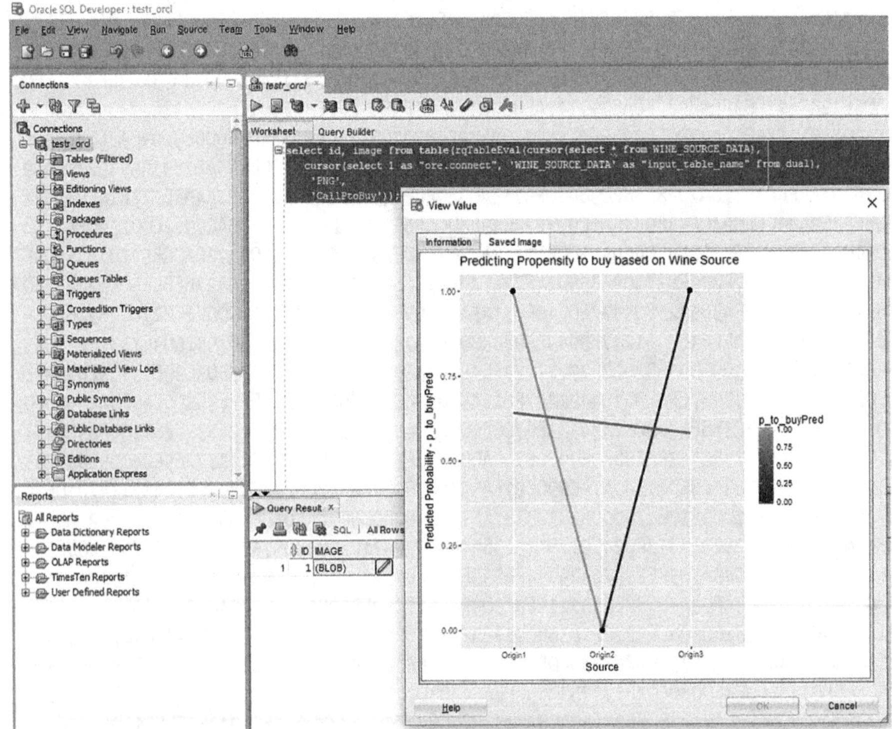

Figure 6-7. PNG output of the logistic regression model to predict propensity to buy wine based on its source

Another graph we are interested in for the GLM machine-learning algorithm is the AUC curve. This code is shown in Listing 6-6.

Listing 6-6. GLM-Based Logistic Regression Model to Build and Score Propensity to Buy Based on Wine Source That Plots the AUC Curve

```
begin
--   sys.rqscriptDrop('BuildandScoreptobuyAUC');
   sys.rqScriptcreate('BuildandScoreptobuyAUC',
'function(table_name) {
ore.sync(table=table_name)
ore.attach()
winedata <- ore.pull(ore.get(table_name))
winedata$ID <- 1:nrow(winedata)
sapply(winedata, sd)
xtabs(~propensity_to_buy +Source, data=winedata)
xtabs(~propensity_to_buy +origin, data=winedata)
label <- winedata[,23]
library(caTools)
s <- sample.split(label, SplitRatio=3/4)
train_set <- winedata[s, c(2:20, 23)]
test_set <- winedata[!s, c(2:20, 23)]
sp.tab <- table(train_set$Source, train_set$propensity_to_buy)
train_set$Source <- factor(train_set$Source)
logitM <- glm(propensity_to_buy ~ Source, data = train_set,
family="binomial", control = glm.control(maxit=100))
library(aod)
head(data.frame(test_set[,c(1:19)]))
p_to_buyPred <- predict(logitM,  newdata = data.frame(test_set[,c(1:19)]),
type="response")
p_to_buyPred <- ifelse(p_to_buyPred > 0.5,1,0)
misClasificError <- mean(p_to_buyPred != test_set$propensity_to_buy)
p_to_buyPred[as.integer(rownames(p_to_buyPred))] <- p_to_buyPred
res <- cbind(data.frame(test_set[,c(1:19)]), PRED = p_to_buyPred)
res1.df <- data.frame(res[,c(1,2,19,20)])
library(ROCR)
pr1 <- prediction(p_to_buyPred, test_set$propensity_to_buy)
class(pr1)
prf1 <- performance(pr1, measure = "tpr", x.measure = "fpr")
class(prf1)
plot(prf1, colorize = TRUE) # , text.adj = c(-0.2,1.7)
res1.df
}');
end;
/
```

The code for calling this R function is shown in Listing 6-7.

Listing 6-7. Code for Calling the BuildandScoreptobuyAUC

```
begin
sys.rqScriptDrop('CallPtoBuyAUC');
sys.rqScriptCreate('CallPtoBuyAUC',
'function(dat, input_table_name) {
    input_table_name <- "WINE_SOURCE_DATA"
    ore.scriptLoad(name = "BuildandScoreptobuyAUC")
    res1 <- BuildandScoreptobuyAUC(input_table_name)
    res1.df <- data.frame(res1)
    res1.df
  }');
end;
/
```

Executing the following SELECT statement to call the function in Listing 6-7 and gives the graph shown in Figure 6-8.

```
select * from table(rqTableEval(cursor(select * from WINE_SOURCE_DATA),
cursor(select 1 as "ore.connect", 'WINE_SOURCE_DATA' as "input_table_name"
from dual),
 'PNG',
 'CallPtoBuyAUC'));
```

The AUC shows an inverted L, which means the GML model built and scored is ideal for the data in context. The larger the area, the more perfect the model.

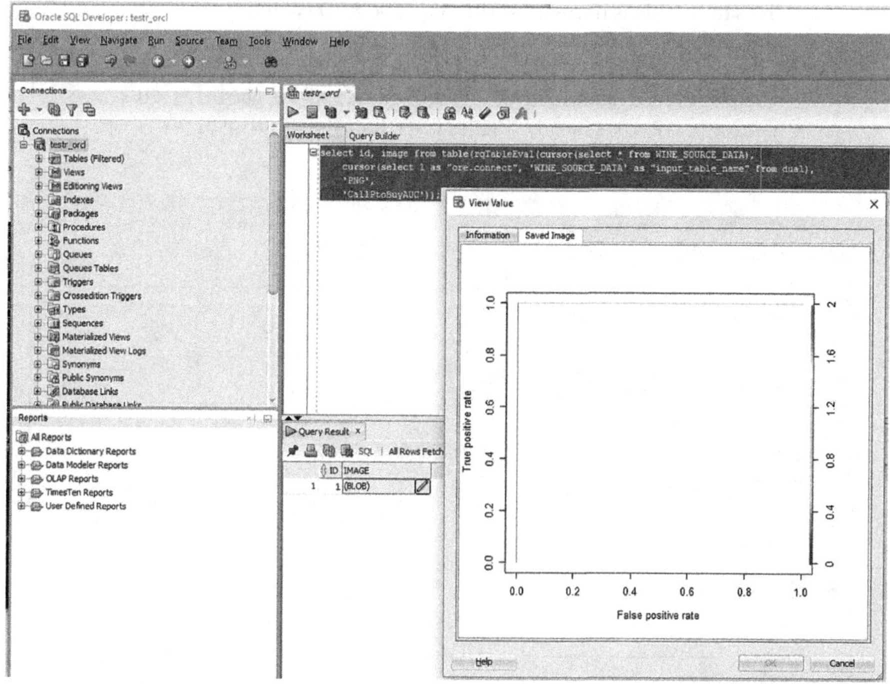

Figure 6-8. *PNG output of the logistic regression model shows the AUC for predicting wine propensity to buy based on its source*

Integrating PNG Output with the OBIEE Dashboard

Following the steps outlined in the subsection "Integrating the PNG Graph with OBIEE" in Chapter 3, the PNG image shown in Figure 6-7 can be integrated with OBIEE. Once the image is integrated, an analysis and subsequent dashboard can be created in OBIEE. Here we list the primary steps involved; some steps have already been provided in Chapter 3.:

1. Create a new physical table of type SELECT in the Physical layer (using the OBIEE RPD downloaded from the WebLogic server and opening it offline in the BI Administration Tool). We already have the connection pool created from Chapter 3. The query used to generate the PNG output of the machine-learning algorithm for logistic regression is used as the initialization string value for the SELECT-type table. This is shown in Figure 6-9.

This new table is named `CallPtoBuy`. The RPD can be downloaded using the following command:

```
datamodel.cmd downloadrpd -O obieenew.rpd -W Admin123 -U
weblogic -P <password> -SI ssi -S localhost -N 9502 -Y
```

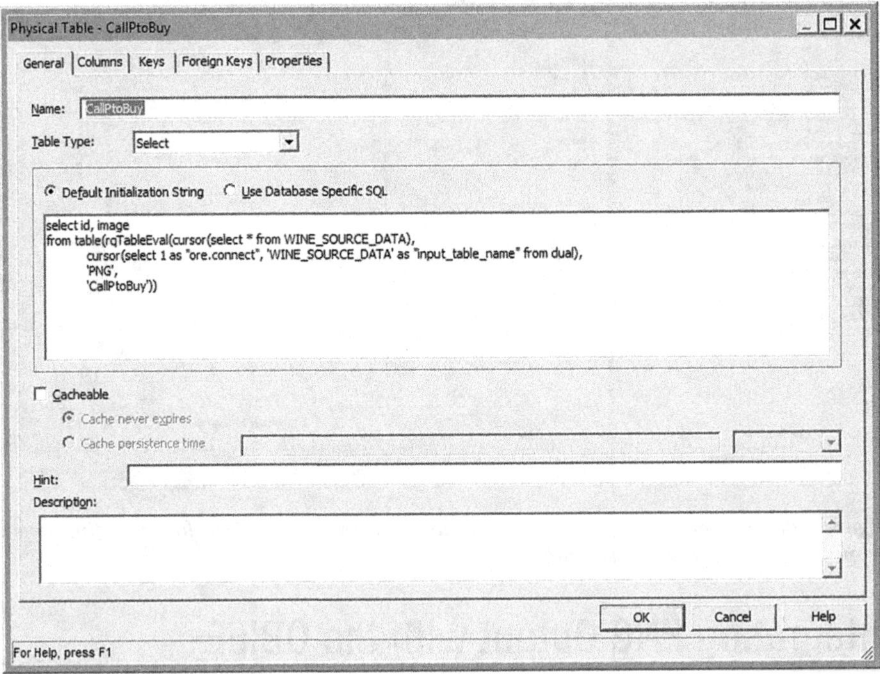

***Figure 6-9.** Physical table properties created in OBIEE RPD for the Propensity to Buy PNG graph to be integrated with OBIEE12c*

2. Add the new table to the Business Mapping and Modeling layer. The dialog boxes in Figures 6-10 and 6-11 show the logical column properties and the expression to be built for the `ID` column and the `IMAGE` column.

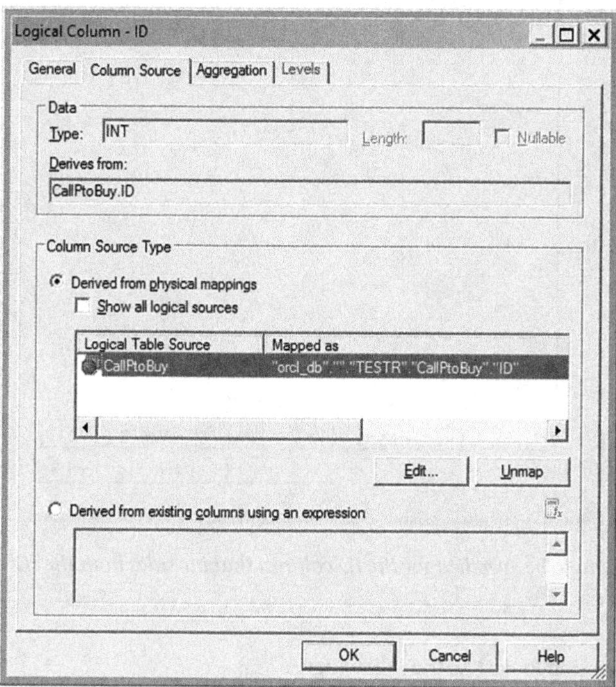

Figure 6-10. *Logical column ID properties*

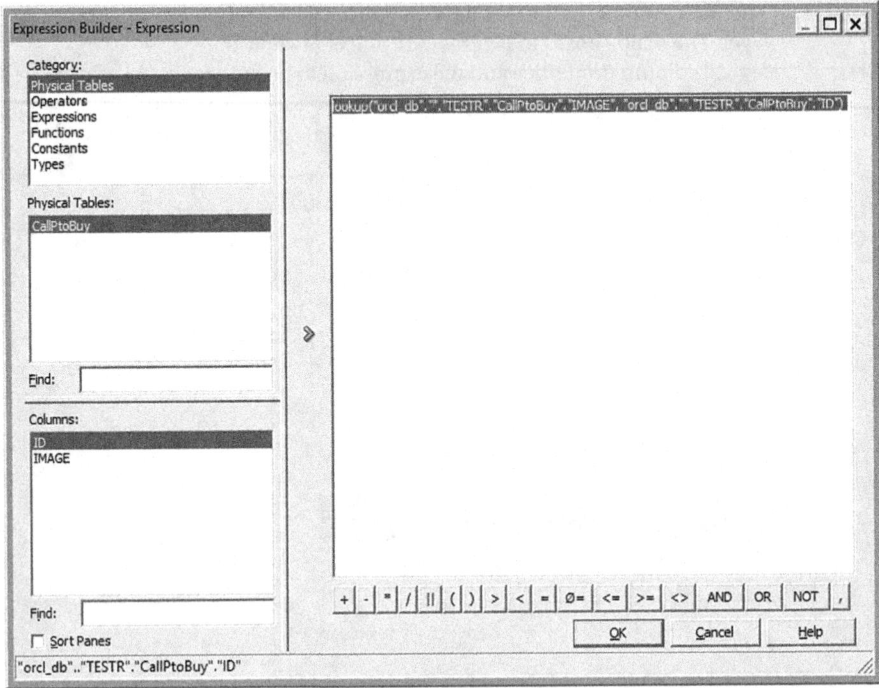

Figure 6-11. *Logical expression to be specified for the ID column that includes both the ID and IMAGE column*

The logical expression looks like the following:

```
lookup("orcl_db"."".""TESTR"."CallPtoBuy"."IMAGE",
"orcl_db".""."TESTR"."CallPtoBuy"."ID")
```

3. The modified RPD needs to be uploaded to the WebLogic server by using the following command:

```
datamodel.cmd uploadrpd -I obieenew08062017.rpd -W Admin123 -U
weblogic -P <password> -SI ssi -S localhost -N 9502
Service Instance: ssi

Operation successful.
RPD upload completed successfully.
```

4. Restart WebLogic Server.

    a. Log in to OBIEE12c using the URL `localhost:9502/analytics`.

    b. Click Administration ➤ Maintenance and Troubleshooting.

    c. Then click Reload Files and Metadata.

    d. Under Analysis and Interactive Reporting, click Analysis.

    e. Select the TESTR subject area.

    f. Expand `CallPtoBuy` in the Criteria tab. Then drag and drop the `ID` and `IMAGE` columns under the Selected Columns area to its right.

    g. Click Results.

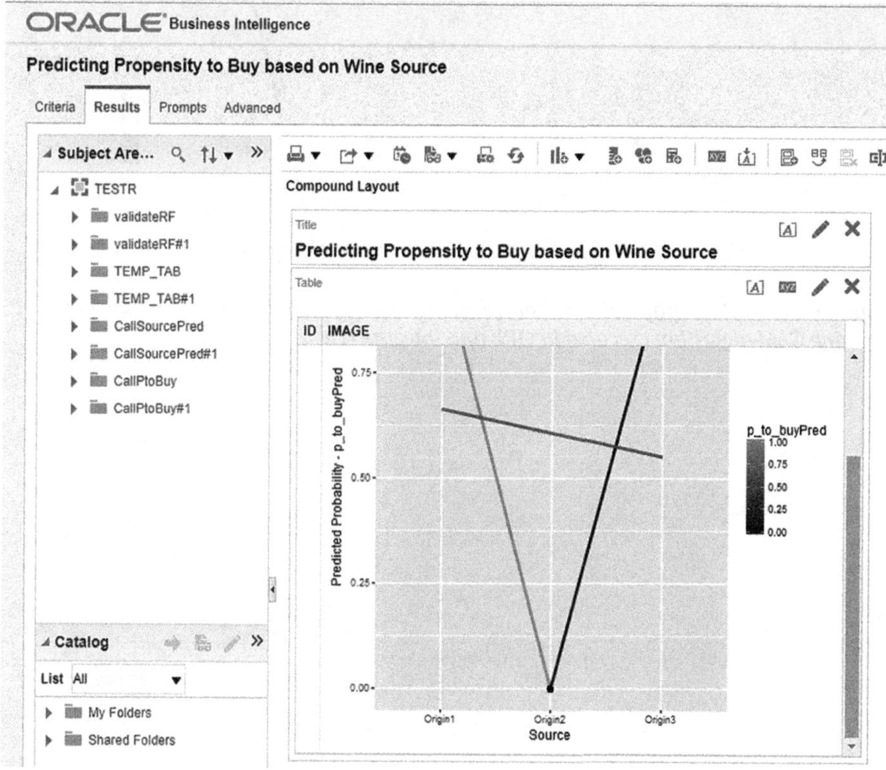

Figure 6-12. *Output graph of wine source vs. predicted probability based on machine-learning GLM algorithm executed in ORE and integrated with OBIEE 12c*

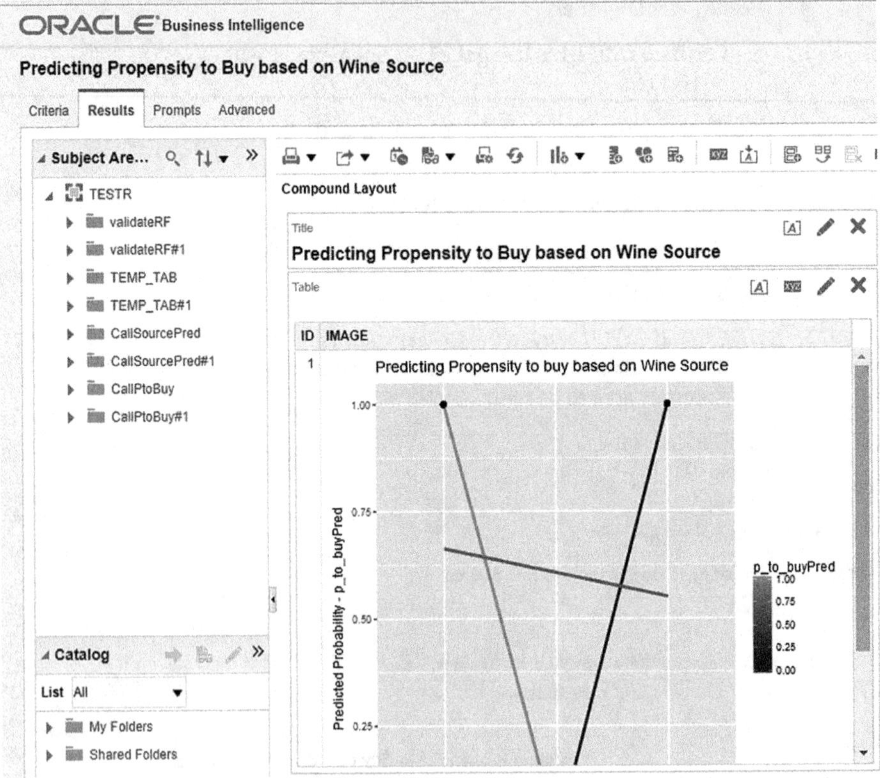

Figure 6-13. *Output graph of wine source vs. predicted Probability based on machine-learning GLM algorithm executed in ORE and integrated with OBIEE 12c*

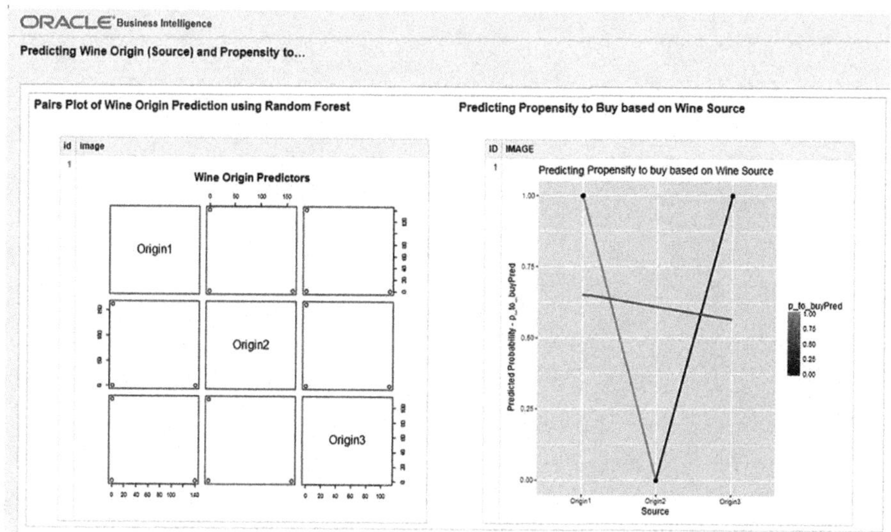

Figure 6-14. *Dashboard showing the pairs plot of predicting wine origin and using it to predict the propensity to buy*

h. The graph of Source vs. Predicted Probability (`ptobuyPred`) appears as shown in Figures 6-12 and 6-13.

Figure 6-14 displays the final dashboard showing the pairs plot of predicting wine origin and then using the origin to predict the propensity to buy.

Summary

This chapter covered the implementation of machine learning in OBIEE 12c. Starting with a brief description of a business problem and solution, it detailed how the machine-learning algorithm of logistic regression, based on the GLM model, can be used to predict the propensity to buy a wine based on its origin. The chapter then showed the various options of the model output via XML, structured tabular results, and a PNG graph. Finally, it outlined how the PNG image can be integrated with an OBIEE dashboard and merged with the Wine Origin Prediction graph to result in a final dashboard that shows both side by side. Executable code and its output of execution were provided wherever necessary.

Index

R. Abellera and L. Bulusu, *Oracle Business Intelligence with Machine Learning*, https://doi.org/10.1007/978-1-4842-3255-2

C

D

E

F

G

H

I, J, K

L

M

N

O

Printed in the United States
By Bookmasters

Printed in the United States
By Bookmasters